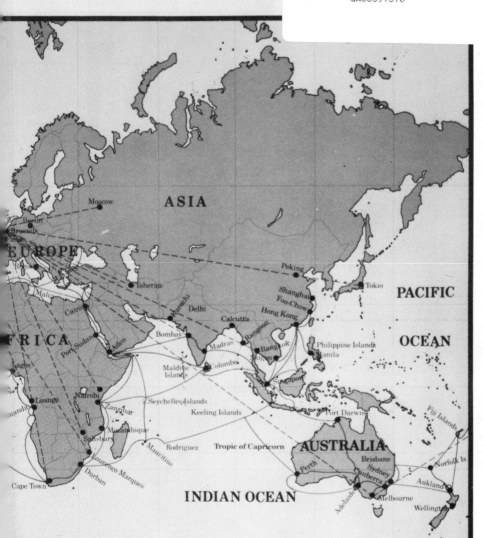

INSIDE AN INTERNATIONAL
Forty Years in
'Cable and Wireless'

INSIDE AN INTERNATIONAL
Forty Years in
'Cable and Wireless'

by

J. F. STRAY

Regency Press (London & New York) Ltd.
125 High Holborn, London WC1V 6QA

ISBN 0 7212 0612 3

Printed and bound in Great Britain by
Buckland Press Ltd., Dover, Kent.

To Sylvia
who died January 1981
aged nearly 84

CONTENTS

Foreword

The story of the British Overseas Cable Service, reaching back as it does to the middle years of the last century, is part of our Imperial history—indeed its spurts of development were often in response to crises in the Empire such as the Indian Mutiny of 1857. A definitive history has recently been published by Cable & Wireless Ltd—the successor to the old companies which mushroomed as the technologies of telegraphy, and later of radio, developed.

But it has fallen to Mr Stray to write the human story behind the technical and organisational history. And amid the welter of detail about technical developments, company formations and mergers, vacillations in government policy etc, it is only too easy to forget that this chapter in our history is essentially a human story of men and women of many races who served in remote corners of the Empire—often in the most primitive and dangerous conditions. Men and women who by their dogged courage and inventiveness girdled the earth with submarine cables.

Mr Stray was one of them. At the end of the day he can look back on a working life devoted to enabling nation to speak unto nation.

He has now performed an inestimable service both to the archives of Cable & Wireless Ltd and to British history by recording his experiences before they are lost down the stream of time.

His book should find a place on the shelves both of the serious historian and of all who are enthralled by the romance of global communications.

The Rt Hon The Lord Glenamara, PC, CH
Former Chairman of Cable & Wireless Ltd.

LIST OF ILLUSTRATIONS

LIST OF ILLUSTRATIONS

CHAPTER ONE

Training Schools

My father died when I was twelve years old, and at prep school. Two years later my mother married again (to Mr Michael Urwin, a chartered accountant) and I was sent as a boarder to Derby School and remained there until the end of 1914.

Derby School was a grammar school but had a few boarders in the School House run by the headmaster. He had been assistant headmaster of the Royal Masonic School Bushey, and a friend of my mother.

I had wanted to be an engineer and had been told that I would be apprenticed to some firm as my parents could not afford to send me to college or university. In 1912 I had met Phil Alfieri who was staying with his aunt two doors away from us while attending the London Training School of the Eastern and Associated Telegraph Companies. He was four years older and was keen to become a wireless amateur. His aunt had a grown up family of four so in her house he had not much room.

So Phil used to spend his spare time at our house and we made a wireless crystal receiver and a small spark transmitter. At prep school I had become friendly with a boy called Donath Harcourt whose father was a well-known artist (George Harcourt, RA). Donath also built a wireless set and installed it in his house a mile away at Bushey Heath and we used to communicate with each other. We had licences from the GPO (in our parents' names) and were authorised to transmit on 180 metres wavelength. Everything was morse in those days and we used to listen to the Eiffel Tower, Poldhu, and other stations. But one day in 1914 we heard someone talking. It was a "Lepel" arc station, near Slough, testing radiotelephony.

When war with Germany broke out in August 1914, Phil had gone off to the cable station at Porthcurnow. Donath and I practised our morse sound reading so that we could join up as wireless operators. We wrote to the Admiralty, and they replied bleakly that if we were over twenty-one and had a Postmaster-General's certificate of proficiency in wireless telegraphy, they would accept us; we were only fifteen and a half.

After I left school my mother asked me if I would like to join the Eastern Telegraph Co like Phil Alfieri. She said it would be doing a job for the war, and there were prospects of an interesting life abroad with engineering work later.

My step-father knew the chief accountant of the company and soon I was filling in my first application form. I was sent to take the entrance examination which I passed all except writing and dictation. I was recommended to take lessons in these and come back again in a month as I was not yet sixteen—the earliest entry age. This I did and was accepted in April 1915.

The first day I joined the LTS I was put with eleven others to learn the morse code under Mr Schaefer and Mr "Daddy" Atkins. Mr Schaefer was a large red faced man and Mr Atkins looked like his nickname.

The school was in the basement of the old Electra House in what was then Finsbury Pavement (now Moorgate Street). This was the Head Office of the Eastern and Associated Telegraph Companies which comprised three main companies, the Eastern, the Western and the Eastern Extension, Australasia and China telegraph companies, together with various subsidiaries with a system from England to the west coast of South America, to South Africa and the Mediterranean, and east through India, Malaya to Manila in the Philippines and to Australia and New Zealand. It controlled 150,000 miles of submarine cable with stations all over the area outlined above.

We had weekly lectures on telegraph procedures in a room on the second floor, an interesting place with pictures, specimens of cables, and one of the axes belonging to the German cruiser *Emden* which had been sunk after raiding the cable station at Cocos Keeling Island in the Indian Ocean. Little did I think that one day I would go there after another war.

A large room, with pillars, in the basement full of tables and telegraph instruments, held most of the probationers (as we were called). Other rooms were occupied by the superintendent Mr Percy Burrell, the assistant superintendent Mr J. H. Stephens, and there were instrument laboratories for electrical examinations of senior men and a maintenance workshop.

Electra House, Moorgate, the old headquarters of the Cable Companies from 1902-1943.

We started under Mr Schaefer learning hand sending with double recorder keys and reading cable code signals from slip (paper tape) and later were taught punching (making holes in paper tape to represent the letters of messages which could then be fed through automatic transmitters to send on the signals). All cable working was on tape. There was no sound reading.

I remember having trouble with a siphon recorder which traced on tape the signals sent by hand into it. I told Mr Schaefer that my machine had gone wrong. He came over and said very severely, "It is *not* a machine; it is an instrument."

We had an hour for lunch which we took in ABC, Lyons, or Express Dairies. We wore business suits with bowler hats in winter and straw hats in summer. Later I sported spats which were very fashionable.

One of the probationers often had lunch with me during the first six months. He was a very superior person and turned up one day in a topper. He introduced me to an old fashioned eating house in Coleman Street where we sat in pews and had beef à la mode and vegetables and suet pudding and treacle all for a bob. But I could not afford this every day. However, after six months in the school, if we passed the prescribed tests, we got our first pay, ten shillings a week.

The school had a sports ground at West Hampstead. I went there a good deal on Saturday afternoons in the summer to play tennis, with another probationer called Pearce who was a cheerful handsome chap. I also went to quite a few theatres in London mostly to Saturday matinees in the winter. Phil Alfieri's cousins, the Wilsons, introduced me to this and we went to the pit at 2/6d. having to queue for seats.

The assistant superintendent, Mr Stephens, gave a course of evening lectures and practical experiments on cable telegraphy and we probs were invited to take it at a cost of one pound. This would be refunded by the company if we passed the exam at the end. Before I left the school he invited several of us to go to the Institution of Electrical Engineers in Savoy Place to hear a lecture by a Mr Harrison on telegraphy. I was much impressed by the lecture theatre with its panelled walls and busts of Faraday and other eminent electricians. The lecture was interesting, particularly at the end when the usual discussion took place. Our own chief engineer, Mr Judd, took part, together with several other well known telegraph engineers including a Mr Murray who had invented his own system of printing telegraphy. The lecturer had not referred to the cable-code, used on most submarine cables. This code enabled the maximum amount of information to be transmitted in a given time—greater than by morse or the teleprinter code, as submarine cables had a very limited capacity which it was essential to use to the full.

After learning hand-sending, punching and writing off messages, we graduated to where Mr Dallas ran an automatic transmitter circuit with three men punching tape for it, a transmitter clerk and sheet-keeper who entered the messages on a sheet with times of transmission. This transmitter sent messages from downstairs to a receiving instrument in the B room upstairs. Here the tape was gummed on forms—one for each message—and the words counted. These message forms were then passed to three hand senders who sent them back to three instruments downstairs where they were written off. There were no printers or typewriters in those days, hence the insistence on good hand writing. We used a script which enabled one to write the whole alphabet without taking the pencil from the paper.

For practice we used old cable messages sent home once a month on a random date and checked to detect operators' errors. If you were debited with more than one error in a thousand words, you were likely to lose your next annual promotion. A most unusual message of twenty to thirty thousand words was from a newspaper correspondent in Albania describing his experiences with brigands and other strange characters and places.

We had monthly tests to show how we were improving our speeds and accuracy, but the six-monthly (for your first pay packet) and the twelve monthly (for transfer to Porthcurnow,) were the real hurdles. If you failed these you got another try a month later, but a second failure meant the sack.

My mother came up to have a look at the school and was courteously shown round by Mr Stephens. She told me that she had been amused when he had solemnly warned her of the dangers young men ran from taking too much alcohol when they went overseas. Perhaps he thought I looked a prospective alcoholic.

In the B room Mr Madsen sat at a desk on a raised dais and supervised checking. This was done by working in pairs to enable errors made in sending and receiving messages to be detected and debited against the learner operators. One day Wootton and I were doing this. We did not feel much like work that morning, so we initialed a lot of messages which we had not checked at all. Madsen must have been watching us because he had us up before him separately and showed us some errors he had found in messages passed by us. We confessed and he gave us a severe wigging but we were not punished, financially.

All this time the war was going on. With my step-father I joined the local defence corp. We wore armbands with GR on them and were irreverently called the "georgeous wrecks." We got Bedford cord breeches which we paid for ourselves and later green uniform tunics. Then early in 1916 the night air raids began on London and we saw lots of damage when we arrived in the city in the morning. The old Royal Mail Steam Packet Co's office was gutted from top to bottom. Then a bomb fell in Moorgate Street just outside the tube station and made a large crater in the road. Splinters from it or another bomb cracked the glass window of the public cable office counter in Electra House, producing a decorative pattern effect. One day after an evening theatre show, I entered Charing Cross station late at night and a hospital train had just arrived and hundreds of ambulances were taking casualties from it to nearby hospitals. The sight of them gave some very sobering thoughts. Lots of young men older than myself whom I knew had joined up. The ones in Bushey mostly joined the Artists Rifles or the HAC; many were later commissioned and went to France but few had been killed or wounded. Later we had Zeppelin raids until one or two were shot down which discouraged them. We also had the splendid story about the Russian soldiers seen in trains "with snow on their boots", who were coming from the north to fight in France!

I passed all my twelve months' tests, and the dozen probs in my month were given two weeks leave before being sent to Porthcurnow.

We all met at Paddington station to catch the Cornish Riviera Express for Penzance. We had an exciting trip. As the train, non-stop to Plymouth, was entering the outskirts of Newton Abbot we hit a goods van which was being shunted on an adjacent line and was, for some reason, slowly moving on to the main line. Fortunately it only overlapped our line by about a foot when we arrived at fifty miles per hour. Our steam locomotive's window of the cab on the left side was broken and the projecting lookout window of the guard's van was torn off. Most of the corridor windows of the first passenger coach were smashed but fortunately no one was hurt.

We were met at Penzance station, as was customary, by a gang of probs from Porthcurnow who had come in to rag us. They confiscated any town articles such as gloves, sticks or bowler hats using the latter as footballs. We were put into a large horse brake and driven the ten miles to Porthcurnow cable station.

As you came down the valley, first there were a few houses for married staff, then the superintendent's house on the left in a large garden, then two tennis courts with the main office above and on the right the mess and staff quarters, school, engine room and recreation hall. Just beyond the tennis courts was a hut for the military guard during the war.

Everyone had a bedroom of his own and there was a mess room, general sitting room and two other sitting rooms (called the wardroom and the gunroom—naval fashion) for the instructors and junior operators respectively.

Newly arrived probs had to suffer a good deal of ragging. They arrived on a Monday and were not spoken to by anyone during that

Stray and Skelton at Porthcurnow Cable Station and Training School.

week but had plenty of apple pie beds made for them. On the Saturday evening they were introduced one by one to an initiation ceremony-cum-concert. Each newcomer had to stand on a table and sing. If he could not or was bad (most were) he was de-bagged and anointed with some concoction. He was then declared a member of the Exiles Club and joined the audience. Most got de-bagged, including myself. But Woollett, one of my month, had learned a splendid tongue-twisting song which he delivered with great verve and quite brought the house down. After the new probs had been dealt with, any nearly-new, i.e. last or previous month's prob who had got above himself in the opinion of the seniors might be hauled up and made to perform, warned or "executed".

For three months after arrival, we worked in the school which was open from 8 a.m. till midnight. We did eight hours in shifts of four hours including Saturdays, though on that day the late afternoon and evening shifts usually got off a couple of hours early unless you were on a black list with lost privileges. The instructors had to do similar duties. There were four of these, who lived in houses up the valley; the bachelors and a couple of army officers lived in quarters like ours. There were the superintendent, Mr "Jackie" Marsden, the assistant superintendent, Mr Hood, the chief electrician, Mr Sinclair, and four supervisor engineers who worked in shifts in the main office.

Life was very pleasant at PK (the telegraph code for Porthcurnow), at least in the summer. We could bathe in the bay at the bottom of the valley, go for walks and picnics and take part in organised games, cricket, rugger and soccer. There were dances and concerts in the recreation hall.

We played cricket and football with teams from nearby villages and went there in the horse brake. We cycled into Penzance occasionally for the day, by special leave, or could go to Lands End, about four miles away, and have a beer or a port and lemon at the last pub. We organised snake hunting expeditions to kill adders of which there were quite a few amongst the rocks and bushes. And there were church services at St Levan Church, in the next valley to the north.

One Saturday evening there was great excitement. Word came that a big shoal of pilchards was coming into the bay, and watchmen from the two fishing villages nearby were posted on the headlands. The villages decided to pool their resources and two boats took up station at the entrance. Just at dusk, the fish came in and the boats quickly surrounded them by paying out nets and rowing hard. It was too dark to do any more and they lay to for the night, hoping the wind would not get up. Next morning they had a stiff struggle with their consciences as to whether they ought to work on a Sunday, but after church they decided it was too risky to leave it until the next day as it seemed as if a "blow" might come up and take the fish and their nets away. So they set to work driving the fish into one corner of the nets and then putting down others till they could dredge them all out into the boats. They got the lot in, except for those eaten by gulls who came over in clouds. They were taken to market in Penzance where they fetched over £2,000, a lot in those days, and the vicar had to go and preside at the share out between the villages. We got a few and had them for meals in the mess—very good they were too.

I became friendly with a chap called Bullen and we did many walks and expeditions together. We nearly got drowned together by bathing in the next bay to PK one day when the sea was very rough, though we were both good swimmers. There was a heavy surf and we went in too far and got bowled over. We managed to get back to the beach completely winded.

After three months we were promoted to working four hours a day in the main office and four in the school. There were six men plus the CC (clerk-in-charge, i.e., engineer/supervisor) on duty.

The building contained the administrative offices on the ground floor. The instrument room occupied the whole of the top floor and here were all the relay circuits for the six telegraph cables which went to Gibraltar, Alexandria, Carcavelos (near Lisbon), Vigo, Spain and two to St Vincent, Cape Verde Islands—one via Madeira and one via the Azores. All were worked cable-code except the Alexandria circuit which was morse. There were landlines from London rented from the GPO.

The six men wound up the tape records on which were the incoming and outgoing signals and watched for faults. All the circuits worked what was known as duplex, that is signals passed in both directions simultaneously. The morse circuit to Alexandria had a sounder which clicked away at thirty words per minute. Mr Armstrong, an ex GPO man who could sound-read, would catch us out if we did not promptly report any remarks or stoppage to him.

I was interested in the engineering side, and was listed to do four hours daily in the engine room one week and the next in the office workshop. K. D. Anthony, then a junior operator, was in charge of the engine room and lived in a part of the quarters which was over the school. It was called Cubes because the rooms appeared to be in the form of largish cubicles. He was supposed to get up before 6 a.m. and start the oil engine, but when he acquired an assistant (me), he left him to do it, and dozed on until about 7 a.m. There were two engines, the smaller 12 hp and the other 20 hp. The former had to be started by hand which meant pushing the flywheel round after heating up the combustion chamber with a blowlamp. I always expected the heavy leather belt would come off and wrap itself round me, but it never did. The small engine was used in the morning and the large one (started by compressed air) in the evening by an engine man.

I had learned that one had to do ten years as an operator before sitting for the exam which qualified one for promotion to supervisor, and enabled one to be a real engineer. The only way of avoiding this was to volunteer to serve on a cable repairing ship as a cable electrician. To qualify for a cableship, one had to swot up morse sound reading and

wireless theory in one's own time. The company would give you a
month at a wireless school before you sat for the PMG's wireless
operator's certificate. You had to have this certificate before you could
be sent to a cableship because the latter did not carry wireless operators
as such; the relatively small amount of this work was done by the cable
electricians. So I volunteered for this and with a few others practised
morse and wireless theory.

The first World War was still going on, but at PK we were cut off
from it. We had a military guard at the office, and on the beach where
the cables landed and used to see a naval patrol ship steaming up and
down but that was all. We were instructed to go into Penzance and
attest at the recruiting office. This meant registering for military service
and taking the oath, prior to being called up at eighteen and a half or
nineteen years.

In September I qualified as a junior operator and was appointed to
the staff as from 1st October, 1916. The superintendent, "Jackie"
Marsden sent for me and said it was proposed to send me to the wireless
school in Marconi House, London, for a month and then I must sit for
the PMG's exam. Could I get through in a month as head office was
not amused when the two men sent previously had taken two months? I
said that I would do my best.

So I left PK, reported to head office and was given a letter to the
superintendent of the Marconi school. There I found the basement of
Marconi House crowded with young men learning to be wireless
operators and being sent to sea almost the day after they had passed
their exams. Owing to the German submarine menace, hundreds of
ships were being fitted with wireless and needed operators.

Our class worked in a large room which was a demonstration room
for showing off Marconi equipment and contained three complete sets,
5 kilowatt (for shore stations or very large liners), $1\frac{1}{2}$kw for ordinary
ships and a $\frac{1}{2}$kw set for small vessels, all arranged against wood
panelling on one side to show off to customers. For our purposes, there
had been added another $1\frac{1}{2}$kw set which we experimented with and
which was used by the post office examiners. There were desks for us
fitted with a buzzer and headphones, and morse key for practising. I
spent a month in Mr Penrose's class, took the exam and got through.

After a few days leave, I went with my step-father to head office and
signed my employment agreement and the company's secrecy form. The
former stated that my salary was to be £72 per annum plus the foreign

service allowance of my station and that the agreement was for five years when I would get leave and sign for further service. I do not remember being asked to sign a further agreement until 1930 when the merger with the wireless companies took place and we all signed transfer agreements. In December I sailed for Gibraltar in a British India Steam Navigation ship. Prior to my joining the London training school, my step-father had paid a premium of £30 to the company. This was refunded to buy an outfit which included such exotic items as a dinner jacket suit and cholera belts. The company supplied a list of what you needed.

CHAPTER TWO

Gibraltar

On the ship I found that I had Miller and Capron as my companions. Miller was a quiet, fair-haired chap whom I liked very much. Capron was a flamboyant young man. We were in the second class as only seniors of over ten years' service travelled first class. The submarine scare was on but convoys had not yet been organised so we went miles out into the Atlantic and took a week to reach Gibraltar. It was my first ocean voyage but I do not remember anything of note about it, except that I was seasick for several days. We arrived at Gib on a brilliantly fine December morning.

The cable station had a large staff at that time; over a hundred foreign service plus twenty or thirty local staff. These were men which the company recruited at stations abroad and trained as operators, but occasionally as mechanics for their maintenance workshops. The third category of staff was called supernumeries and consisted of messengers, etc.

We, called the F1 staff, had six grades, the first grade being superintendent of a large station and so on down to sixth grade for operators. You did so many years in each grade, getting an annual increment and then had to wait for promotion to the next grade. To reach the fourth or supervisors grade, you had to pass qualifying exams.

The juniors and a few young seniors lived in the Mount Pleasant quarters with the mess and office on the opposite side of South Barrack Road. Mr Carlisle was assistant superintendent and the chief electrician was Mr Sinclair who had been transferred from PK with Mr Ivor Hall as his deputy. There were four supervisors and a number of watchkeeping electricians of whom Cardwell was one. The other seniors including some over ten years service who were unticketed (not passed the exam for the supervisor's certificate). They did jobs such as filing and the daily check to prevent loss of messages, attending to service messages and in charge of cable circuits.

The mess for the young bachelors was run on similar lines to that at PK. We each had a bedroom and there were the usual three sitting rooms. They all had balconies with splendid views of the bay. There was a library with about 3,000 volumes, a billiard room, writing room and entertainment hall with a piano. There was a matron, Miss Pinkham, who had her own sitting room and bedroom, a small sick-bay and a surgery in the mess building where Dr Gill, came regularly. We had organised cricket, rugger, soccer and hockey, and played the Gibraltar Cricket Club and army and navy teams.

We had a large house, "El Cobre" in Spain where we could go for a day or two. It was at the entrance to a valley in the hills about four miles behind Algeciras.

It was looked after by a Spanish caretaker and his wife, and was run as a club with a small monthly subscription of two shillings. Beckinsale, a senior bachelor, was chairman and was christened "El Presidente". He had learned Spanish and we shall come across him later during the Spanish civil war of 1936.

Gibraltar had two rowing clubs and a yacht club apart from service clubs. There was also a golf club at Campamento about three miles into

Gibraltar in 1918, from the north west.

Spain. On the North Front there was a race course and the Calpe foxhounds had kennels on an estate in Spain and hunted in the district. The name Calpe came from the early Roman name of Mons Calpe. Later the Moors over-ran southern Spain under the command of an individual called Tarik. The Rock became known as Jebel Tarik, (the hill of Tarik) which resulted in the present name.

We worked a nominal seven and a half hour day with half hour off for a meal, but most of the shifts were a straight six or seven hours. We did a five week round, changing duties each week. There was a good deal of overtime which increased as the war went on, and we did six hour Sunday shifts three Sundays out of five, with a double shift on one of them. Overtime was paid at time and a quarter, and Sunday duty at time and a half. At PK my pay had been £4 a month and at Gib £6 a month plus £2 foreign service allowance. The mess bill was £3.15s a month, plus drinks, tobacco, subscriptions (5/- for sports and 2/- for El Cobre). We got all our main needs, board/lodging, etc., provided free and were left with only a pound or two in our pockets at the end of each month. This was a good system as it did not give much scope for going off the rails. We were not allowed to sign for alcoholic drinks in the mess, until we were twenty-one years of age but on Christmas morning there were free drinks for all, paid for out of the bar profits. One Christmas one of the juniors got drunk and was incapable on duty. He was sent home on the next ship as being drunk on duty was the inexcusable sin.

Each shift organised itself into a group who got on well together, as we could apply to change shifts. After night duty the one I joined used to go over by the 9 a.m. ferry to Algeciras, hire gharrys (open horse cabs) and spend the weekend at El Cobre. We took with us two large baskets full of food and drinks from the mess, alcohol being allowed on these occasions. We used to have walks up the valley behind the house. We could bathe and sun-bathe in the garden, eat oranges off the trees in season, and have sing-songs round a big fire in the evenings in winter. Very jolly it was after a week's night duty, and we thoroughly enjoyed it. These weekends were known as long offs. Married staff and children could use El Cobre from Tuesdays to Fridays.

J. H. Robinson, who was about a year or two older than I, had his mother and young sister come to stay for a few months in Gib. She was a widow, her husband having been the company's superintendent in Colombo. Robinson invited me to come for a couple of midweek days

*Gibraltar staff spending a weekend at "El Cobre" near Algeciras in Spain,
Hughes, Robinson, Blunden, Bowen, Crosland, Payne and Drucquer.*

at El Cobre. We had both to be back for duty by 7 p.m. on the second day.

Our gharry bringing us to Algeciras was late and we missed the 6 p.m. ferry the last one each day in wartime. As usual we never had much cash in hand, certainly not enough for an hotel. Mrs. Robinson had also brought Joy Hall, the four year old daughter of Ivor Hall. Robinson and I went to see the manager of the Anglo Hispano Hotel who readily agreed to letting us have two rooms and meals for the night and morning, on payment later. We now had to arrange about our evening duties in the office. There were no telephones from outside Gib in those days, so we went to the Algeciras telegraph office, and in the best Spanish that we could muster, told the men on duty that we were brother "telegrafistas" and would they break into the Gib to Cadiz wire circuit, so that we could send a message to our office. They agreed and we reported to the CC and asked him to get two men from the mess to do our duties, to be repaid later. On our return to the hotel, we found poor little Joy Hall in tears because she could not see here mummy that evening. Mrs Robinson was able to pacify her and the next morning we all got back to Gib.

In the summer I played cricket regularly and in my second year was elected vice-captain of our team. Nash Prosser our Captain was probably the best cricketer ever amongst cable men. He was a first class batsman and bowler, and easily up to English county standards. H. R. Cox was a tall dark-haired, handsome man who was a good all-rounder. He had a good singing voice, was a good bridge player, and had been educated at Christ Hospital. We had quite a few Christ Hospital men; they were nearly all good at rugger. Cox told me that when the company opened its station at Colombo about five operators, of whom he was one, had been specially picked to go there because they were good all-rounders at games. It was desired to make a good show amongst the young tea planters in Ceylon.

It was rightly thought that games made for better morals and physical fitness in tropical countries. A high standard of both integrity and fitness was called for and you were expected always to maintain the company's good name. Occasional wildness when young was tolerated but not encouraged.

I had a mishap when playing cricket. The Gibraltar Cricket Club's ground was not properly fenced, only a number of posts with a wire rail. When running after a ball, I ran into the wire and was knocked flat on my back. I got up, said I was all right and went on fielding. However, it seems that I looked groggy and, as we won by five wickets, was not sent out to bat. Later I was found wandering in the quarters asking where my room was. Matron was called and put me to bed. I woke up next morning quite all right but could hardly remember anything since lunch the previous day. It was slight concussion, and I was kept in for a couple of days.

At Gib there was a man called John Palmer who was three or four years older than I. He had been at Alexandria when the war started and, with several others, had wanted to join the army. The company told them that their services were needed where they were and they must not break their contracts. Some stayed, but one or two, of whom Palmer was one, got passages on ships to England. The company was in touch with the government and when Palmer's ship got to Gibraltar, he was taken off by the army and told to work in our office there, and fined one year's seniority. When the war was over the company relented and

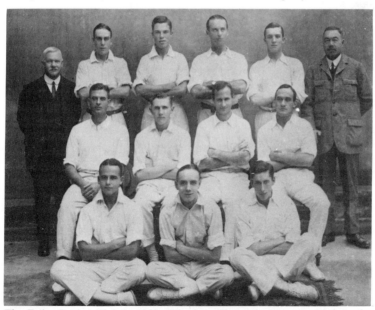

The Exiles Cricket Club in 1918, Gibraltar. The author is second left in the middle row.

gave him back his lost seniority. I met him briefly in Cape Town some years later. I heard afterwards that he came into a baronetcy on the death of some relation and left the company's service.

Cecil Webb proposed that he, Miller and I should jointly buy a riding pony. We had recently been given a war bonus of £8 a quarter so were more affluent. I said that I had never ridden before, but Webb said he would teach me. He was a good horse-man and had been riding in the local races on a horse owned by one of our senior bachelors called Johnnie Burnet. So we bought a black pony called Antonio from an Army Vet., and under Webb's tuition, I did learn to ride moderately well, though I fell off a good many times. For ten shillings a year to the Jockey Club, we could use the cinder track round the race course for a gallop. Later we bought a trap (dog-cart) painted yellow and blue, and hitched Antonio to it and drove about Gib and into Spain. At this time one drove on the left in Gib and on the right in Spain, changing over at the Spanish Lines as the frontier was called on the other side of the neutral ground. We kept the pony and trap at the stables of a cab driver who lived just above the quarters on the Europa Road. With three of us, we could arrange to exercise him every day.

Stray on Antonio, Gibraltar.

We went walking a good deal in Spain as well. It was known as "spadging". Drucquer and I did a lot of this together. We went to Algeciras one day by ferry and walked to Carneiro Point at the west end of the bay where there was a lighthouse and a stone Martello tower.

On another occasion we climbed the hill a few miles north of Gib. On it is another Martello tower known as the Queen of Spain's Chair. Legend has it that the Queen of Spain was to watch the storming of Gibraltar by the Spanish army in the eighteenth century. The garrison had seen the preparations for the attack, and just before it was due they sallied out one dark night and destroyed the whole of the Spanish lines. The event was commemorated by an annual public holiday, called Sortie Day. Even at that time the Spaniards wanted us to return Gibraltar to them, and there was talk of swapping it for Ceuta on the Moroccan side of the Straits.

Drucquer and I decided to visit Ronda in the mountains about fifty miles from Gib, not far from Jerez where the sherry comes from. The company's rule was that we had to have the superintendents permission to go away from Gib. further than El Cobre, and we learned that someone had recently been refused permission to visit Ronda. We were doing a lot of overtime which might be called for at any time, so we planned to give out that we were going to El Cobre and actually go to Ronda. We went by train from Algeciras after night duty on Saturday and returned on Tuesday, having arranged for someone to work our Monday evening shift. If anyone wanted to change duties or get a shift worked, details were entered in a book in the instrument room and signed by all concerned including the supervisors. We stayed at the Reina Victoria Hotel in Ronda. It belonged to the hotel company which owned the larger Reina Christina Hotel at Algeciras (now owned by Trust Houses Forte), and had a British manageress. It was perched on the top of a 500 ft cliff overlooking the Tajo or gorge of Ronda. The town is on the top of a hill, half of which appears to have been removed in prehistoric times, and straddles a narrow stream which falls over the cliff into the valley below. It is a spectacular site. There are three bridges, Roman, Moorish and Spanish, though only the latter near the edge of the cliff is ordinarily used. We thoroughly enjoyed ourselves and got back to Gib. without being found out.

There was a bullring at La Linea and also at Algeciras and the famous matador, Belmonte, came to perform, so some of us went to see him. While admiring the skill and bravery of the bullfighters, most of us were revolted by the bloodshed and cruelty, especially to the poor horses who got gored.

There was a brothel in Gib familiarly known as HQ. It was tolerated or possibly approved by the military authorities and reported to be regularly inspected by them. A few of our men patronised it as they did some of the similar establishments in Spain. I once went to see HQ but was quite put off by its tawdriness and the not very inviting inmates.

In the summer we bathed practically every day and at Camp Bay we had a changing hut for bathers. To get there one had to pass through the naval victualling yard and we had what were known as Rock passes to enter various localities including most of the upper Rock guarded by sentries. At the end of the pier we had a diving board and about a quarter mile seaward was a moored cable buoy. This was for cable ships to tie up and lie stern towards the cable tanks in order to ship cable.

Most days there was a number of our men there in the summer, but on one occasion I was there alone and, the weather being quite calm, I decided to swim out to the mooring buoy. I hung on to it for a few minutes and then noticed that the army sentry at our cable hut was gesticulating in my direction. So I set off to swim back, he told me that a large shark had been observed entering the bay round Europa Point. That was the only time I heard of a shark in Gib bay. There were a few small octopus and a large one seized a man's foot when working in the Admiralty harbour, and he might have been in trouble if he had been alone.

In those days hardly anyone wore shorts except for football, hockey, etc. We had grey flannel trousers and blazers or sports jackets which we wore summer and winter, but often went without coats when spadging. A few bought white duck trousers but only wore them about the mess and office.

I was too busy with games, riding, walking and swimming to go in much for what was called poodle-faking , that is social calls.

I was asked to go to a tea time salon and was introduced to Commander Frewin, RN who was King's Harbour Master and Commander of the Yard. In World War II I met his son, Lt J. B. Frewin, RN in the far east and we exchanged dinners. He was later Sir John Frewin and C-in-C of the Home Fleet; he died in 1975.

We did not mix much with army and navy officers though I met a few. This was because we could not afford their standard of living. The Garrison Library, Rosia Swimming Club and Sandpits Lawn Tennis

Club, were almost exclusively service clubs.

Our own mess was run like an army mess. We had guest nights and there were concerts, dances and amateur theatricals in the hall, and we drank the loyal toast. It was managed by a committee, mostly seniors, the principal officials being the mess president and his vice, wine caterer and mess caterer. The latter was allowed time off by the company and did a permanent four hour duty. We got our whisky and sherry in casks, the first, from Scotland, and the latter from Cadiz, and bottled it, this being the main job of the wine caterer. Cardwell had this post and I occasionally helped him to mix over proof whisky with distilled water in a spare cask. It was then drawn off into bottles and corked with a machine worked by one of the waiters.

Whisky cost 2d. per peg, either with water or soda, and Capstan cigarettes were 10d. for a tin of 50, there being no duty. We juniors, as I have said, were not allowed the former, except to take a bottle or so to El Cobre for our long off parties there, but we smoked a good deal and cigarettes were often used as counters when playing cards.

Like PK the office was an oblong building of two storeys. Administration, workshop, etc. were on the ground floor with the instrument room on the whole of the top floor. Owing to the declivities of the Rock, the office was about fifty yards from the mess, down a slope, and our sitting room balconies looked over its flat roof. Below the office were the South Barracks where a British regiment was quartered, the 2nd Battalion of the Welsh Fusiliers. Their commanding officer, Col Arnold, was a keen cricketer and in the garden of his house, above Barrack Road, there was a practice cricket pitch with a net which he let us use.

The instrument room had long tables on either side, one end against the wall and extending so as to leave a wide central aisle.

Each cable circuit was on one table, with automatic transmitter and punchers on one side and siphon recorder tape receiver on the other. We changed over from transmitting to receiving half way through a shift or duty. It took another year or more before one became a really good operator and was promoted to faster and more important circuits. I discovered that I could punch messages automatically while occupying one's mind with other thoughts. We had been issued with a name/date metal stamp. This had rollers for changing the date and was used to stamp each message dealt with. When punching while day dreaming, one might fail to stamp a message. Later the transmitter clerk, whose job it was to time each batch, would hand this message back to you and say, "Did you punch this?" You looked and could not for the life of you say whether you had. To relieve the monotony when we got on to important circuits which dealt with thousands of words of cipher telegrams in war time, we competed as to who could punch the most words without errors or erasures. The highest ever achieved was by Saunders who did 20,000 words of cipher.

In the middle of the instrument room was a sort of lectern with two large black books on it, irreverently called the bible. These contained a complete list of all telegraph offices in the world even down to village post offices, showing which country they were in, issued by the International Telegraph Bureau at Berne. It's official name was the Nomenclature of Telegraph Offices, or Nomen for short. The clerk-in-charge had a desk on a dais in the centre aisle with the watch electrician at another nearby.

Of the four CCs, Farrant was a tall dark good-looking man with a quiet manner. A typical strong silent man, respected and liked by the staff. I remember one night when two of us had been punching hard for two hours to keep up with a fast auto and it was sticky in September when the famous Levanter cloud hung over the Rock. Farrant came up behind me and said, "you can go outside for ten minutes for a breather," he took my place and started punching. When I got back he did the same for the other man. He was transferred to Athens in 1917 and remained in Greece for the rest of his career, becoming the company's divisional manager in Greece. "Agony" Payne was younger than the others, and often came to El Cobre with us youngsters and entered heartily into our fun. Menzies was rather corpulent and could swear like a trooper but was very efficient. He was feared but not much liked. The fourth CC, "Dickie" Trounson was the butt of the staff. He was a mild little whiskered man and he got ragged a lot. He was a kindly man, but I'm afraid not much respected.

At Christmas the mess gave a children's party in the hall, having had about £20 worth of toys sent out by Gamages. Like the free drinks, it was paid for out of the bar profits. Someone dressed up as Father Christmas and distributed presents from a decorated tree in the usual fashion. All the married staff, their children and those of friends outside were invited.

We used to walk up the upper rock and enjoy the splendid views over the bay. St Michael's Cave, on Queen's Road which ran along the rock

about half way up was not then open as it contained a dangerous
vertical shaft down which someone had fallen. Our Rock passes had
various letters of the alphabet on them and we could only pass sentry
posts if that post's letter was on the pass. On one occasion I came to a
sentry post near the south end of the rock and found that I could not go
through. Some weeks later on walking south from another part of the
Rock, I found myself the other side of the same sentry post and could
not go past it!

The PT sergeant was allowed to use the garrison gymnasium for
private classes, so our shift formed itself into a group to do gym. We
paid him 30 shillings each for a course of lessons. It was good exercise,
and we played basketball there as well.

There was a cableship, the CS *Amber* of 1,043 tons stationed at Gib.
She was rather old having been built in 1888, but in good condition. She
had all her cable tanks forward of the engine room which put her funnel
a long way aft, unusual in those days. My friend Irish was third
electrician and the second electrician was a chap called Briggs. In war
time cableships worked under dangerous conditions as they might be
stopped in one place for hours whilst splicing cable and were a natural
target for submarines. Strong escorts of three or four small warships or
armed merchantmen were provided to prevent attacks.

There were rarely any large warships at Gib but there was a flotilla of
old torpedo boats built in the 1890s. They were small and had a couple
of guns, and were what were known as turtle-back boats from their
curved forecastles. They patrolled the Straits day and night.

One stormy night one of them capsized in the Straits with heavy loss
of life, a sad disaster. Larger ships did pass through the Straits, one was
the Russian cruiser *Askold,* unique in having five thin funnels. She was
christened "the packet of Woodbines" by our navy. We later had a few
MLs, large fast motor launches with one gun which patrolled to harass
submarines.

The defences of Gibraltar were very much on the alert throughout the
war. There were 9.2 inch guns mounted near the summit and lower
down batteries of 6 inch guns. All night searchlights played from
Europa Point across the Straits to the north African coast about thirteen
miles away and others were mounted on the moles of the harbour
directed to cover the bay. The guns had practices against towed targets
both by day and night and one could clearly see the fall of shot. There
was no blackout of the town's lighting as it would not have been of

much use, but one night about 8 p.m. we had a scare. All lights were suddenly cut off by the power station and numerous guns stared firing into the bay. This went on for over twenty minutes, and then the firing ceased and the lights came on. We were never told officially, but it was believed there was a German submarine in the bay.

In 1918 a naval balloon section was set up on a sports ground near the naval officers' club in the dockyard. The balloons were captive cigar-shaped ones and were used by escorts of convoys who towed them so that observers in their gondolas had a large field of vision for spotting German submarines. One broke its cable, rose rapidly and was whisked by the wind over the top of the Rock and out into the Mediterranean. Fortunately it was not manned at the time.

In the summer of 1918 we had an epidemic of dysentery, which had a decisive effect on my career. I was the first to be affected, although it was only severe diarrhoea. Then I heard that others had it, and Mr Carlisle, the assistant superintendent came to my room with an army doctor who cross-examined me about where I had been lately and what I had eaten.

About a month later I caught Spanish influenza which was beginning to sweep all over the world. There were hundreds of cases in Gib both among the services and the local population, and many died. I was soon out of bed again but the doctor kept me off duty for another week. Miss Pinkham, the matron, had been there for about twenty years, and I liked her. She knew hundreds of our men who had been stationed there over the years and was very popular. She managed the maid servants who cleaned our rooms, etc., working with the mess president and mess caterer who managed the men servants.

The Spanish peseta had gradually increased in value against the pound sterling until the latter was only worth 15.90 instead of the normal 25 pesetas. As we got all our food in Spain, our mess bills had soared and were now £9 per month. The result was that unless we did lots of overtime, we could be in the red at the end of the month, as I was when I was off duty sick.

So there was a meeting of the staff at which all the juniors suggested going on strike and all the seniors objected to this. A committee was set up to meet the superintendent and write a letter to the company about our woes. It was announced that we would in future be paid in pesetas at the pre-war rate of 25 to the pound. We could then exchange our pesetas down town for 16 to the pound, or use them to pay expenses.

While I was still down with diarrhoea, head office instructed the superintendent to send me to the CS *Amber* to relieve Irish who was to be transferred to the cableship *Levant II* based at Malta. I was interviewed by Mr Carlisle who told me that the *Amber* had to go to sea for a few days and the doctor said I was not fit enough. My colleague, "Boy" Gates, had studied wireless, had the PMG's certificate and was eligible for service on cableships, so he was sent instead to the *Amber*.

On 8th November 1918 HMS *Britannia,* a battleship, was torpedoed in the Straits off the Spanish coast, and several hundred men were drowned. The bodies recovered were brought to Gib for the funeral. The news of the armistice came through about 9 a.m. on 11th November but the Governor suppressed it until the naval funeral was over.

At 1 p.m. the news was announced and all the ships in the harbour started sounding their sirens and the noise was deafening. An American ship of 10,000 tons, loaded with petrol in drums and some ammunition, caught fire about this time but failed to get attention on account of the noise. They towed her out of the Admiralty harbour and beached her towards Campamento to the north where she burnt furiously for four days amid occasional explosions of ammunition.

The practice was for newly qualified operators from PK for the Eastern company to be sent to one of four overseas stations, Carcavellos (near Lisbon), Gibraltar, Malta, and a few to Marseilles. Those for the Western company went to Madeira or St Vincent (Cape Verde Islands), and those for the Eastern Extension company to Singapore. In the Eastern after about two years at one of these four, you were transferred to either Alexandria or Suez for another two years, and might finally go to Aden to complete your five year tour abroad.

Doré left to go to Malta on a cruiser in 1918. About a week later I walked into the mess room for lunch and found him there. He told me the ship had got about half way and then been ordered back by wireless and had dropped him off before going elsewhere.

In December 1918 my brother who had taken the army entrance exam from Derby School and got a place in the Indian Army, wrote me that he was sailing for India. He went to Wellington Army College in India and was gazetted into the 22nd Punjab Regt, later changed to the 3rd/Fourteenth Punjab Regt in the re-organisation after the war.

In March 1919 I was informed that I was being transferred to the cableship *Levant II* at Malta and would travel on a warship. I was told to pack and report at 9 a.m. the day after to HMS *Sweetbriar,* a sloop lying alongside in the admiralty harbour.

When you were transferred your parents were notified by head office in London. This was also the case if you had a bad illness and if it was serious, daily bulletins would be sent to London by the superintendent and passed on to your parents. Later, if married and your wife was not with you, such information would also be sent to her.

CHAPTER THREE

Cableship "Levant II"

I soon found out all about HMS *Sweetbriar*. She was doing a ferry run, Gib to Malta and back, carrying naval stores and passengers. But during the war she had been a Q ship. These were small merchant ships or specially built ones fitted with concealed guns and manned by the navy. They were to trap and destroy submarines who would think they were merchant vessels. *Sweetbriar* had been specially built and could do 16 knots. She had four 4″ guns, two on each side inside the superstructure. They were concealed by steel plating which was hinged and could be suddenly let down making wide openings for the guns to fire through. She also had a tube through the bottom of the ship right aft, down which depth charges could be dropped to explode when she was far enough away. There were no depth charge throwers in those days.

The captain was a pre-war retired post captain who had been recalled to the Admiralty and after organising Q ships had asked to command one. I was given a cabin under the poop and lived in the wardroom with the officers. There were the first lieutenant and two other officers, the two senior ones being Royal Naval Reserve men and the junior was RN as was the engineer officer. There was a young RNVR doctor. They were all nice and jolly and I liked them.

We went to Algiers where we spent the day and I went ashore with the first lieutenant and engineer officer. We had a bit of rough weather and I was very seasick. I decided that as I was going to live on board a ship, I had better get over this so I stayed up and went to every meal possible. It did not do much good and I found out later that I could never entirely get over being seasick.

From Algiers we went to Bizerta and here we picked up three more passengers for Malta, all British army officers. We finally got to Malta and tied up in Dockyard Creek in the Grand Harbour.

I went ashore in a dghaisa (pronounced disar), the two-oared local harbour boats with raised stem and stern posts, like gondolas. I had been booked into the Osborn Hotel in Strada Mezzodi as the *Levant II* was away at sea.

I went across the Marsamuscetto Harbour on the other side of Valletta to the suburb of Sliema and then on to St Georges beyond where our main cable office and ship-shore wireless station was, and called on the superintendent Mr Barwell. He said that the *Levant II* was expected back in a few days.

Unlike other company's stations, there was no bachelors' mess and quarters at Malta. A quarter's allowance was paid and the staff sorted itself out into small groups of from a dozen to twos and threes. Each group rented a furnished house and was catered for by a Maltese messman who charged so much a month for food and service. There were four company furnished houses for married men including the superintendent who had a big flat over the main office building. There were plenty of these as several Maltese firms made a business of providing them. They took them on long leases, often from the Roman Catholic church, furnished them and they were let to army and naval officers and our men.

Many naval ships had Maltese messmen who thus became trained in this job out of which they made a good profit.

Cableship Levant II.

Bullen, my PK friend, had been sent to Malta two years previously and we had corresponded while I was in Gib, I went to the house in Sliema which he shared with a few others and was told he was out sailing for the day. I never saw him as I learned that he and another man had gone out in a sailing dinghy and were both missing. An air and sea rescue search was made by the navy for a week or more, but they were never seen again. It was a very sad beginning to my acquaintance with Malta.

In a few days the *Levant II* arrived and tied up at the company's cable tanks at Hay wharf in the Marsamuscetto harbour near Floriano, just outside Valletta. I reported to Captain Lawson and learned that Irish was to be transferred to the *Sentinel* (470 tons) also based at Malta, and she was expected to arrive shortly.

There were three cableships at Malta, and another, the *Levant I* at Piraeus in Greece. The *Levant I* was the smallest, being a converted trawler of 141 tons and worked in the Greek Islands. The *Levant II* was not much bigger, being 283 tons and was intended to replace the *Levant I* eventually. The *Sentinel* and the two *Levants,* only carried two cable electricians. The *Amber* at Gib and the other ship at Malta, the *Electra* of 1,236 tons, had three.

As soon as the *Sentinel* came in, Irish transferred to her, and I left the hotel and went on board *Levant II*. She had five officers and one petty officer (the cable jointer) and a Greek bosun and crew. There was Captain Lawson (actually a chief officer who was acting as captain), Hannaford, chief officer; H.R. (Bob) Spratt, chief electrician; myself, second electrician; Alec Henderson, chief engineer; and Bristow, the cable jointer.

Between the bridge deckhouse and the forecastle was a largish hatch way and then a large winch with 5ft diameter drums (wide flat pulley wheels) on each side which were used to haul cable or rope by putting four or five turns on them. The bows had the usual large sheaves arranged in a clipper bow, characteristic of all cableships.

All cable repairing work was done from the bows of cableships. Only large cable laying ships had sheaves for paying out cable over the stern. The reason is that a ship can be handled or manoeuvered better this way.

Most cableships had three or four large round tanks for coiling stock cable for use on repairs. But the two *Levants* only had holds which held two coils of cable. The foremast had a derrick for hoisting out cable

Cableship Levant I at Syra.

buoys, the latter being lashed, one on each side, to the foremast shrouds (rigging). The older ships often had a cross yard on the foremast used for handling buoys. Wire and hemp rope, grapnels, etc., were stowed in space below the crew's quarters in the forecastle. A steam engine and dynamo supplied electric light for cabins, navigation lights, etc. In such a small ship accommodation was very limited and every inch of space was used for stowing something. One got used to this and also to the necessity of seeing that all loose objects were what is known as chocked off, that is either fastened down or otherwise secured, as in the slightest rough sea the ship danced about a lot.

Captain Lawson was an able cableship man. He eventually went to head office and after being in charge of the marine department, became a general manager. Hannaford was a nice man and I met him again in another ship. Old Alec Henderson was a character. He was married to a Greek lady who lived in Malta, and spoke Greek and some Italian. When we had finished a job and were going to put on full speed for the next one or our home port, he would walk to the engine room skylight and shout down to his Greek assistant: "Fir-r-re oop". As we had no purser or chief steward like the larger ships. we were given 5/6d. a day messing allowance and ran our own mess. This was done by our Greek steward, Apostoli, supervised by one of the officers and Bob Spratt acted as wine caterer.

No sooner had I joined the ship than she had to go into dry dock for scraping, painting and minor repairs which took two to three weeks and we could not live on board. I had been meeting people on our Malta staff whom I had known before, and one of them, Bruford, suggested I should join their small mess. The house faced St Julian's Bay the other side of Sliema and was one of a row of terrace houses known as "Sunstroke Terrace" because it was very hot in summer.

I stayed there while the ship was in dry dock, going each day by ferry to Dockyard Creek. Bob Spratt initiated me into the considerable amount of clerical work my job entailed. Numerous copies of cable repair data had to be made on a hand written Gestetner copying frame and there were letters and reports to be typed. Cable data was circulated to all our ships, ten of them, and head office required three or four copies of everything.

The ship was soon finished in the dockyard and we were sent to repair one of the two short cables linking Malta and Pozalla in Sicily which was broken.

Practically all submarine cables then consisted of one copper conductor, usually stranded, i.e., made up of a number of thinner twisted wires, and insulated with gutta percha. This was covered by a layer of copper tape to keep out the marine teredo worm which likes to eat gutta percha. Over this was a serving of jute or hemp, and then a number of steel wires as armouring. Finally a tarred tape was put on the outside. The overall size varied from just over one inch for deep sea cable to three or four inches for double armoured shore ends for rocky coasts.

To find out where a break or fault was, tests of electrical resistance were made from both ends by the shore electrician, but sometimes by the ship's. If a cable was broken the measured resistance consisted of the cable conductor plus the end resistance which depended on how much of the copper conductor was exposed to the sea water. Various methods of finding out this end resistance were used. One good one had been invented by an elder brother of my former instructor, Mr Schaefer of the Training School. Having obtained the electrical resistance to the break, inspection of the splice sheets of the cable showed which piece it was in. These sheets were a list of all the pieces of which the cable was made up together with the electrical values of each piece. Reference was then made to the cable charts. They showed by blue lines the position of all the cables, with small circles at splices with ship's name and date. On the chart the position of the break was then marked.

On the ship's arrival at this position, if out of sight of land, a mark buoy would be put down close to the line of the cable. It would have a flag on it and if required two lamps showing white lights. Sun and/or star observations were then made to fix exactly its position and it would then be used as a fixed point for subsequent manoeuvres.

A grapnel on a wire rope was lowered to the bottom on one side of the cable line and dragged by the ship as slowly as possible — about 2 or 3 knots — across the line. This would be repeated until the cable was hooked. To detect this, the officer directing operations sat on a small piece of hard board fitted with battens the other side to enclose the wire rope near the ship's bow. He could thus feel with his behind that the rope was dragging over the ocean floor. On hooking, this feel disappeared and the strain increased. The grapnel was then hauled up to the bows and two men were lowered in bosun's chairs to make fast chains and ropes on each side of the cable. It was cut, and the two ends pulled on board. Usually one end was short, i.e., to the break, the other going to the shore on one side. Deck testing wires were connected and each tested in turn. The ship would communicate with the shore with instruments in the test room and report progress by service telegram to head office. The shore end would then be attached to a buoy and let go, and the short end picked up.

The other end would then be grappled for and raised in the same way. Ship's stock cable would then be jointed and spliced on to the end to the other shore, and the ship would steam at about 4 or 5 knots towards the buoyed end, paying out the stock cable. A boat was lowered which attached a rope from the ship to the buoyed end. After testing this end again, the ship's stock cable would be cut and the two ends of the cable spliced together and let go. While each splice was being made a max/min thermometer would be lowered to the bottom on a piano sounding wire and the depth and bottom temperature recorded. The depths would be sent later to the Admiralty Hydrographic Department. The temperature was needed to calculate the exact electrical resistance of the piece of new cable laid in. The resistance of copper varies considerably with temperature.

There were lots of variation of the above procedure, the cable might break when being hauled up or it might be buried near the mouth of a big river. You had then to move along it till it was strong enough to be picked up, or was not buried. In-shore it might be too shallow for the ship and you either had to use the ship's boats or hire a small tug and/or lighter. The work was made interesting by its unpredictability. Sometimes you had a fault which came and went or was otherwise difficult to locate and you might have to cut into the cable to make further tests. It was here that an experienced chief electrician was so valuable. As repairs and stock cable cost a lot of money, such men were very valuable to the company.

The two *Levants* and the *Sentinel* were too small for deep water repairs, i.e., over 500 fathoms (half a mile). When the larger ships had to hook an unbroken cable in deep water there would not be enough slack to bring it to the surface. So a special grapnel was used which gripped the cable on one side and cut it automatically on the other. You had to grapple for the other end, but at least you got one end at the first hook.

The common accuracy of testing was about half a nautical mile and the navigational accuracy in those days was of the same order. So usually you were not more than a mile out altogether which is pretty accurate for the open sea. Where you could take bearings and ranges from fixed points on land greater accuracy was possible. Range-finders

Group photograph Stray, Bristow, Hannaford, Spratt, Lawson, Henderson and the dog old Bill.

had not been fitted in 1919 but they were supplied in the next couple of years. The larger ships had searchlights mounted in a crows nest on the foremast.

The strains on ropes and cable were indicated by dynamometers with scales marked in tons and cwts and the large drums on the cable engines used for picking up and paying out had revolution counters from whose readings the lengths of rope and cable were calculated. When on cable work the junior electricians, and sometimes the senior jointers, kept continuous watch with the ship's navigating officers and recorded in a log book everything that happened; lengths of rope used, cable picked up and paid out, etc. This log book, together with the test room log was used by the chief electrician when compiling the report which was read by the captain in case he wished to add anything.

According to the company's rule book, the captain and chief electrician had to consult together as to each step in the work. The co-operation was quite good, but the captain could have the last word.

We returned to Malta and after taking coal and stores, left for the Messina Straits. There were five telegraph cables across these straits belonging to the Italian government. Under an agreement with our company they were maintained by us in exchange for the landing rights of the two Malta Sicily cables. Before I joined, the ship had been in the Messina Straits repairing them as they had all got broken or faulty during the war, and it had not been possible to mend them.

Bob Spratt and I went ashore with testing gear to the cable-house to locate the faults in the three cables still to be mended. They ran across the narrowest part of the straits at the north end, the Scylla and Charybdis of classical times. At the Messina side (Charybdis) there was a martello tower the ground floor of which was used as a cablehouse.

The next day we started repairing the cables and were there about two weeks, returning to harbour at night.

We went several evenings to performances of comic operas at the local theatre, taking a box for the five of us.

The Italian cableship *Citta Di Milano* was working in the Straits. They operated their ship differently to us. She was classed as a warship in the Italian navy and manned by naval officers and crew. But she also carried cable electricians, jointers and odd cable hands who did the actual cable work but were civilians from the Pirelli cable factory at Spezia. They were led by Signor E. Jona, an eminent cable engineer, who was over sixty years of age.

Bob Spratt told me of an interesting occurrence on the *Levant II's* earlier visit to Messina. Having hooked one of the broken cables and buoyed the good end, she was picking up to the break when suddenly all sorts of flotsam in the shape of clothing and pieces of wood came to the surface and a heavy strain was registered which suddenly was released and the end came on board. This looked as if it had been cut with some sharp instrument. On enquiry from the Italians, it was learned that a ship had been torpedoed near there during the war. It seemed likely that it went down on top of the cable.

During these repairs I landed at Bagnara on the Italian mainland where the cables came on shore. This has a beach with the road and railway to Reggio on a ledge of the inland hills just north of Scylla. It was on this beach that the British army has twice landed, once during the Napoleonic wars and again under General Montgomery in 1943.

In due course we completed the repairs to these cables and returned to Malta. Soon after we read in the newspapers that the *Citta di Milano* had sunk with the loss of over twenty lives including Signor Jona. We were naturally shocked with this news.

A week later we were told by head office that the *Levant II* had been chartered by the Italians to do a number of repairs for them and we were to proceed to Palermo in north Sicily to pick up their representative, Signor Del Grande, who would have the charts and cable data. Head office said that as we had no room on board for him, he would have to return on shore each night.

After coaling we set out for Palermo where we arrived the next day. There was no sign of Signor Del Grande and we got involved in an imbroglio with the Italian Customs who demanded to see our manifest of cargo. It was explained that we did not carry cargo, only stock cable. They then said: "Ah you are a cable ship and belong to the Navy." We said: "No, we are a merchant ship." They said: "Then you must have a manifest." Complete deadlock and they put a guard on the ship, while the captain and Spratt went ashore to find Del Grande. They returned with him and the matter was cleared up.

Signor Del Grande was a short, slightly stout man. He spoke little or no English but knew French which Spratt could get along with, and Alec Henderson helped with his Italian. He had been on board the *Milano* when she sank but was rather reticent about what exactly happened.

Next day we went out of Palermo harbour and anchored off a beach to the west, called Mondello, where the cable landed. We had to renew the beach end and trench it from the cablehouse to the water's edge. This was rather fun as the beach was crowded with bathers of both sexes who were interested in what we were doing, and came and talked to us as a good many could speak English.

The ship went from there to the island of Ustica, a convict settlement about forty miles north of Palermo. We arrived on a Sunday afternoon and soon a boatload of local inhabitants, men and women, was rowing round us, so we invited them on board.

One of them was an Italian soldier in a smart grey uniform and cape with a red lining. He addressed us in fluent English with an American accent and told us he had lived for two or three years in New York. We gave them some wine and had a good party.

Alec Henderson used to buy a red wine produced in Cyprus and sold in Malta in large jars. A jug of it was always on our table at lunch and dinner for anyone to help themselves. After we returned to Palermo the steward came to me and said a man had brought a dozen large bottles of white Chianti for us. It turned out it was a present from Del Grande.

We carried out several repairs to cables in the Lipari Islands and went ashore on some of them. One, called Vulcano, had the hillside covered in yellow sulphur with smoke rising from it. The whole area is volcanic with two major volcanos, Etna on Sicily and Stromboli on an island north of the Messina straits.

We then went to the south of Sicily to repair a cable from Mazara to the island of Pantelleria, 140 miles north east of Malta. This proved troublesome as the fault was difficult to locate. While grappling for it, we raised a cable and decided to underrun it. A large sheave is lowered over the bows on a wire rope and the cable put into it. The ship then steams along slowly with the cable running over the sheave and back into the water, so that every yard can be examined. This can only be done in shallow water, say 20 or 30 fathoms, and fine weather. This cable began to go in the wrong direction and we realised we had got the wrong one. It was our own Gibraltar to Malta No. 3 cable and not the Italian one at all. We radioed Malta and they reported it was working normally so we hastily dropped it and were lucky not to have damaged it.

The charting of cables in the wrong place happens now and then. It is usually due to the original laying vessel being inaccurate in its navigation owing to bad weather and/or ocean currents. One of my later chiefs told me of the prize case of this in the Greek islands. There was a short cable between two islands. Between them was a small automatic lighthouse on a rock. The chart showed the cable running north of the lighthouse but it was subsequently found that it ran on the south.

We had nearly run out of coal, water and food. We only had a large ice chest so we soon finished our fresh meat. Our steward opened a large tin of corned beef and Del Grande's eyes almost popped when he saw it. He told us that in Milan where his home was they only got meat one day a week. The ship returned to Malta to replenish and Bob Spratt took Del Grande to see the local sights, as he had never been there before.

At Naples I took a ship's boat with testing apparatus to a small bay to the north where the cables landed. It was lucky for me not to have gone to the *Amber;* the reason was that as the *Levant II* had only two navigating officers, we electricians (and especially me, the second) often took charge of boats. In the larger ships the second or third officer would do this. So I soon learned how to steer and handle oared cutters going ashore and coming alongside the ship in all weathers, experience one did not get elsewhere.

Having set up the test gear in the cable house, I returned to the ship. Owing to Naples having an electric tramway system, we could only test cables at night. This was common near all towns with trams. Leakage earth currents upset our delicate galvanometers.

Soon after we left Naples and went to the island of Capri. It was found that the chart of the cable we had to repair had not arrived from Spezia, so Del Grande took the ferry back to Naples to see about it and we had four days at Capri with no jobs.

The first evening Alec, Spratt and I went ashore for a walk and then to a café in the lower town. We were sitting at a table when a gentleman came over and said: "Hello Spratt, what are you doing here?" Spratt explained and introduced him as Mr Mackenzie. It seems they had known each other in Greece during the war. Spratt invited him to lunch on the ship. After he had gone Spratt said: "You know, that was Compton Mackenzie, the novelist".

He had lunch with us the next day and invited the five of us to dinner with him the following evening. He explained that as his house was three or four miles away, we would dine at a large café in the upper town.

We went by the funicular railway to the upper town and found the café. He introduced us to his wife, Faith, and two other ladies. One a

Mrs Campbell and the other a pretty American girl, the wife of the American vice-consul in Naples. We had aperitifs on the verandah and dinner in a private room. I do not think I had laughed so much for many years. Our host and his wife, ably assisted by Spratt, Lawson and the others kept up a continuous flow of amusing and witty conversation throughout the dinner and evening. I remember being introduced to octopus as a dinner dish but did not think much of it, and still do not. We eventually got back on board rather late. We were not able to return the Mackenzies' hospitality but Spratt did send him several bottles of gin — then in short supply in Capri.

The next day I was bathing from the ship after tea when Alec suggested I come with him in a hired boat to see the Blue Grotto. So I went as I was, and when we got inside by pulling the boat through the opening, dived into the water and swam about. The blue lighting effect comes from light which goes down into the sea outside and is reflected upwards from under the hanging outer wall of the cave.

Finally we said goodbye to Del Grande in Naples. I had learned from him a lot of Italian technical terms about cable repairing. I had had to do a great deal of calculation as all the Italian cable data was given in international ohms whereas we used the British Association ohm. The two ohms are only fractionally different, but it makes a difference when you have a lot of them.

While at Naples we saw H.M.S. *Iron Duke*, flagship of the Mediterranean Fleet and other British Warships, and the town was full of sailors in the evenings. On our return to Malta the port authorities said we had to be quarantined for a week on account of smallpox at Naples. So we asked them whether they had quarantined the *Iron Duke* which was also back. This seemed to upset them — perhaps they had tried to — and eventually they allowed us to go ashore.

After our Italian tour we were sent to the Greek islands to do repairs there and passed through the Gulfs of Patras and Corinth and through the Corinth Canal. This is about five miles long but has very steep and, in the middle, high sides subject to landslips. It can only take ships of up to about 4,000 tons. It was started in the Roman Emperor Nero's time but only finished in the last century.

We called at the Piraeus, the port of Athens, and then went on to the island of Syra. This was our largest station in Greece with cables radiating to the Dardanelles (for Constantinople), Salonica, Crete and Egypt, and other places.

The company's extensive Greek system was controlled by a divisional manager who had a minature head office in Athens. When cableships from elsewhere went there, they came under his orders. At that time the divisional manager was Commander Cottrell RNVR.

Our superintendent at Syra was Mr Hastings who was also British consul. His wife was a sister of Bob Spratt and we were hospitably entertained at their house. The Spratt family was very much a company one. Bob's father had been superintendent at Gibraltar before Hodgson, and of his older brothers, one was the company's representative at the cable factory at Greenwich of the Telegraph Construction and Maintenance Co who supplied most of our stock cable, and the other was a supervisor.

On our way back to Malta we went to Zante in the Ionian islands off the west coast of Greece, where there are many estates growing the small grapes which are dried and exported as currants for our Christmas puddings. When Corfu and the Ionian islands were returned by the British to Greece in the 19th century by Gladstone, he went to Corfu to hand them over and is reported to have made a speech in Greek which none of his audience could understand — it being in classical Greek.

Mr Sergeant was British vice consul at Zante and he and his Greek wife invited us to their town house. Sergeant made some splendid wines from the grapes grown on his country estate and gave us some whenever we visited him.

The inhabitants of Zante are very proud of their beautiful island

Zante, Ionian Islands.

which they described as "Zante, fleur de Levante". On the nearby island of Cephalonia there lived an Irish family called O'Toole who made a fine brandy from the local grapes and we were able to obtain some.

At Corfu I was taken on a country walk by Hannaford to One Gun Battery which looks down on a bay with a small island with a church on it, called Ulysses Island. The people of Corfu still play cricket and have a ground almost in the town.

When we got back to Malta, Captain Lawson was relieved by Captain Sherwood, a tall handsome man. He was very pleasant and I liked him. While at Malta I was able to have one or two games of cricket by invitation from the shore staff, and I joined a small tennis club in Sliema. The cableship *Electra* was often in Malta at the same time as we were and I became friendly with her second officer, Howard, a rather lanky, fair-haired young man. "Driver" Briggs from the *Amber* was also in the *Electra,* Captain Smythe, a rather stout jolly man, commanded her.

While in Malta we heard the story of a row between *Electra* and *Sentinel.* The former had commenced a repair and buoyed one end of the cable when head office ordered her to leave it for a more important job. The *Sentinel* was sent later to finish the repair. When picking up the *Electra's* cable buoy, the mooring rope parted. Captain Hunter of *Sentinel* sent an irate message to *Electra* complaining that her buoy rope was rotten. In reply Captain Smythe sent an ironic message saying, "Congratulate you on smart repair." This form of message was occasionally sent by head office to a cableship which had done an especially rapid repair.

A number of the shore staff had been with me in Porthcurnow and Gibraltar and invited me to their messes so I had a busy social life. The shore staff always seemed to think that we ship's men made whoopee when we came ashore. Perhaps we did. At sea life was very austere which they probably did not appreciate. We often had to work long hours with no over-time pay. So we were given a good deal of leave when in port, as long as we did the work needed there.

Soon after we got orders to go to Suez to lay some new shore ends. This was unusual for *Levant II* but it seems the Red Sea ship, the *Cambria*, was very busy down south and out in the Indian ocean.

We had about five days passage to Port Said and went through the Suez Canal to Port Tewfik at the south end. I sat up half the night as I did not want to miss anything, and the night passage with a searchlight

"Cable at the bows", on sliding-prong grapnel.

Putting on chain "stoppers".

Heaving cable on board, Chief Officer Hannaford.

Back: Greek engineer and Bristow; front: Three of Greek crew.

installed by the canal company at our bows intrigued me very much. Ships travelled singly in those days and not in convoy as they do now. We had to tie up to the bank once to let the homeward bound P & O mailship pass, but we passed one or two smaller ships without stopping.

On arrival at Port Tewfik we learned that we were to assist Captain Patterson to shift five shore ends from near Suez Town to a new cablehouse two or three miles further south round the bay. A new harbour was being built for oil tankers to discharge and load close to the two refineries south of the town.

We were at Suez for two or three weeks and most days were out in the bay laying new shore ends and transferring the Red Sea cables to them, one at a time so as not to interrupt the cable traffic. I spent nearly every evening at the Suez staff mess which was similar to the one at Gibraltar, and had a jolly time. Captain Sherwood's father-in-law was a canal pilot living at Port Tewfik and we were invited to his house and also went on a moonlight picnic in the desert when I escorted Queenie, a sister of Mrs Sherwood — a very pretty and jolly girl of about my age. There was an RAF station at Suez and we met several of their officers at our mess and had one or two rowdy parties. Prosser, my old Gibraltar cricket captain, was in Suez and I met him and his wife again there.

We finished at last and went back through the Canal to Port Said, taking with us Sherwood's father-in-law, and making the trip all in one day. The canal is ninety-nine miles long, and pilots are changed half way at Ismailia.

We got orders to mend the broken Port Said to Alexandria cable. Spratt sent me ashore with testing gear to set it up in the cable house and I had my first tussle with the customs who were doubtful whether this was allowed. I explained it was all coming back on board the next day and they gave in.

After finishing this repair we went to Alexandria and tied up in the harbour. The British port police — three officers — came on board and over drinks told us there had been quite severe rioting in the town the previous day with crowds throwing stones at them.

The captain gave me a letter to take to the superintendent, so I went off in a cab from the docks. The rioting had ceased but it was necessary to keep to the main streets.

At our office I was ushered into Mr W. E. Pender's office by Mr Cambell, the assistant superintendent. Mr Pender was one of the most senior superintendents at this time. He asked me what I was going to do and I told him of my wish to visit the mess. He warned me not to wander alone about the streets.

We left the next day for Syra and ran into very bad weather and I was, as usual, very seasick. Cableships can only mend cables in good weather and in bad weather in the *Levant* it was impossible to do any clerical work or even serve proper meals, so we ate sandwiches, etc. and drank Turkish coffee.

After loading some cable at Syra, we went back west through the Corinth Canal and the gulfs of Corinth and Patras into the Adriatic to repair a cable between Corfu and Otranto in Italy. During the war the Navy had laid an enormous net, with mines attached, right across the southern end of the Adriatic, a distance of about sixty-five miles and a small one about three or four miles long between Corfu island and the Greek mainland. When the war was over these nets had been abandoned and allowed to sink to the bottom of the sea. Unfortunately, the big one was almost on top of part of our Corfu-Otranto cable, but the present repair was north of and well clear of the mined area of the net.

We grappled there for over a week and found the cable in such poor condition that it broke each time, and we soon had a gap about ten miles long. We reported to the divisional manager in Athens and were told to go to Patras and take some stock cable which was stored there. On arrival we found it was in short lengths and had to be spliced up, so we were there for two or three days.

The superintendent at Patras invited us to his house and on arrival for an evening party we were surprised to be offered pink gins. The common aperitif in Greece is oyzo (pronounced ouzo), a colourless spirit which turns white when water is added. Our host explained that he had served on the west coast of Africa which is undoubtedly one of the homes of pink gins. It also turned out that his wife was English having been born in Yorkshire.

We returned to Corfu and Captain Sherwood and Spratt went ashore to see Commander Cottrell, the divisional manager in Greece who had been on leave to England, and was on his way back to Athens. They felt that we should never have been sent on this Corfu-Otranto repair, it being too large a job for our small ship. Commander Cottrell must have agreed because two days later we were told to leave it for another job.

This next job was on a cable from Corfu town up the straits between the island and the mainland to a small island called Fanu, north of

Corfu, where the navy had had a base during the war and from which there was another cable to Otranto. These had been joined through at Fanu after the base was evacuated to provide a second Corfu-Otranto link. The present repair was in the middle of the straits between Corfu and the main-land.

During this job we hooked the anti-submarine net referred to above. This short net was not mined and was harmless but we had rather a job disentangling our grapnel which brought up a bunchy tangle of heavy wire netting.

From Corfu we went to Zante again and spent Christmas there. Mr and Mrs Sergeant invited the five of us to Christmas dinner with them, together with MacTaggart and his wife. MacTaggart was quite a character. Born of Scottish parents in Greece, he had joined the company's local staff.

He had been to school in Belgium and spoke French and Greek fluently, and also some Italian. His English still had the Scottish accent of his family. It was a jolly party and towards the end we all danced round the room holding out our handkerchiefs while we held hands in the Greek manner.

We were also invited to MacTaggart's home, and while there his wife suddenly said, "Look," and pointed to the hanging electric light in the centre of the room which was swinging slightly. It was a very mild earthquake shock. They had a severe earthquake in the 1950's which destroyed half the town.

From Zante we went to Syra and were ordered to take part in the laying of a new cable from Syra to the island of Tenedos, near the entrance to the Dardanelles. We had to lay twenty miles from Syra northward and buoy the end, the rest to be laid by the *Electra*. We completed this job and returned to Syra where we met both *Electra* and *Levant I*.

She had a Greek captain and crew but the ship was commanded by the chief electrician, Herbert Finnis. There were three Finnis brothers. Their father had been chief accountant to the divisional manager at Athens and they had all been born in Greece but educated at English schools and had joined the company. Arthur was then at Syra. Alfred had been at Gib while I was there, but was sent to Athens to work in the DM's office. Herbert had a man called Simmonds as his second electrician in *Levant I*. Simmonds, like MacTaggart, was a Britisher who had been born in Greece and joined the local staff.

With three cablehips in Syra the younger officers made considerable whoopee with various parties on board and on shore. There was a Greek comic opera company there at the time and we went several nights to it.

"Tickey" Eastwood who had been at Porthcurnow with me was now in *Electra* and "Driver" Briggs and Howard were still there. After the theatre we would meet at a local café for drinks and dancing into the small hours.

One night I returned to the ship about 11 p.m. to find it was blowing very hard. A Greek island steamer of about 1,000 tons was moored stern on to the quay next to the *Electra* and we were on the other side of the latter. The Greek ship was dragging her anchor and being blown onto the *Electra* and she down onto us.

I saw Captain Smythe leaning over *Electra's* rail above us and he told me to wake up Captain Sherwood at once. We got several sailors up and put out more ropes to hold the ship from being forced aground on our side where it was shallow. The Greek ship which had caused the trouble had some crates of oranges as deck cargo. Next morning a lot of *Electra's* crew were eating oranges.

We got orders to return to Malta, and that Hannaford was to transfer to *Electra* as chief officer and Lawson was to come to us for the passage there. We left Syra and set out for Malta, and had a very rough passage.

On arrival in Malta we learned that the ship had to be docked for repairs, and when finished she was to return to Greece to relieve the *Levant I* which was to be sold.

Captain Sherwood and Alec Henderson were to stay with the ship during the refit. Then the latter was to go to the *Sentinel.* Bob Spratt was to go to Zanzibar to join the *Sherard Osborne,* Lawson was to return to England and I was to go to Capetown to join the cableship *Britannia.*

In the meantime there was a lot of clerical work for me to do, making out the data for recent repairs. We had done over fifty jobs in the last eleven months, that is more than one a week and steamed about 20,000 miles. A busy time but good experience for a beginner like me.

Spratt was courting so I did not see much of him. Eventually I ran out of work because he got behind with writing reports. When I asked him about this, he said, "Oh you write them. You know how I always do it," I did for I had been typing them up for about a year. So I set to work and wrote up the last few. He read them, altered a few words, sent them to the captain, and I had them back to type.

Meanwhile I asked if I could go to Capetown via the UK so that I could see my parents, and Captain Sherwood passed this on to head office. But they thought otherwise and cabled our station at Carcavellos, near Lisbon, who booked me on a Portuguese ship from there.

The *Levant* had to go to the dockyard so I moved to the Imperial Hotel, Sliema, a quiet hotel at that time. At the next table in the dining room an elderly lady and her daughter were often joined by a young RN lieutenant who was evidently the daughter's fiancé.

I was told I was to travel to Gibraltar on the SS *Teutonic,* a White Star liner now a troopship, and thence by rail to Lisbon. I found that the lady's daughter had been married to her lieutenant and her mother, Mrs Lyndsay, was going to England on the *Teutonic.* So I asked if I could help her with her luggage as I was going to engage a flat cart (commonly used in Malta) to take mine to the Grand Harbour and hers could go as well.

However a Naval Commander approached me and said he had intended taking Mrs Lyndsay and her luggage direct from Sliema in a naval steam picquet boat and going round to the Grand Harbour to put her straight on board the *Teutonic,* and would I care to come too. This is a very handsome way to go on board a ship with lots of sailors to handle your baggage, and we arrived alongside in great style.

CHAPTER FOUR

Cableship "Britannia"

The *Teutonic* was a White Star liner of 15,000 tons and she had held the Blue Riband of the North Atlantic.

There were about 200 passengers in the first class, mostly army officers and wives, and a handful of civilians. She was fitted as a troopship with accommodation for about 1,600 men.

On the after end of the wide promenade deck, a wooden structure had been built to serve as a hospital. It was occupied by about twenty subalterns and I was allotted a berth there.

I am afraid we were a rather noisy lot in that hospital and being the only one not in uniform, I was rather conspicuous in my one and only blue suit. The weather was fine all the way to Gib and I spent a lot of time playing chess in the smokeroom with a young officer who was keen on the game but not much good. I know this because my brother, Miles, had become a good chess player while still a schoolboy. We used to play during holidays and he always beat me.

We arrived at Gib about 6 p.m. and moored at the south mole in the Admiralty harbour. After dinner I got a pass from the purser to go ashore and climbed up the hill to our quarters and called on "Chutney" Hodgson, my old superintendent.

He had been advised that I was coming and told me to go to our town office in the morning and they would get me ferry and rail tickets for Lisbon from Thomas Cook's.

I had met a handsome army captain and his pretty wife on the ship who told me they were disembarking at Gibraltar and going by train to Paris. He asked how I was going to get my baggage to the town — a mile or so from the south mole gates which were themselves about a quarter of a mile from the ship. I was not sure myself but had an idea. In the Gib. dockyard there were a number of two-wheeled carts each drawn by a mule with a Spanish driver. I accosted two drivers with

Albatross caught unharmed and later released.

empty carts and offered them some cash to ferry our luggage to the Dockyard gates. We hired two cabs, put all the baggage in them, ourselves took a third and drove to the Bristol Hotel where they would stay the night.

I collected my Cook's tickets to Lisbon and went to Algeciras on the ferry about 4 p.m. I found the Anglo Hispano hotel was full and they told me that the large, posh hotel, the Reina Cristina was also full. But they said they could get me a room for the night at a Spanish pension. I caught the train early next morning for Seville.

It was a slow one, stopping everywhere, and we got to Seville after dark, where I put up at the hotel Ingleterra. The next day I got the train for Badajoz on the Portuguese frontier. There was a night train leaving for Lisbon at 8 p.m. so I caught that after telegraphing our superintendent at Carcavellos. There were no sleepers and I had to sit up all night in a crowded carriage.

At Lisbon there was a company's messenger to meet me and I was taken to the Angleterre Hotel, and afterwards to our Lisbon branch office where I met Mr Mellish, the officer-in-charge. He replenished my purse and told me that my ship to Capetown was not expected to leave for about a week.

At the hotel I met a young man about two or three years older called Jackson. He took me to an English tea shop the next day and who should come in but Mellish who said, "You haven't taken long to find this place." It seemed to be a haunt of English businessmen in Lisbon of whom there were a good many.

The next day I took a train to Carcavellos to see our superintendent. It is eight miles west of Lisbon on the north side of the Tagus estuary and was an important cable station.

It was one of the best stations in the company as far as the staff was concerned. There were facilities for most games and a good bathing place, and one could get into Lisbon town while living in pleasant country surroundings.

Lisbon is a handsome city. The main square is paved with coloured flag stones in such a way as to make them look like the waves of the sea. It was known to the English as "Rolly Motions Square", and is said to make some people feel seasick.

After eight days I embarked on the Portuguese ship *India* with several others in the hotel. She was 8,000 tons and carried eighty passengers in first class.

Besides Jackson and myself there were two other young men about our age. One was going out to be accountant at the Carlton Hotel in Johannesburg, and the other was a South African who had been at college in England and was going home. Then there was a Englishman and his wife who belonged to the Bank of London and South America and were going out to a bank job in Lourençomarques, the capital of Portuguese East Africa. I met him again in 1930 when I went there myself. There was the Moreillon family. He was a bearded Swiss missionary doctor, his wife was English and they had three delightful little girls who ran about the ship chattering in both French and English. They were going to a mission station in East Griqualand in South Africa. There was a rich Portuguese planter from Angola returning there with his half-and-half wife, rather a pretty woman and several children, and an assortment of other Portuguese going to either Angola or Mozambique. There were two American engineers, one a thin gaunt man representing a firm making tractors, and the other worked for the Rapson Company who made lifts and office equipment.

I shared a cabin with a fat German engineer who had been running a sugar refinery in East Africa before the war. He had been interned and was returning to a similar job. He suffered from an inferiority complex vis-a-vis the British, the result, I suppose, of Germany losing the war.

After leaving Lisbon, our first port of call was Madeira where we stayed about two days.

Beyond Madeira we stopped for about an hour off the Salvage Islands about half way to the Canaries. We landed a couple of passengers by a boat which came off from the shore. We then went on the Las Palmas where we stayed two days.

I went ashore with a party from our ship and we explored the town, visited the Cathedral and saw all the sights — not many of them in those days as few tourists stayed there. However, hordes of men came down to the ship selling the local wares, mostly lace, linen, jewellery and similar things. I bought a handsome drawn thread bedspread which I sent home to my parents. They asked if we had any gold sovereigns to sell and offered us thirty shillings each for them — a good price in those days.

We left Las Palmas and had a long trip round the West African coast and into the Gulf of Guinea until we reached the Portuguese island of San Thomé. The ceremony associated with crossing the Equator was apparently not celebrated in Portuguese ships. I had my 21st birthday but that was not celebrated either.

San Thomé is a small island which grows a lot of cocoa. It is covered in tropical vegetation. Our company had two subsidiaries, the African Direct and the West African Telegraph Companies which had a chain of stations on the coast from Bathurst in the Gambia to the north, down to Angola in the south, and San Thomé was one of them.

At San Thomé we took on board 200 Africans as deck passengers. They had been recruited in Lourenço Marques for work on the cocoa plantations and were being sent back home.

After leaving there we came to Luanda, the capital of Angola. The town is at the south end of a lagoon two miles long and half a mile wide, enclosed by a narrow sand spit running parallel to the shore with the entrance at the north end. It makes a splendid harbour and is deep enough to take ships up to about 15,000 tons. There were no piers or quays there in 1920 and we anchored off the town to discharge passengers and cargo.

After a couple of days we left for Lobito Bay. This is the terminus of the Benguela railway, and the harbour is similar to that at Luanda, being a long wide lagoon with a sand spit on the seaward side, but it is even larger and has a small pier where we went alongside to unload cargo. The small town consisted mostly of railway workshops and bungalows for the staff. The railway was built by the British and still had many British engineers in 1920. About eighteen miles inland is the town of Benguela, through which the railway runs, and on for about 600 miles to the Katanga border.

We stayed here about five days and were able to bathe in the lagoon at an enclosure made for the railway staff with stout nets to keep out the odd shark.

About 400 miles south of Lobito Bay and just south of the border between Angola and South West Africa, is Cape Frio. After passing this the water temperature falls rapidly due to the Benguela current running north from Capetown and the Antarctic.

We arrived in Capetown on Good Friday and I was met by Stevens, my old acquaintance from the cableship *Amber* in Gibraltar, who was third engineer of *Britannia.* My new chief, Mr Hancock, appeared, and we all went on board where I was taken down to see Captain Boyd, an elderly bearded man, who then said to Hancock, "We will sail tomorrow at 8 a.m."

I learned that during my lengthy journey from Malta, various new arrangements had been decided by head office. I was originally to relieve Last, the third electrician. But, meanwhile, it had been decided that the cableship *Transmitter* (of 900 tons, built in 1914) normally stationed at Freetown in Sierra Leone, should come to Capetown for a refit. Her chief electrician, H. E. N. Evans, was due for leave. As she was expected soon, Perry the second electrician of *Britannia* was ordered to stay in Capetown to relieve him. I was now to relieve both Perry and Last, and another junior electrician would be sent out later.

However, the Capetown-Mossamedes cable was broken about 200 miles north of Capetown and they had waited for my arrival to go on the job. Stevens suggested we should have a bathe after lunch. He took me by hansom cab to where the tramway ran round the coast on the west side of the Cape peninsular. There was a hackney carriage stand with old hansom cabs near an old wooden jetty. The other side of it was used by the harbour tugs, as it had no cargo cranes on it like the other berths in the docks.

We went on the single-decker tram to Camps Bay about five miles south where there was a built out open air swimming pool heated by the cooling water of the tramway power station. Outside the pool the sea water was very cold, about 50 degrees F. The sea was always cold on the west side of the peninsular on account of the Benguela current. On the east side, in False Bay, it was quite warm, at least in the summer.

I found I had a most palatial cabin in *Britannia*. She was an old iron ship of 1,525 tons built in 1885 for the Telegraph Construction and Maintenance Co and sold to the Eastern Telegraph Co in 1904. Her deckhouses were made of teak, unlike the usual steel ones.

The dining saloon ran right across the ship aft and from it a wide central alleyway ran to the stern with two cabins on each side. On the starboard side were the captain's day and sleeping cabins with bathroom, and on the port side were the chief and second electricians' cabins. Mine was the one at the stern and right over the port propeller. It was almost square and had a settee bunk, desk and wardrobe with the usual folding washbasin.

Forward of the saloon there were two alleyways with cabins on either side, nearly to the bows. The cable test room was forward amidships on the same deck, called the main deck. The wireless cabin and chartroom and a tiny sea cabin for the captain were in a deckhouse under the bridge on the upper deck. She was a well arranged and comfortable ship to live in. She had three cable tanks and the cable engine was on the main deck under hatch covers — taken off when in use to disclose the tops of the cable drums and controlled from the upper deck which was open except for awnings amidships and aft. She had the usual clipper bows with sheaves in it and a long cross yard arm on the foremast for handling cable buoys. All our cableships were painted white with yellow funnels and looked very yacht-like.

Britannia left Capetown as planned and we arrived at the cable repair next day.

As we had only two electricians, Hancock and I had a strenuous time for the next ten days or so. Except on two occasions when the weather was bad it meant we had to work shifts of 4 hours on and 4 hours off, and we got pretty tired. Our jointer called Fleming was competent and helped with some of the dock watches while grappling to get hold of the ends. We had to do hour after hour of this, day after day, as we found the cable was so rotten that it broke time and again. From previous records this might be expected as the ocean floor on this stretch of coast had large amounts of sulphur on the bottom and this corroded the cable sheathing wires so that sections had to be renewed about every twenty years. The original cable had been laid about 1889 to connect Capetown with the West African system, laid some years before.

On watches I soon got to know the deck officers. Captain Boyd was a bachelor and near retiring age, but very sociable and loved entertaining.

Unrigging a cable buoy, note sailor removing oil lamps.

If you had a guest to dinner who might be older than you, or perhaps a lady, the captain would appropriate him or her and take over the party. At least it would save your ship's wine bill a bit. He had one regular habit. Every morning he would put his keys in his left trouser pocket. At eight bells (8 a.m.) the 2nd Officer would report to him, "Chronometers wound, sir." He would then transfer his keys to his right hand pocket. No doubt he had long before learned that accurate navigation depended on the chronometers having a steady rate and this is achieved by the same person winding them at the same time each day. He had had a very long career in cableships. He told me that years before when he was a young officer, Lord Kelvin, who had played a considerable part in early submarine cable work, came for a voyage in his ship.

Kelvin invented the type of magnetic compass which became standard on most ships (it was called the "standard compass") and also the sounding machine known by his name.

The chief officer, Gooch, was a shortish man but cheerful and competent. The second officer, Dillon, was also not very tall. He was a South African who had originally joined the Western Telegraph Co's cableships before World War I and served in South America. He was on leave when the war broke out and immediately joined the army. Later he was sent to India and someone found out he had been a cableship officer so they sent him to the Persian Gulf to Basra in the Government cableship *Patrick Stewart*. When the war was over he returned home to Capetown and got a job in *Britannia*.

The third officer, Clark, was a tall thin man. He was married and had a wife in Capetown. Hancock also had his wife there as had May, the chief engineer, a very staid but good looking middle aged man. Taylor was second engineer, Stevens, my friend from *Amber*, third engineer, and there were two young men as fourth and fifth engineers. The Doctor was called Anderton, a cheerful rubicund man in middle age, and a good doctor as I found out later.

Then there was Perryman, the purser, a tall young man, very cheery and mad about fast motor bikes. We had British petty officers — a bosun, carpenter and bosun's mates and a cable engine driver and Fleming, the jointer and his mate, O'Hehir. They had a small mess of their own. The crew, sailors and stewards, were all from St Helena and a few firemen, known as kroomen from an African tribe in West Africa who came for a year or two.

When the weather was fine and we were grappling at slow speed, Perryman and the young engineers amused themselves by catching albatross of which there are many in these latitudes.

If you trail on a line over the stern a six inch metal triangle — like a motor road sign — with corks attached to make it float and a piece of fish or meat on it, an albatross will grab it. His beak having a curved end, gets entangled and he can be hoisted on board. They seem unable to fly off the deck at all—they have webbed feet. We did not hurt them, though they used to make savage pecks at us. We held their wings open to show their size, six feet or so, took photographs, and then dropped them overboard. Once on the water, they could fly off easily. It is supposed by sailors to be very unlucky to kill them.

We finally got one end of the cable and spliced on and paid out ten miles and buoyed it to make sure of having one good end. We had a further thirty miles of new cable to lay to close the gap before we got the job finished.

On returning to Capetown, we found the cableship *Transmitter* had arrived and berthed at No. 1 jetty. We tied up near her in the morning. Hancock told me that we had to take some cable from her and it would take until midnight. One of us would have to be on watch throughout. After coaling and taking stores we were ordered to proceed to St. Helena so as to be in a more central position to cover both ships' beats which together stretched from Cape Verde to Capetown. All I wanted was to buy a few toilet necessities and Mr Hancock said he would relieve me from 4 p.m. to 6 p.m. His wife being there, he wanted to get home as we would be away for a month or two.

I went over to *Transmitter* and met Izard, my opposite number and we arranged about watching the cable transfer which was just starting. Mr Hancock went ashore and returned at 4 p.m. to relieve me. Just as I was going ashore, Dillon appeared, said he was going too and would I like him to show me around the town. So we took a hansom cab and arrived in Adderley Street, the famous main street of Capetown. Shopping finished, Dillon suggested a tram ride to Wynburg, a suburb a few miles north. The trams had overhead wires and while the route was mostly double tracked, there were stretches of single track. As we neared the end of one of these, we saw a tram coming in the opposite direction which, instead of stopping at the double track, come on straight for us, the driver shouting that he could not stop. We stopped but before the conductor could pull the trolley arm off, the two trams met head on though the other was slowing down. Dillon and I were on the top open deck and we braced ourselves for the crash but it was not severe. Our tram then pushed the other tram into its place on the double track, reversed and went on its way. As we did so we saw the other driver try to re-start which brought flames out of his controller box.

The next day we sailed for St Helena where we arrived in eight days, a distance of 2,000 miles. The west coast of Africa cable route had been completed in 1889 and ten years later — at the time of the Boer War — the company had laid a direct route to Capetown via the Cape Verde Islands, Ascension and St Helena. The speed or word capacity of telegraph cables varied inversely as the square of the length, so island relay stations were used whenever possible.

Everyone knows what St Helena is famous for, but it is an out of the way spot so its other aspects are not so well known. Jamestown, the capital, is situated at the seaward end of a valley in the rocky hills which form most of the island. There is no harbour, only an open anchorage with a landing place near the castle. This is an old fort built many years ago which has a moat on the seaward side. It then conveniently accommodated two hard tennis courts. On the right looking from the sea, the hillside is called Ladder Hill, because there is a wooden ladder which runs straight up its steep side with 499 steps. The main street with houses, a few shops and the government administration buildings, leads straight up the valley and ends in a road which gradually climbs up the left side. There is a fork road to the right which goes up Ladder Hill with hairpin bends. The left hand road comes, at a height of about 500 feet, to a small cluster of buildings which constitute the Eastern Telegraph Co's cable station. The superintendent's house, called "The Briars", was where Napoleon spent his first few days in St Helena. There was a bachelors' mess and tennis courts, and one or two houses for married staff. From here one had a splendid view down the valley to Jamestown and the sea.

Apart from growing vegetables for local consumption, a great deal of flax was produced, especially during World War I. Later on when world prices dropped, there was considerable distress among the islanders, and the British government had to make grants in their aid. They are very multi-racial. There were many negroes brought from Africa, and they mixed with the military garrison so that the colour of St Helenans varies from nearly black to white. They were a cheerful crowd and much devoted to cricket. There were several teams who competed in a league.

We soon met Mr Soloman, a business man who grew flax, was Union Castle Line agent and our shipping agent. The Union Castle Line's intermediate steamers used to call there once a month each way. In the old days sailing ships called regularly and the remains of a wrecked one was visible in the anchorage.

Mr Soloman, a tall rather handsome man of about thirty-five, was a good tennis player and we soon started playing regularly in the castle moat. Down the wall there was a ladder like a ship's accommodation ladder from the quarters of the resident magistrate, Mr Stephens. He was a sort of Pooh-Bah of Jamestown as he was also postmaster, with savings bank, and held various other government jobs. He came to watch us playing tennis and invited us to his quarters for drinks. So I invited him to dine on board a few days later.

One morning I was talking to Dillon and told him I intended next Sunday to take some sandwiches and climb a rather conspicuous hill on the western edge of the island called, from its shape, Sugar Loaf Hill.

We set off and after reaching the top, stopped for lunch and then continued until we reached Longwood Plain. We called on the Diesens who ran a farm and they gave us tea, and we returned to Jamestown via the hill road. After that Dillon and I did other walks on Sundays. We even walked up the ladder on Ladder Hill.

There were no motor cars or even motor bikes on the island in those days, only horses and a few carriages. I decided on Sunday to try riding so I hired a horse from Mr Warren who kept the chemist shop in Jamestown. He also had a country house and kindly invited me to tea. I had a good ride up to Longwood and then on to his house at tea time and later rode back to the town, but some of the going was very steep.

Our stay in St Helena came to an end when we were ordered to proceed to Principe Island in the Gulf of Guinea; and repair the cable broken nearby. This was a run of 1,500 miles.

We found the job involved repair of the end near the beach. This was in a narrow creek with palm trees and tropical vegetation all around, and we took two of the ship's boats. A Portuguese planter appeared and told us he ran an estate where they produced cocoa. He showed us the pods from which it is extracted which were growing on surrounding trees. It was all very interesting to me as this was the first time I had been on a tropical island.

When we had finished we returned to St Helena. But we only had about a week there before we got orders to go to Luanda in Angola for another repair. This was a run of 1,350 miles. After completing the job, we had a couple of days in Luanda, coaling and getting fresh provisions. Our officer-in-charge there took us to play tennis on two new cement tennis courts, and it was noticeable that they had been laid with a slight but definite slope to one side. This had been done to allow water from showers to run off rapidly and let the surface dry quickly. I have never seen this done elsewhere. One would think it would affect one's play but it did not seem to make much difference.

To the south side of the town there was some rising ground and they had made a deep cutting through the hillside. This was to allow the prevailing southerly winds to blow through and keep the place cool.

From Luanda we got orders to return to Capetown, an 1,800 mile run. Dillon asked me whether I would like to go up Table Mountain. He had a friend who went up frequently on Sundays and knew all the ropes, and he would arrange for us to go with him.

Capetown has the most splendid situation of any town I have seen, not excepting Naples of which it is said, "See Naples and die." I have seen pictures of Rio de Janeiro and San Francisco but I do not think that they beat Capetown. It is the massive size of the main flat topped mountain with its two flanking hills, Devils Peak on the left and Lions Head on the right, overshadowing the town, harbour and bay, to a height of 3,550 feet, that makes it so impressive. The town creeps up the lower slopes to a belt of woodland and above that the mountain rises almost sheer. About the centre of the cliffs, there is a deep cleft running parallel to the front and hardly noticeable unless pointed out. This is Platte Klip Gorge and is the only way up the face unless you are a rock climber with a rope.

We left the ship about 6 a.m. and got a taxi to the residence of Dillon's friend, Douglas Cairncross, a good-looking, wiry chap about 6 feet tall, aged about twenty-six years.

Behind the main north face of Table Mountain, it stretches back for some miles in a succession of ridges with shallow valleys in between. On the west side these ridges stand out as twelve bluffs, called the Twelve Apostles which face the Atlantic. Running along the hillside just below the bluffs is a footpath known as the Pipe Track because buried next to it is a large water main. This takes water from the reservoirs at the back of the mountain top down and through the cleft between it and Lions Head to two open reservoirs above the town.

Cairncross, Dillon and I walked up to this cleft, known as Kloof Nek, and then along the Pipe Track to the second gap between the Twelve Apostles where we started to climb up it. It is called Blinkwater Gorge, but jocularly known as Stinkwater Gorge. About half way up there is a waterfall, Cairncross warned us to be careful as someone had fallen and been killed there recently.

We followed an upward path and soon reached the top of the mountain which is flat. We went to the front edge and saw the magnificent view of the town, docks and Table Bay below with Robbin Island and its north shore in the distance, and the Blauwberg Hills beyond. To the left was Lions Head, the top about 1,500 feet below us and Signal Hill stretching from it towards the Bay.

Near this point there is now a large concrete building which is a restaurant and the upper station of the cableway. Two passenger cars ascend and descend simultaneously in about ten minutes. So you can now get to the top by the motor road via Kloof Nek without walking at all. But in 1920 and for nine years afterwards, if you wanted to see this

A picnic on the slopes of Table Mountian. Jack Stray, Douglas Cairncross, Frank Smythe, Sylvia and Dixie.

Walking round the coast road with Douglas, Jack, Sylvia, Frank and Effie Smale.

splendid view, you had to walk all the way up.

We went along the two mile flat top to the eastern end where there is a mound of stones called Maclear's Beacon which is the highest point, 3,550 feet above sea leavel.

When there is a south east wind a white cloud settles on the flat mountain top and hangs down for several hundreds of feet over the face, resembling a tablecloth hence the name. The south east winds also sweep down into the town with great force. There is a fable about the table cloth according to which there was a Dutch farmer called Van Dyck who lived on the slopes of Devils Peak. He used to sit on his stoep and smoke a great pipe. The Devil visited him and they had a competition to see who could keep his pipe going the longest, and the smoke settled on the mountain, causing the tablecloth. As neither won, they are still smoking.

After a picnic lunch we explored some of the small valleys at the back of the mountain before returning. We began our descent down Platte Klip Gorge which is very steep. The lack of proper nails on the soles of my boots caused me to slip and more than once to land on my back. We got to the bottom of the gorge at last and entered the woods. There one could see hundreds of fireflies, each one a tiny sparkle of light, which was fascinating.

We reached "Beech Hurst", where Cairncross lived and he said we must come in and have a sundowner before returning to the ship. The house had a drive with two entrances, and as we reached the eastern one, we saw a car enter the other. I was introduced by Cairncross to his sister, Sylvia, and her companion Percy Bowyer.

We all went inside and up to Cairncross's room, which adjoined that of his sister and mother. "Beech Hurst" was then a private hotel. It was built in the lower part of the grounds of a larger house called "Leewenhof", a very old Dutch house built in the 17th century by Van de Stel, the governor of the Cape. I learned later that it had been the home of the Cairncross family until the death in 1918 of Lt Colonel T. W. Cairncross, the husband of Mrs Cairncross. Some years later both houses were bought by the South African government. They pulled "Beech Hurst" down, renovated "Leewenhof" in the old Dutch style, and it is now the official residence of the administrator of the Cape Province.

Sylvia Cairncross was a girl of twenty-three years of age, very pretty with golden hair. We all had drinks and I was invited to visit them again later. I learned that in 1914 Sylvia had been at Cape Town University studying for a medical degree, but had immediately joined as a VAD (mis-stating her age) and went to East Africa on active service until the end of the war. She was now working in the office of the Child Life Protection Society.

Not long after Dillon and I went up to "Beech Hurst" in the evening to see the Cairncross family. Douglas and I became friendly and he said he had promised to take two girls up the mountain and asked me to go, together with another young man called Smythe, who worked in his office. We went up the same way via Stinkwater but it was rather a wet and dull day.

On the way back from Luanda I had had a radio contact with the mail ship *Llanstephan Castle* and chatted (in morse) with the chief wireless officer. He invited me to visit him when we both got to Capetown, which I did.

As we had neared Capetown I overheard someone talking on a radio-telephone and using most unparliamentary language. I later saw in the newspaper that the Marconi Company had opened a branch office in Capetown and that the manager was a Mr Penrose. So I went to see him and, sure enough, it was my old instructor from Marconi House four years before. As we were talking a man came in and I was introduced to Pritchard, a Marconi engineer demonstrating field-service radio-telephone sets. He was the man I heard talking and I told him what he had said. We soon became friends.

Dillon was relieved as second officer by Arthur Cole, a thin rather red faced young man, very jolly. Dillon left Capetown for England and I never saw him again as he resigned from the company. He went to America as chief officer of the cableship *Restorer* owned by the Commercial Pacific Cable Co which had laid cables across the Pacific from California to the Philippines and Shanghai.

I introduced Arthur Cole to the Cairncross family. Douglas and I frequently went up Table Mountain on Sundays. There were some splendid wild flowers, heathers of many kinds, and a red orchid called disa. Many were protected by law and it was an offence to pick them, but we used to gather some of those allowed. There is a mountain club which has a hut near the top and one could get tuition in rock climbing, but though we joined the club, we were more interested in scrambles and walking.

Cole and I were invited to become members of a mixed party to spend the weekend at Kommetje, a small seaside place on the west side of the Cape peninsular, about sixteen miles south of Capetown. The "Mrs Grundy's" of Capetown were, of course, horrified that young men and girls should go off for the weekend together! The girls had one room and the men another and we made picnic expeditions, walking up to sixteen miles climbing and bathing, played games and it was great fun.

Sylvia Cairncross had two special girl friends, Dorothy Dixie and Effie Smale. Then there was Effie's sister, Nell, and Mavis Kemp who lived with her parents at "Beech Hurst" and occasionally others. Most of the girls had jobs in banks and offices. The men were Douglas Cairncross, Percy Bowyer, Arthur Cole, Fred Smythe and myself, with others now and then. Sylvia Cairncross told me that a party of them were going on an expedition at Easter and left Capetown in two cars. As they went down Adderley Street they noticed crowds of people lining the pavements. Dillon's brother who was sitting in the back of one of the cars next to her, suddenly remembered that the newspapers had said that Harry Lauder was due to arrive that day. So he seized her tartan rug , draped it over his shoulders, stood up in the car and waved to the crowd. They, of course, thought the great man had arrived and cheered wildly until the two car cavalcade turned out of the main street. She said they put on all speed in case they were followed.

Britannia was noted among our ships for having long spells in port but we eventually got orders to mend the cable from Luanda to San Thomé island, and set off north up the west coast. Before we left a young man called Lumsden arrived from England as third electrician. He was a Scotsman from Dundee who had qualified as a wireless operator and volunteered for cableships.

The cable was faulty but not broken and we went to Luanda to test for the position. Hancock and I went ashore and met J. E. Broadbent, the officer in charge; this was the title at small branches where there was only one European. The fault proved difficult to locate and after spending most of the day and evening on it, we were put up for the night by Joe Broadbent. He was most helpful in supplying us with nourishment, both liquid and solid. He was a stout man with a moustache and usually looked very solemn, even pompous, but suddenly you noticed his eyes twinkling over something that had been said, and you realised that he had a keen sense of humour.

We went north from Luanda and eventually picked up the fault. It was found at a kink which we recovered. How it had got kinked was a mystery as it was forty miles from the nearest splice. It must have been caused by the original laying ship in 1879. We then returned to Capetown and resumed our rather jolly life there.

We occasionally made up parties of six or eight and had dinner at the railway station restaurant, a good one at that time, and went on to a show at the Tivoli Theatre afterwards. The Cadarga Hotel, in Mill Street, had Saturday night dances, and we used to go there now and then.

We also had a few games of cricket. Several of our St Helenan crew were good, and we formed a team with them and some officers. The snag was that white South African teams would not play against teams containing coloureds (as our St Helenans were classed). But the cable office foreign service staff had no such inhibitions and we had a few games against them. H. A. (Beery) Merchant—well known in the ETC—was their Captain, a most cheery and popular man who became a superintendent before retiring.

Another incident was the damage to the mailship *Saxon* in Capetown docks. She hit the coaling jetty with here stern owing to the second engineer putting the engines astern when the order from the bridge was to go ahead. She was unable to take passengers, and after temporary repairs was filled up with coal for the UK as there was a coal strike on there.

Sylvia Cairncross said she would show me how to surf so we went to Muizenberg one afternoon where there is a splendid beach and rollers, on the east side of the peninsular in False Bay, and I began to learn. It was this afternoon that we suddenly realised that we should both be very sorry when I went on leave next year.

The ship again left for the north to repair the cable near Banana at the mouth of the Congo river. We had to grapple for it in the mouth of the river where the current and tide run very strongly, and the poor old *Britannia* was difficult to handle under such conditions, as she was so slow. However, we got the job done and went into Banana for one night. This is a small port mainly for pilots who take merchant ships forty miles up the river to Matadi. In our company's staff rule book there was a section at the end giving details of requirements and recreations at branches abroad. Recreations in Banana were listed as "walking along the sandspit". We had only one European there. It must have been the worst station with nothing to do except your job—and walking along the beach.

On our way south we called at Luanda again for coal and provisions and then set on for Capetown. The following day two of our stewards went sick with measles, and soon after I got it. An emergency sick bay was made with canvas screens on a forward hatchway on the main deck for the stewards, two more of whom also got it, and I was confined to my cabin. Ships' doctors often do not have enough to do. Our doctor used to collect marine life which came up on the cables, dissect it and sent specimens to museums. Now he had his hands full. After we berthed at Capetown the stewards were sent to the isolation hospital for quarantine but I was allowed to stay on board, and soon got up. I was obliged to stay on the bridge only, or my cabin, so as not to infect anyone else.

We soon had some changes. We got a fourth officer (additional), Duncan Best who had recently been axed from the navy. Captain Boyd went on leave prior to retirement and was relieved by Captain Lear whose wife came with him. Later my chief, Hancock, went on leave and was replaced by H. E. N. Evans, nicknamed by his initials.

Britannia's electrical staff got an unusual job. The two submarine cables from the north landed on Robbin Island in Table Bay and were connected to our office in St Georges Street (parallel with Adderley Street) by two separate four-core bay cables. One landed near the pier at the foot of Adderley Street, and the other at Grainger Bay, west of the docks. This was an insurance in case one got damaged by a ship's anchor, which could easily happen in the severe gales often experienced there.

An underground cable from Grainger Bay to the office went faulty and HEN Evans told the shore chief electrician that he would tackle it. This we did and it was interesting as another kind of cable work. The cable was rubber insulated in a lead sheath and we hired a local plumber to make lead "wiped" joints in the sheath, using a small piece of moleskin to mould the molten lead.

I do not remember much about the festivities of Christmas 1920 except the weather was cold by Capetown standards, it being the middle of the summer.

About a fortnight after Christmas Sylvia Cairncross and I went for a walk after tea in the woods behind the house. We sat on some flat stones at a place known locally as the slippery rocks and I asked her to marry me, and she said, "Yes". Later we broke the news to her mother and brother who received it with much enthusiasm and at once produced drinks to celebrate the occasion.

The company frowned on any one getting married with less than ten years service. No housing allowances, ship's passages or other married privileges were given until then. Later this was reduced to eight years. But in the ships, officers did not at that time get any marriage privileges at all.

However ships' electricians, seconded from the shore staff, got higher salaries on special scales going up to second grade. I was well aware that I could hardly afford to support a wife for at least another year or so and Sylvia was told about this. I proposed to volunteer after leave for a year in *Transmitter* where I could save up and then we could get married.

Soon after we had to do a repair to the St Helena cable near Robbin Island and one fine morning we were grappling for it. The water was clear and two sharks, each about 8 or 10 feet long, appeared and started rubbing themselves against our wire grappling rope.

Soon after this we had a dance on board *Britannia* and invited all our lady friends. It was then that Sylvia suggested that we should get married before I went on leave and that after our honeymoon she would continue with her job until I had finished my time in my next ship, when she would come to England to join me. I agreed, and applied to the company for permission to spend two months of my leave in South Africa before coming home to England.

In March I was relieved by "Tickey" Eastwood who had been with me at Portcurnow.

I went to see the padre of Sylvia's family church, the Presbyterian church in Orange Street. He said he was acting for the normal incumbent and was not sure whether he was legally licensed to perform marriage ceremonies but would find out, and it was arranged we should be married on 24th March. On the 19th we both went to the Magistrates' Court to get a licence as I was not officially resident in South Africa. After waiting we were ushered before the magistrate and before we knew what was happening, we found we were actually being married! His clerk had evidently not understood that we only wanted the licence. Well, we did not stop him, and in view of the padre's licence question, perhaps it was a good thing. I had not yet got the ring so we went and bought it. This was on a Saturday. We told no one though our usual gang of boys and girls, with us, went on a picnic on the Sunday and to pull our legs kept on addressing Sylvia as Mrs Stray.

But on the Saturday afternoon I got a shock as I received a telephone call telling me to come back to the ship at once. I thought at first we might have got orders to go to sea. Eastwood was only arriving on the Monday. But when I got on board I was told to report to Dr Anderton for vaccination against smallpox. That morning two new Kroo firemen had arrived on a ship from West Africa to relieve two on board. After reporting to the second engineer, they were told to go to Dr Anderton's surgery as he kept medical records of all the crew. Anderton looked at one of them and said: "Are you feeling all right?" He said he was feeling sick so the doctor carefully examined him and decided he had smallpox.

Sylvia and I were married in the church, and her mother had a reception at Beech Hurst. We left later by train for Worcester, about 109 miles up country where we stayed the night at the local hotel. The next day we continued by train to a place called Robertson where we had been invited to stay with Sylvia's elder sister, Mercy, and her husband, Netlam Miller, who was a bank manager. Sylvia had two married sisters, both more than 20 years older than she.

We had a pleasant stay at Robertson. One day Netlam took me on a long walk to some hills nearby to gather nerines—beautiful pink flowers with silver pollen.

We then went on by train to Graaff Reinet in the Karroo district, about 600 miles from Capetown where we had been invited to stay with Sylvia's other sister, Gertrude, who was married to a lawyer called Arthur Steer. The railway goes via Mossel Bay and we arrived there the following morning. While the train waited we got out for a walk up and down the platform, when who should we see doing the same but General Smuts and an ADC. He was the Prime Minister and his coach had been attached to the back of our train during the night.

The line climbs up the Montague Pass, 2,350 feet, through the Outanique Mountains with numerous tunnels and sharp curves. It was hauled by two locomotives, and in places one could see both ends of the train without leaning out of the window; it is a most spectacular ride.

Travelling in the long distance trains in South Africa was very comfortable. Though the gauge is only 3ft 6 inches, the carriages appear as wide as those in England. Two and four berth compartments are provided, the berths being folded during the day. The restaurant cars are particularly noted for their good cuisine and excellent service. If the train is not too full a tip to the conductor can get two of you a four berth compartment.

We were welcomed at Graaff Reinet by Gertrude and Arthur Steer and taken to their bungalow. Sylvia, of course, had been to Graaff Reinet many times before. The town is sited within almost a circle of hills with the Sundays river winding round, and is very picturesque. It was a very early Dutch settlement, in 1786. As it has a regular water supply, there are numerous gardens, orchards and vineyards.

At the north end a large dam, 1,100 feet long was being built across the river at what was called Van Rynveldt Pass to make a lake to conserve the water. It was completed in 1924. The Karroo district, like many parts of South Africa, has a small rainfall but when heavy rains do occur, the rivers become raging torrents. Sheep farming is the main industry but there is little or no grass and the sheep—only running at one to the acre—subsist mainly on the so called Karroo bush.

Gertrude and Arthur Steer had lived there about fifteen years and had a large circle of friends both Dutch and English to which we where introduced, and a very pleasant community it was. Arthur had recently been largely instrumental in getting a new modern hospital built, of which he was secretary. He was a good tennis player and took me to the club to play. He was organist of the English church and could play almost anything on the piano or organ by ear. I have never forgotten hearing him play the Intermezzo from *Cavalleria Rusticana* on the church organ one day when he was practising. It was marvellous. In fact, he was very gifted all round. Gertrude was also capable both as a housewife and in organising social affairs, and they were obviously popular members of the community.

So we had a very pleasant stay there and were sorry to have to return to Capetown.

Sylvia and I stayed at an hotel in Capetown until my departure. I was booked on the mailboat *Walmer Castle,* and so we had to say goodbye and did not see each other for about eighteen months.

The day I left she introduced me to a young man called Bobbie Bird who was travelling in the same ship. He had been trained as a dentist in the USA and had got engaged to an American girl. He was going back there now to marry her, via the UK. The owner of the Cadarga Hotel, Mr Boden, his wife, son and two daughters were also passengers. Young Boden, Bobbie Bird and I spent a good deal of time together on the voyage and incidentally played a lot of deck cricket and other games. I won a prize—a silver cardcase which I still use—at the fancy dress dance by making a toga out of a sheet (with the help of the Boden girls) and posing as a Roman citizen. The mail run to Southampton took sixteen and a half days then, with a few hours call at Madeira.

As we approached the dockside, the younger Boden girl, known as "Tommy", looked at the dock workers on the quay and said: "How funny, there are no black men." She had never been outside Africa before.

We went by special train to Waterloo and I reported to head office. As I was a shore staff man seconded to the ships, I had to see both the staff and marine departments. Mr Crow was the staff superintendent in those days. One also had to see the company's doctor who sent a report to the Staff dept. Off my own bat, I also visited the electrical department and met Mr Leslie Smith who was most kind to me, a most junior electrician, and took me to see the electrician-in-chief for a few minutes. This was Mr Schaefer who invented the cable testing method referred to earlier, and the brother of my instructor at the training school.

I caught a train for Newcastle and then a local train for Warkworth where my mother and stepfather had been living for about two years. They had bought a house called "Southville" a quarter of a mile above the village and not far from the ruined castle owned by the Duke of Northumberland who was the principal landowner in the district.

Warkworth Castle is picturesquely sited on high ground above the river Coquet which runs past it and then bends round to enclose the village below the castle. It is a good salmon river, and apart from fly fishing, salmon were also netted regularly just below the old narrow stone bridge at the bottom of the village main street.

I played golf and tennis and had a pleasant holiday with my parents. The governor, as my brother and I called my stepfather, had bought a Singer touring car and we went for drives at weekends.

Head office informed me of my appointment to the cableship *Transmitter* with departure for Sierra Leone about September. In August they sent me a telegram asking me to go a month earlier owing to sickness. They said I could have a month's extra pay or a month's extra leave next time.

I was invited to stay a week with Sir William and Lady Turpin who were old friends of my mother. They had a house and farm just outside Bushey. Sir William was a retired official of the Treasury. Mother arranged to get a fresh salmon for me to take in a bass bag as a present for the Turpins. The train from Newcastle arrived full, as the rail strike had ended the day before, so two extra coaches were attached. As they were not connected by corridor with the dining car I got out at York and walked up the platform. When I returned at a later station my carriage had been taken off and my suitcase and precious salmon had disappeared. I got another seat and went to see the guard who found my luggage *and* the salmon safe and sound in the van.

I reported to head office, where I met Hannaford, my old chief officer of *Levant* days who said he was coming to *Transmitter* with me, and a week later caught the special train from Euston to Liverpool and embarked on the Elder Dempster Lines mailboat *Abinsi* for Freetown, Sierra Leone.

Before leaving London for Sierra Leone, I paid a visit to the London Training School. This had been moved from the basement of head office in Electra House, to Hampstead. The company had bought a building in Shepherds Walk, near the top of Haverstock Hill.

In addition to being a school for operators, they had started two year engineering courses for selected men with four or five years seniority. This was a reversal of the original policy of not allowing men to do electrical work until they had ten years seniority, except for those who went on cableships.

I asked the staff superintendent if I could take this two year course but he said: "No. You are required on cableships. You volunteered for them."

CHAPTER FIVE

Cableship "Transmitter"

The *Abinsi* was a passenger ship of 10,000 tons and we had a smooth passage to Freetown, calling at Las Palmas on the way.

The senior wireless officer was a chap called Sutton and I spent a lot of time talking to him in the wireless room adjacent to his cabin.

Before breakfast one day he gave me the news bulletin just received and in it was all about the enquiry into the stranding and loss of the P & O liner *Egypt* which had happened not long before. Later he told me to keep it under my hat as the captain had decided to cut that item out of the ship's daily newspaper—presumably so as not to upset the passengers.

Two days before we reached Sierra Leone, he was very busy sending and receiving messages, and told me that the Union Castle mailboat *Saxon* was on fire in the bunkers and proceeding to Freetown. He had been busy relaying messages between *Saxon* and the *Kenilworth Castle,* the next week's mailboat just out from Southampton, which had been ordered to call at Freetown. General Smuts and his staff were on board *Saxon* and the *Kenilworth Castle* was to take them off and on to Capetown.

Abinsi arrived at Freetown early in the morning and there was the *Saxon* with smoke coming from her sides. Hannaford was relieving Jock Turner, whom I met briefly.

We signed on at the Port Captain's office and *Transmitter* sailed at 6 p.m. for Bonny at the delta of the Niger river in the Gulf of Guinea.

Next day Jock Turner went to Elder Dempster's office about his passage home, and they said: "You have got a Master's certificate, haven't you?" He said "Yes". So they asked him to survey the *Saxon* as the fire had been put out, and give her a seaworthy certificate to proceed to Capetown. He went on board and examined her. The fire had only been in the bunkers and the damage was not serious. So he signed on the dotted line and got the ten pounds fee, and the *Saxon* left Freetown.

My new ship, *Transmitter,* was quite different from both *Levant* and *Britannia.* Of 900 tons, she had been built in 1914 at Goole. She was not popular with those who had to live in her, being badly designed. She had a raised forecastle, then a well-deck where the cable engine was placed, and then a raised shelter deck to the stern with cabins under it. Amidships at the forward end of the shelter deck was the dining saloon, but as she worked in the tropics, this was not used as there was a long table on the quarterdeck where all meals were served. The chief steward used the saloon as an office. But the testroom, amidships under the shelter deck, was near the stern. We had no telephones and the testroom should have been where the saloon was, so as to be near the cable work. The captain's cabin was under the bridge above the shelter deck and there was a central gangway over the well deck from here to the forecastle head. The well of the engine room skylight was so narrow that the tops of the three cylinders of the main engines practically filled it. So the engine room was so hot (in the tropics) that the engineer on duty was dripping with sweat five minutes after starting his four hour watch.

The Captain who was tall and rather thin on top, used to say, "Damn the man who designed this ship!" every time he bumped his head after

CS Transmitter off Gravesend, 1914.

visiting us in the testroom. Ten years later she was sold to the French Government and renamed *Arago.* I hope they liked her.

The passage to Bonny enabled me to meet all my shipmates, several of whom were not new. Captain Sherwood (ex *Levant II*) was in command, and Clark the third officer and Dr Anderton had come from *Britannia.*

My new chief was "Driver" Briggs whom I had known in Malta in *Electra.* Head office had decided to send a third electrician (me) to *Transmitter* which up until then had only two. Then the chief electrician went sick and they hurried me out there. He had left for home before my arrival, leaving Briggs as acting chief. He was easy to get on with and extremely popular with everyone. He was good at his job, too, and taught me a lot about testing, as he had developed one or two methods of his own which were very effective.

We arrived at Bonny and anchored in the river, part of the delta of the Niger. Our officer-in-charge, Pyle, came on board and about noon he, Briggs, Dr Anderton and I went ashore. We had the usual pink gins before lunch and then Pyle regaled us with a magnificent meal, the pièce de résistance being palm oil chop. This is the West African counterpart of Indian curry. It consists of chicken (or it was said, missionary for early Africans) and vegetables with lots of hot peppers, all cooked in palm oil. Served with it is a sort of suet pudding. It makes a very good meal but you really need to take a siesta afterwards.

Soon after we went on a series of repairs for the French government. They had no cableship in West Africa and we did jobs for them on the cables connecting their colonies from Dakar in the north to Conakry, Ivory Coast, Togoland, Dahomey and Libreville in the south. We went to Dakar to mend their cable to South America which was broken off Cape Verde, the most westerly point of Africa.

Dakar was quite different to all the other places we went to in West Africa, being a large modern town with a fine harbour with numerous piers and quays. At most of the other ports we had to anchor and go ashore in a surfboat. These were heavily built wooden boats 20 to 30 feet long, manned by a dozen or more African paddlers, a row on each side, and steered by a large oar. At French ports the surfboats were provided with what was called a Mammy chair. This was a four-seater wooden box with steel posts meeting overhead. You sat in it and were paddled to a pier running out from the beach, which had a crane on it. This hoisted the Mammy chair and occupants out of the boat and landed them onto the pier. The tricky bit was the return journey to the surfboat, dancing in the heavy swell. We were told that the Africans would be fined ten shillings each if a passenger were drowned, which was very comforting.

At Dakar, Briggs and I were taken by car about fifteen miles to the cablehouse at Yoff, north of the lighthouse on Cape Verde. We had to walk the last mile in loose sand as there was no road. Next day we went out and hooked the cable and repaired it, but found the shore end was faulty. It was decided to renew it, so Hannaford, a couple of sailors and myself were landed on the quay at Dakar early next day, together with a mushroom anchor, large snatchblock and shovels, etc. and we went by lorry to Yoff. We found the African natives hired by the French to carry all this heavy gear had gone on strike and we could not get it moved over the mile of sand near the cablehouse. I saw an African with a camel nearby and he agreed to hire it to us. This is the only time, as far as is known, that a camel has been used for cable work.

When we arrived at the beach the ship was already in the offing. We buried our mushroom anchor in the sand and attached the snatchblock. This is a large pulley the side of which can be opened to put a rope in. Mushroom anchors look as they are named, and are very heavy. They are used to anchor mark buoys at sea; their round shape prevents a cable getting caught on them. The ship sent a boat ashore with the end of a thick manila rope which was passed through the snatchblock and taken back to the ship. The new cable shore end was fastened by the ship to one end of the rope and slowly pulled ashore by the ship's windlass heaving on the other end.

By the time we got the end into the cablehouse it was getting dark. Next day Briggs and I went back by road and collected all our gear, again with camel transport. It was very hot and exhausting work.

We had a short spell at Freetown after this. It is so-called because it is the home of the descendants of many African slaves repatriated from the West Indies. The town is a non-descript place with wood and galvanised iron roofed houses and bungalows and the stores of the trading companies. There were no proper shops with windows for displaying goods at that time. The streets are wide and many are lined with flame-of-the-forest trees which look very picturesque with their red blossom. On the 1,200 ft summit to the west towards the sea, is a colony of bungalows, known as Hill Station. The senior officials lived there and went up and down by light railway. Two roads—one way—were being built for motors but were not yet finished.

The cable station was on a small cliff overlooking the waterfront. Below it was a ship's depot with cable tanks and between were two 100 ft self supporting lattice towers for the aerials of the ship/shore coast station run by the company. There was also a large bungalow at Hill Station for the superintendent and staff to spend weekends.

The superintendent was a Mr Stilwell who was well-known for running the Cable Derby Sweepstake for many years. He had a house next to the office and there was a bachelors mess over the latter. It was estimated that he had an income from the sweep of not far short of £1,000 a year—a lot in those days—but it involved much work as tickets were distributed all over the world.

I became friendly with one of the shore staff called Pesket. He had originally been in the Eastern Extension Company in Malaya and had resigned to become a rubber planter. When the war came he joined the army and after it was over he got a job with the African Direct Telegraph Company, which, as a subsidiary of the Eastern Telegraph Company, ran most of the west African cable stations.

We decided to take sandwiches one Sunday and climb Sugar Loaf Hill to the east of the town. After getting to the top, about 2,500 ft., through thick bush, he proposed we walk on to a place called Charlotte Falls on a small river where we had a bathe and ate our lunch. It was a lovely picnic spot with a succession of small falls and many trees which gave shade.

Briggs and the second officer decided to have a picnic and camp out for the weekend at a place called Lumley Beach which was on the seaward side of Hill Station. They borrowed a tent and set out, but they were invaded at night by land crabs, some of them over a foot across.

Near the entrance to the estuary was the wreck of a ship which had been torpedoed during the war, and beached on a sandbank. The second engineer and some others took a boat one Sunday and visited it, but all they found were rats and some oysters.

The ship then went on a series of repairs to the French cable between Dakar and Conakry. Head office instructed us to go to Dakar and pick up a French representative who would remain on board during the work. This is common practice when cable ships are chartered to foreign governments, but had not happened here for some years. But we soon found out why. The representative turned out to be the director general of the French cable system in West Africa, an affable and pleasant man of middle age. We learned that he was going to translate Mr H. D. Wilkinson's well known (in the cable service) book on cable laying and repairing, published in 1908, into French and had applied to his government to come on a trip with us to see how it was done. We got the impression that he thought we sometimes took longer than necessary over repair jobs.

One funny incident happened. Dr Anderton tried one evening to drink the DG under the table but the latter remained much the more sober of the two. We were finishing a job and at about 1 a.m. slipped the final splice. This is done by attaching first two and then one manila ropes and slowly lowering it down to avoid a kink. The rope is finally cut by an axe on a block of wood. Anderton said to the DG in rather thick accents that this was what he called "The Mary Queen of Scotchsh act" and he must come and see it on the ship's bows. But it is doubtful whether our guest knew what the hell the doctor was talking about.

Later the ship arrived at Conakry about 120 miles north of Freetown. To save time we started grappling for the cable just outside the anchorage.

We found a new shore end had to be laid and to splice it up, the ship's boats were used as it was shallow. While waiting for the joint to be finished, we suddenly saw a huge column of smoke rise from the ship a mile away. We watched and in a couple of minutes it disappeared. When we got back we heard it was due to a bucket of hot oil from the engine room catching fire. Campbell, an African engine storekeeper naturally dropped it, and it ran all over the well deck, but the Bosun soon put it out with a hose. Campbell was badly burned up his arm and was attended to at once by Dr Anderton.

When getting the end ashore it was necessary to have a long trench dug, but the French superintendent said as it was lunchtime on Saturday, nothing could be done till Monday morning. The DG however, disappeared in a taxi and returned about an hour later with a warder and a gang of convicts and the trench was dug forthwith. He said the prison governor was an old school friend of his.

It was typical of the French superintendents of their West African stations that they had little authority to incur local expenditure. On one occasion he said he would have to telegraph to Paris for authority and it would be at least a day and probably two before he got a reply. As they paid £300 a day for the ship, such delays were expensive—for them. Compare this with the company's system. As our ships worked all over the world, day and night, there was a duty officer in head office, London, who was either in his office or could be contacted by telephone, and could make decisions and give orders if necessary in reply to telegrams, thus saving time—and money.

On our return to Freetown HEN Evans arrived (from *Britannia*) as chief electrician and Briggs reverted to second and myself to third. Briggs was swotting to take his promotion exam and used to get up at 6 a.m. and put in a couple of hours' work. He could have taken a purely electrical exam which would qualify for promotion on the ships only, but he was determined to take the full shore exam which involved learning all the shore cable station rules, both company's and international, law, accounts, administration, etc. So when in Freetown, he used to spend a lot of his free time ashore in the office. He had acquired a large quantity of notes in a foolscap book which he said he would send to me if he passed his exam.

Not long after he was relieved by a man called D. K. Smith who was three years senior to me. Briggs left for the UK where he took his exam, passed, and sent me his notes as promised. They were used to take my exam some years later, and then passed on to someone else.

We had been invited to dances on shore in Freetown by Elder Dempster's staff mess and others. Captain Sherwood suggested we hold a dance on board, which was done very successfully. There were only about twenty-two European ladies who lived in or near the town—all wives of various officials and employees of business firms, so it was not a large affair and we did not have a great deal of space. But we cleared the quarterdeck which had canvas screens that could be let down round it, and fixed up a few coloured lights and our hand gramophone provided the music, with a supper from the galley. It went well, as a ship's dance was a local novelty for the small community. We had another later on, but this nearly ended in disaster as a tornado came up and some of the guests got rather wet going ashore by our ship's boats. There were no quays at Freetown and we had to anchor hundreds of yards from the pier.

Tornados in West Africa were small but very violent cyclones. The wind went round and round a point which moved onwards rapidly but erratically, tearing off house roofs, uprooting trees, and causing general damage but soon passing over. Often and especially at sea, they were accompanied by lightning like great ropes of fire and deafening thunder.

Soon we had to go to Accra in the Gold Coast (now Ghana) to lay shore ends into a new office. There had been outbreaks of influenza at West African ports. Dr Anderton made us all parade daily and have our throats sprayed to try and avoid infection, and it seemed to work.

Accra from the sea appears as a long line of low cliffs with white houses, warehouses, etc., and a boat harbour enclosed by a small breakwater. There is heavy surf all along this coast which runs west to east, which is not surprising as the South Atlantic stretches as far as the south polar continent. Ships have to anchor about two miles from the shore, and you proceed to the boat harbour by surfboat, being then carried up the beach if you do not want to wet your feet.

When we got there the port doctor was reluctant to let any of us ashore on account of the influenza but finally said Hannaford and I could go to supervise the landing of the shore ends. The ship moved to a position, about a mile offshore, and the end of a manila rope was brought ashore by surfboat and a gang of a hundred African labourers were assembled to haul on it. The ship attached the cable and an empty barrel to the rope and we started pulling. At intervals stops were made for more barrels to be fastened on to keep the cable afloat while we pulled. It was a slow job and a slight current tended to drift the cable sideways, but eventually we got the end ashore and enough slack to reach the office about 200 yards inland.

The next job was to cut the barrels adrift so the cable would sink. A surfboat did most of them but, as we had none of our own sailors with us, Hannaford and I got very wet in the surf showing some Africans how to do this.

The new building was called Broderick House after the family name of Lord Middleton who was chairman of the African Direct Telegraph Co. It had offices on the ground floor, a flat for the superintendent and a bachelors' mess on the upper floor, a handsome building for Accra.

We repeated this job by laying the second new shore end in the same way and then had to cut the cables, east and west, and join up the new ends.

While we were at Accra some of us were invited to play tennis. When we left to go back on board about 6 p.m. two shore staff came with us to dine and sleep on board. We got to the boat harbour and were carried to our surfboat on the beach. Then the African in charge would not put off. Eventually a small European in gaiters, with an African servant carrying a tin trunk, appeared and were put on board our boat. He introduced himself as the Bishop of Accra and apologised for delaying us but said we were the last boat available and he wanted to go to Sekondi, the next port 100 miles west, by the mailboat leaving that night.

By this time it was getting dark and rather rough. We got along-side our ship and all scrambled aboard and left the Bishop to continue to the mailship about half a mile away. We were lucky. A swamped surfboat with about twenty-five men in it would have meant several would have been drowned, as it was nearly dark with a heavy sea running.

We went to Sekondi where the company had a branch. A couple of miles on the west side of Sekondi is Takoradi which now has a large enclosed harbour with quays for ships to go alongside. But in 1922 it had not been built. There was much argument on the coast as to the wisdom of spending the £11 million it was estimated to cost, but it turned out to be a good investment and was invaluable during the last war when fighter aircraft, brought by carriers, were landed there and flown across Africa to Egypt and the Middle East, thus saving the long haul round the Cape.

Our next job was rather unusual. Before World War I the Germans had laid cables to Monrovia, the capital of the African Republic of Liberia, and then on to Lome, the capital of the German colony of Togoland.

After the war Togoland was divided, a small strip in the west being joined on to the Gold Coast (Ghana) and the rest, including its capital, Lome, mandated to France. The Accra-Lome cable was declared jointly owned by France and Britain. It subsequently went faulty and then broken. So the British Government sold their share to France and they wanted it picked up and re-laid in the opposite direction, i.e. easterly from Lome to Cotonou, the capital of their colony of Dahomey.

We started off Accra, hooking it and then picking up mile after mile, cutting out any faults. When the break was reached, we grappled for the other end and continued picking up until we got to Lome, when we had recovered over 100 miles of cable. We then started paying it out again in an easterly direction towards Cotonou. Here we laid a new shore end and connected it up to Lome.

Nearly all the French cables off the West African coast had rather poor characteristics owing to leakage. This new one had practically none and the French Superintendent amused us by saying he would have to send to Paris for a *bobine de resistance* to keep the electric current down. He temporarily achieved this object by using one old fashioned *leclanche* cell with only an inch of fluid in it as a battery for signalling. These cells are the ones which were almost universally used in English houses to work electric bells until about thirty years ago, being in glass jars with a black painted top.

One afternoon the jointer was busy at his job and the bosun, James, was yarning with his mates. He said that in April 1912 he had been serving on an American cableship at Halifax, Nova Scotia, when they heard about the Titanic disaster. The next day they were ordered to take on board over 100 coffins, proceed to the scene and pick up as many bodies as they could. This they did and returned to Halifax. They were then told to return to the place where the Titanic sunk, grapple for her and fix the position accurately. This was carried out though they had to abandon the rope as it was not possible to unhook the grapple caught on the sunken ship.

During our return passage to Freetown, we were off Axim near the western borders of the Gold Coast and at breakfast someone pointed out a large log of wood floating past. We stopped to pick it up. It was a log of mahogany about 6ft × 6ft and 30 or 40 ft long, very heavy. It was taken to Freetown and declared to the Receiver of Wrecks (the Harbourmaster). It was stated to be worth two or three hundred pounds.

The Governor of Sierra Leone was Dr Maxwell. His wife gave informal afternoon tennis parties to which Smith, Clark and I were invited. We went up to Government House where a dozen basket chairs were arranged in a circle on the lawn. Mrs Maxwell sat on one side of the circle with her husband on the opposite side and tea was served by African servants in white ducks and red sashes. One of them presided over a gramophone discreetly hidden behind a bush, on which soft music was played. Tea over we all went to the tennis court, except the Governor, and made up fours for various sets, while those not playing chatted to Mrs Maxwell who did not play herself.

HMS *Antrim* a light cruiser, visited Freetown and one or two residents took a party from the ship to climb Sugar Loaf Hill. One of the visitors was introduced as Dr Jones. On the way down one man slipped and injured his leg and the leader suggested calling Dr Jones who was a hundred yards away. It was then learned that he was not a medical man at all. The *Antrim* was on a special voyage to test out some new wireless equipment for the Admiralty and Dr Jones was a scientist, seconded from one of the universities.

The wireless sets on most of our ships were made by the Marconi Company in England, except the *Transmitter* which had a German Telefunken set. The company operated ship-shore stations at Freetown and Lagos in Nigeria and these had been supplied by the Telefunken Company. The reason was that, in the tropics, atmospherics, i.e., noises due to lightning, etc., were very bad at night time on the medium wavelengths used then. They made an almost continuous roar in our headphones. The Marconi sets had rather a low note but the Telefunken transmitters had a high pitched note which gave much better reception at night.

We went on a job near Conakry and while grappling the ship was swept down by the tide and grounded on a sandbank. She was stuck for about two hours but gradually went over the bank into deep water as the tide rose.

The ship's crew was all West African natives. One of the stewards who cleaned out the doctor's cabin went sick. Dr Anderton could not find out what was the matter with him and told me that he believed someone had put a juju on him. The doctor could not do anything for him and he had to be sent ashore to the hospital. The sailors usually judged the weight of an object by its size and it was amusing to see three or four of them gather round, say, an empty packing case, prior to lifting it, while when one was sent to fetch a 56lb shot which is only about six inches across and used for depth sounding, he would look astonished when he tried to pick it up.

One type of mishap is a foul in a cable tank when paying out, and this occurs now and then. The cable is coiled in the tank starting at the outside and working inwards. In the case of new cable, the outer covering of which is impregnated with tar, each layer is whitewashed to prevent sticking. When paying out there are one or two experienced men in the tank and they have to be very careful not to get caught up in the cable as, at four or five knots, it can whip out very quickly especially the short inner turns near the centre. The bosun or one of his mates stands by the open top with a whistle. If a foul does occur, usually due to an upper turn sticking to a lower one, he blows his whistle and the bridge puts the engines astern and swings the helm, while the engine driver on the paying out drum puts on the brakes. If a man should get entangled, the brakes are put on very hard and everyone takes cover as the cable may break. What usually happens is the cable gets into a tangle and is damaged. It then has to be cut and spliced up again. You cannot stop a ship of a couple of thousand tons quickly.

While on passage one afternoon, the ship suddenly stopped. Those off duty came on deck to see a boat being lowered. It picked up a small object and returned to the ship. It was Hannaford's uniform cap! The chief engineer was not amused as his boilers with a full head of steam were blowing off from the safety valve.

Two or three of the engineers went on a picnic to Bullom which is the other side of the wide estuary on which Freetown is situated. Later two of them went down with malaria. They had evidently been bitten by mosquitoes as it is damp and swampy there. Lying at anchor off Freetown there were no mosquitoes and generally this was the case along the coast where we anchored about a mile or so from the shore. So we did not normally sleep under nets. Occasionally we got swarms of flying insects, and on one or two evenings they were so bad that we had to dine in the dark. Lights attracted so many that our plates were full of them and they covered the table cloth.

To keep fit we used to throw a medicine ball from one to another around the deck. One day in Freetown about six of us jumped over after the ball until the captain appeared and ordered us all back on board as there could be sharks.

A few German cargo ships were making their appearance on the coast and one day there was one of 3,000 tons at Freetown. She was towing a hulk or very large lighter. The next day there was a fierce tornado in the afternoon and when it cleared, we saw the German ship anchored near the shore about two miles from her previous berth. At the same time our office reported one of the cables was broken. We estimated the German ship was right on it, so Hannaford went over in a boat. They picked up their anchor and, sure enough, the cable was on it. Hannaford attached a rope and buoy and let it go. The company rarely, if ever, sued ships for damaging cables. The facts are hard to establish—usually you do not know which ship was responsible, and it was not forgotten that the shipping companies were some of our best customers for sending cablegrams.

This sort of damage was most common in places like the English Channel where trawlers worked. Later a method of "plowing in" submarine cables in shallow water was developed which helped to prevent damage, and recently midget submarines have been used to supervise this.

Lagos, the capital of Nigeria, our next call, was very different to other places on the coast. It is situated on what is virtually an island. To the east is a large shallow lagoon. On the west side is the harbour, entered by a long narrow channel with short breakwaters at the entrance. As you go up this channel, charming houses and bungalows with trees and green lawns are on your right hand, and then it opens out into a large inland harbour. On the right is the main town. In the centre is a shallow patch, and to the left is a ship channel leading to Apapa on the opposite side from the town.

When *Transmitter* went to Lagos it was usually for coal, and for this we berthed at Apapa near the Nigerian Marine quay. Local coal came by rail and was delivered by native labour, using baskets. Consequently it took a day or more to get our modest 150 tons or so on board. The Nigerian Marine officers invited us to drinks at their mess and canteen and we entertained them on board in return. The Nigerian coal was not of high quality, and our engineers used to say that half of it went up the funnel, meaning it has a high ash content, but it was cheap and readily available.

Ships not at quays anchored at the side of the channel on the town side of the harbour, next to the Marina as the wide tree-shaded road along the channel and harbour front, was called.

Government House and its large garden ran alongside the Marina and our company had recently got a site next door to Government House and were building a new office with bachelors' mess and superintendent's flat above similar to Accra but of quite different architecture. It was finished about the end of 1922 after I left *Transmitter.*

There was a good deal of malaria in Lagos as the whole area is low lying and swampy, and mosquito control was difficult. Apapa was especially bad in those days and there were numerous stegomyia mosquitoes which can carry yellow fever. I was lucky and never got malaria while in *Transmitter,* though I did later in Accra and Lagos in 1947 and 1949.

The ship then went to Libreville in the French colony of Gabon, to mend one of their cables. The town is on the north bank of an estuary about half a mile wide, and is almost on the Equator. It had many tree-lined avenues, and here I saw for the first time touch-sensitive plants. All along the riverside road were green bushes whose leaves curled up at the slightest touch—rather fascinating—it made you want to go on touching them.

To enable us to get better tests of a difficult fault, D. K. Smith was left behind in Libreville for a couple of days with testing instruments, while the ship went about twenty miles out to hook the cable to Cotonou in Dahomey. When we returned to pick him up, he said he had been most assiduously entertained by the French superintendent who had even offered him a temporary wife in case he was lonely at night. D. K. was a rather austere character though good company.

On this trip we had the captain, chief officer, chief electrician and two of the engineers down with malaria. As I was either in a ship or lived on the coast for relatively short periods (up to two years only) I did not regularly take quinine nor did Sylvia. She had one and I had two bouts of malaria in our careers in the company, though we lived for about eighteen years in the tropics.

It was now a year since Hannaford and I had joined *Transmitter* and head office said that our reliefs were on their way.

After finishing the Libreville job the ship went back to Lagos. Our reliefs arrived on the *Abinsi* and our passages home were booked on her.

Our voyage home was uneventful. We called at Las Palmas and finally arrived at Plymouth where passengers for London were landed before the ship went on to Liverpool. We stopped for a few minutes at a small country station where there was a crowd of people, all in their Sunday bests. Some of us got out and exchanged cheerful remarks. You must remember we were all going on our first holiday after at least a year in Africa, but I think the country folk thought we were a bit round the bend.

At Paddington, I said goodbye to Hannaford whom I never saw again. He, poor chap, developed cancer of the throat and died a few years later.

After reporting to head office, seeing the doctor, etc., I caught the train to Newcastle and on to Warkworth where Sylvia had already arrived. She had left Capetown in the *Garth Castle* (Union Castle Line Intermediate ship) about six weeks earlier, and, after calling at St Helena, Ascension and Tenerife, reached London. The governor (my stepfather) went up to London to meet her. My mother told me, with great amusement, that her maid, Jenny, asked before Sylvia's arrival how she would address a black lady. Her idea seemed to be that everyone born in Africa must be black.

We had three months leave, including the month owing to me from

Britannia and spent about two months of it at Warkworth. Sylvia said that everything in England looked very pretty but was very small. When presented with some Brussels sprouts for dinner, she said; "Even the cabbages are small!" She had never seen Brussels sprouts before.

We then went to London and stayed at Meadowbank. The Exiles Club had recently been started by the company who bought the house and grounds on the river at Richmond and rented Orleans Park nearby as a sports ground.

As this was Sylvia's first visit to England we did a round of all the sights of London; the Tower, Westminster Abbey, St Paul's, the South Kensington museums, etc. We also went to Walker & Halls and a wholesale linen warehouse and, armed with "orders" from head office, bought cutlery and linen at a considerable discount, for our future residences.

Head office informed me that I was appointed to my old ship, the *Levant,* now stationed at Piraeus and we were to proceed overland to Trieste and thence by sea to Athens, leaving early in December 1922.

CHAPTER SIX

Cableship Levant Again

Sylvia and I left Waterloo for Southampton and embarked for Le Havre two hours later.

We went by train to Paris and in the evening caught the night train to Milan, having a two berth compartment in a Wagon Lit coach. So we only saw Switzerland from the train, but as it was December, there was plenty of snow on the mountains.

The train went through the Simplon tunnel and soon we were in North Italy running past Lake Maggiore.

Milan is a handsome city and we had a walk round before returning to our hotel. Sylvia spotted some milanese silk underwear and, as the lira was heavily depreciated against the pound, bought a few for about 2/6d. each.

Next day the train took us on to Trieste where we were met by a Mr and Mrs Vincent. He was on the company's staff in our Trieste office and she was one of Sylvia's cousins from Capetown. They were a good deal older than we were but took us for a drive to Miramar and entertained us handsomely.

The next day we embarked on a Lloyd Triestino ship of 2,500 tons for Piraeus. The ship arrived at Venice the next morning and remained there for 24 hours. So we had a whole day to explore the city and saw most of the well known sights.

The ship went down the Adriatic and called at Corfu and I took Sylvia to see One Gun Battery and Ulysses Island which had been visited in 1919. Lying off Corfu was HMS *Coventry,* a light cruiser of the Mediterranean Fleet. It was on this ship at Corfu that Princess Andrew of Greece took refuge with her year old son Philip (now Prince Philip, Duke of Edinburgh) when King George of Greece was deposed in 1922—just before we got to Greece. We passed through the Gulfs of Patras and Corinth, between the mainland of Greece and the Peloponnese.

We arrived at Piraeus and were met by Alfred Finnis, who had been in Gibraltar with me and were taken to the Angleterre Hotel in Constitution Square in Athens. After reporting to the divisional manager, Mr Stevens, he told me the *Levant* was up at the Dardanelles. He said our three cables through the Gulf of Corinth, from near the canal to Patras had been damaged during the gale, probably by ships' anchors and he expected *Levant* would come to mend them.

The next day he said *Levant* was going direct to Corinth and I was to go there by train the following day to join her. There were landlines joining the cables at both ends of the canal and the company had a landline engineer who lived at Corinth.

So at 4 a.m. I said goodbye to Sylvia in the hotel and caught the train to Corinth. There was no sign of the ship and about noon we walked to the canal office who telephoned the other end and reported the *Levant* at anchor nearby.

She arrived about 4 p.m. and sent a boat for us and I was able to have a hearty tea with bully beef sandwiches—the only meat they still had on board. The man I was relieving, Kaye, left for the train from Corinth.

My new shipmates were Captain Goodland and Jock Turner whom I had met in Freetown.

Herbert Finnis, the eldest brother, was chief electrician, and Boudouris, a middle aged Greek, chief engineer. As before, the ship had a British cable jointer and the bosun and the rest of the crew were Greeks. Herbert Finnis was a rather thin faced, dark haired man of middle height and cheerful and we got on well together. He had a vast knowledge of the Greek cable system as he had worked for years in *Levant I* in maintaining it.

We set to work next day to deal with the cables to Patras. One had been dragged clean out of the cablehouse by a ship's anchor. The other two were broken about a mile or so out, no doubt by the Greek steamers during the storm. We soon got them repaired and returned through the canal and on to Piraeus harbour for coal and provisions.

Sylvia had moved from the hotel in Athens to the Phalere Hotel at Phaleron Bay which is about eight miles from Athens on the south coast. There was a very good electric railway from Piraeus town, through Phaleron—about three miles—and then on to Athens where it goes underground and serves three city stations. The trains were like those on the London Metropolitan Line. It had been built by British engineers and gave a frequent and rapid service at modest fares.

Sylvia had met the Captain's wife, Mrs Aimée Goodland and her sister Violette Carew who was visiting the Goodlands. They had a rented house at Phaleron and were young, and good company.

We were soon off again to mend one of the island cables on the east side of Greece. When we got there it was found the cable was faulty some five or ten miles out, but had been cut close to the beach on orders from the divisional manager. I went ashore with Jock Turner in a boat and we fished the seaward end up and connected it to a rubber covered wire of which we had a thousand yards on a big reel from the ship. This allowed Finnis on board to test cables without going ashore and was a great time saver. He had scrounged this drum of testing wire from the navy during the war. It was used by them to explode observation mines and was called torpedo lead.

We now had to lay a new piece of cable from the sea end into the cable house, about 100 yards away. It was getting near Christmas and we wanted to get back to Athens for it. So I suggested to Finnis that if he gave me a boat, three or four men, a jointing and splicing box, and 100 yards of cable, I would joint and splice up this new piece and trench it into the cable house, while the ship could at the same time go out and mend the other fault, thereby saving a day. He consulted the captain who agreed at once. On joining cableships all electricians had to learn how to make cable joints under instruction from the jointers. The main technique was to cover the soldered copper conductor with gutta percha, worked with a hot iron so that not a trace of air was trapped in the joint. Otherwise, in deep water, it would blow the joint under the immense pressure—up to 2 or 3 tons per square inch. Electricians could not be as good as jointers who were trained in the cable factory at home, but for joints in shallow water, they could manage all right. And all the sailors could make the outer splice in the sheathing wires as they were continually doing it under the bosun's supervision.

So we got back to Piraeus a day or two before Christmas and Jock Turner, Sylvia and I were invited to Christmas dinner at Captain Goodland's house in Phaleron.

Soon after Christmas the ship returned to Chanak in the Dardanelles, where she was now stationed while there were no jobs on hand. Turkey under Kemal Attaturk had defeated the Greeks in Asia Minor and occupied Smyrna, and made threatening moves towards Constantinople and the Dardanelles. The latter had been controlled by an Anglo-French Commission since the Turkish defeat at the end of World War I. So the

British Government under Lloyd George had sent a strong military force to the Dardanelles and a large fleet, half of it there and the other half at Constantinople. *Levant* had gone there with the fleet and had laid six cables across the straits for the British Army. She had to stand by there in case of damage to them, and the company's main line cable to Constantinople. If war broke out she was to evacuate the staff and bring them down to Chanak.

Shortly before my arrival, General Sir Charles (Tim) Harrington had been negotiating with the Turks at Mudania, on the Sea of Marmora, when the Constantinople cable broke. The *Levant* hurried back to Chanak from another job and mended it. Admiral Sir John Kelly who was in naval command at Chanak had been much impressed by *Levant's* work. He told Captain Goodland that he had been getting frantic signals from the Admiralty about the interruption of communications between General Harrington and the home government. Thereafter *Levant* was usually greeted on arrival by a special signal from the admiral who was well known in the navy for sending snappy signals.

The company ordered McTaggart (in Zante) to pack a suitcase and take charge at Chanak temporarily. He stayed there for two years, his wife joining him later. He at once set to work to learn Turkish.

There was nothing much to do and it was very cold with occasional snowstorms. *Levant* had a small round coal stove in the saloon aft, one amidships down below, and a third in the forecastle for the men, and we needed them. Just before leaving the ship in 1920 in Malta, a naval signals officer had given me a wireless valve, then just coming into use. It was like an electric light bulb with wires sealed through the glass. I had made up a panel with clips and terminals to use it but now it seemed my successor had not kept it going. So I got some batteries and started using it to receive news bulletins from the long wave (about 11,000 metres) Post Office high power station at Leafield, near Oxford. The signals were weak but it was just possible to write off most of the news daily.

Soon after this the Constantinople cable was broken lower down the straits and we set off to mend it. When making a previous repair a couple of miles away, Finnis told me they found a mine entangled with it and had to abandon a mile or so and lay a bit round the danger area. We kept a good look out but completed the job without seeing any mines. This cable was joined through at a cablehouse on the north side of the straits opposite Nagara Point. It was dark when we got there and I went ashore in a boat. There was a British army post nearby and I reported to the officer in charge. After joining up the cables he asked me in for a quick whisky and told me there was a detachment of White Russian troops from the Crimea which was a bit of a problem for him. He said, "You had better keep clear of them as they are a bit trigger happy and sometimes shoot at people." Needless to say, his advice was heeded.

The Dardanelles was littered with abandoned naval and military equipment and some sunken ships. One fine Sunday morning, Jock Turner and I went with some sailors in one of our boats fitted with sails up the straits. Just on the north side of the narrows leading into the sea of Marmora were two half sunken Turkish ships, sterns high out of the water. We went alongside one and climbed on board. Some of the 3″ teak deck planks had gone but we cut out a lot more and filled our boat with them and returned to the ship. These ships had been Turkish transports and had been torpedoed and sunk by Commander Holbrook, VC who dived under the Turkish nets in his submarine and got into the Sea of Marmora where he created havoc, finally diving back and emerging safely.

As the sterling wages of our Greek sailors were worth a lot in Greek drachmas, Turner had got together a crew in which each one was skilled in some trade. We had a shipwright, two carpenters, two caulkers, a boilermaker and other odd skills. He also used to collect any metal scrap he could find, e.g. cable drums from old empty mines, cartridge cases, etc., and copper from short lengths of scrap cable, normally dumped overboard. This was sold at Piraeus and the money put in a ship's fund from which he bought odd items of equipment for the ship which head office could not be persuaded to supply.

After paying a call on Admiral Kelly, Captain Goodland told us that, as he was leaving, Sir John said, "My next visitor is the young captain of a destroyer which he was unlucky enough to get aground near Tenedos, at the entrance to the Dardanelles. But I shan't be too hard on him because he is a keen and energetic officer." Discussing this later, Jock Turner remarked on the differences between naval and merchant service officers regarding the safety of their vessels. He said that while a merchant service officer should never risk his ship by taking chances, if you force a naval officer to do the same in peacetime, he may fail to take a chance in war time when by doing so he can beat or sink the enemy. So the admiral was wise in not taking too severe a view of the destroyer officer hazarding his vessel.

We soon had another trip to mend a cable near Piraeus and whilst there Axtell arrived from England to relieve Jock Turner, who was appointed acting captain in Goodland's place as he was due for leave. Herbert Finnis also went on leave and was replaced by B. S. Hunt.

We returned to Chanak and Captain Turner said that in future we would anchor in one place and stay there, come hell or high water. Previously we had chopped and changed when it blew from different directions. So we anchored near the shore off an old Turkish fort west of Nagara point. If it blew onshore, one of us kept an anchor watch at night in case we dragged. We invited the senior signals officers mess of three captains to dinner, which hospitality was returned. They were Captains Montgomery, Butler and Straight of the 22nd Divisional Signals. They suggested we run an old piece of cable core to the beach and they would lay a field cable to their telephone exchange and connect us up. This was most convenient as we could now telephone our own office in Chanak and all army units and even a naval visual signal station on the hill nearby which could pass messages to any warship, including our friend, Admiral Kelly.

Butler had a banjo, so he and Axtell on his guitar, performed together. In fact, we got so friendly with them that most days we telephoned to arrange whether we dined with them or they with us. They also took us to army football matches, and invited us to come and help them dig their allotment, a vegetable garden they had started. So life at Chanak was much improved. They lived rather primitively in an old Turkish barracks close to where we were anchored. They had only oil lamps and a heating stove, so they liked coming on board in the evenings as, though cramped, we had electric light and more amenities.

Monty produced a cousin, Lieut Commander Montgomery, RN, on board HMS *Royal Sovereign*. Admiral Kelly had departed in his ship *Marlborough* and had been replaced by *Royal Oak* with Admiral Duff, and sister ships, *Resolution* and *Royal Sovereign,* 13.5 inch gun battleships. Lieut Commander Montgomery had been seconded as liaison officer with the army, and he came to lunch with us. He invited us to lunch, together with Monty, on board his ship. The battleships were on the other side of the straits, about five miles away. So Jock Turner said we would take *Levant* over there, and Monty informed his cousin that he was coming in his private yacht!

We anchored near *Royal Sovereign* and Jock, Axtell, Monty and I had lunch and were shown over the ship, gun turrets, conning tower, bridge, gunnery control room, engine room, etc. They had recently installed a short range wireless set with morse operating position on the bridge for rapid communication with other ships in the squadron. There were no radio telephones in those days.

They presented us with a mahogany plaque about 15 inches high on which was mounted a bronze figure of Mercury which is their badge, together with an inscription stating it was given to the *Levant* by the 2nd Divisional Signal Company at Chanak 1922/23.

In 1964, when the company built an 8,000 ton cable-laying ship named CS *Mercury,* the Royal Corps of Signals presented her with a statuette of Mercury. It was reported in the newspapers that this was the first time Jimmy, as their badge of Mercury is nick-named had gone to sea. A letter from me to the company's magazine *Zodiac* recalled Chanak and this with photographs was published in the royal signals journal.

There were various incidents which we heard about on the service grapevine. One of the battleships was anchoring and the first lieutenant was on the forecastle as the chain was going out. It stopped and he had his toe on it when it suddenly restarted. He lost his balance and disappeared down the hawser-hole with it. Everbody thought he would be crushed to death, but no, he fell into the water and when picked up was found only to have torn clothing and severe bruises; no bones broken, a truly extraordinary escape.

McTaggart gave a party in his flat over our office in Chanak and there were twenty or thirty guests, very multi-national, as there were Greeks, French, Italians and Turks and British army officers, and even the Turkish governor came.

Later the cable near to Besika Bay went faulty. It was unsafe to send the ship in case the Turks fired on her, so McTaggart hired a large launch, borrowed gear from us and set out to mend it. He had to go more than fifty miles and it was very cold so we lent him what the navy called a lammy suit, consisting of a coat with hood, and over-trousers of almost inch thick woollen material. It had been acquired from the navy some years before for our helmsman. He did the job and was back in two days.

Sylvia and I decided we could not afford to go on living at the Phalere Hotel which the low value of the drachma had enabled us to do so far.

We rented a ground floor furnished flat in a street with the odd name of Pezmanzoglou in Phaleron. Even this was expensive as, shortly after, the American financier Pierpoint Morgan arrived in his splendid steam yacht, the *Corsair* which moored near us in Piraeus harbour. He agreed to lend the Greek government some millions of dollars to stabilise the exchange rate. Our pounds sterling became progressively worth fewer and fewer drachmas. This seriously affected our catering on the ship which was done by our steward, Apostoli, and supervised by one of us. The practice had been to finance the mess by borrowing drachmas from the company's money in the captain's safe and replacing it at the end of the month. This was fine while the drachma went on depreciating but did not work when it went the other way. So we started a mess floating fund. Everyone gave in £10 and the money was used to buy stores, listing them at their sterling value and charging them out in sterling on our mess bills when consumed. We got 7/6d. a day messing allowance. When in port we only paid for meals taken on board. This was useful to me, as normally I only had lunch on board and lived ashore with Sylvia.

Ship's officers and men accumulated their pay on the ship's books and one could draw cash when in port but it was charged out at the rate of exchange at the end of the month, now an unknown quantity. So most of us had our pay sent to our bank in London. We cashed sterling cheques at the rate of the day as we needed them. This was easy in Greece where the local population were only too eager to buy sterling cheques. So we had early lessons in what to do when exchange rates fluctuate rapidly.

On reaching the ship one morning Axtell said the captain and Hunt had gone to Athens to see the divisional manager. It appeared that Hunt had orders to relieve the chief electrician of *Transmitter*. When they got back I was told that Hunt was going at once, leaving me in charge and the DM was sending Alfred Finnis as my assistant as we were under orders to do several repairs to our own and Greek government island cables. The government owned all the short cables linking the small islands in the Aegean Sea and had a contract with us for their maintenance.

Acting as chief electrician on the job at twenty-four years of age may be a record. Our first repair was on a faulty cable from Corinth to Patras. We went through the canal to the cablehouse and Alfred Finnis took our test wires ashore. Both reels were used to enable a loop test to be carried out using one of the other good cables.

We hooked about ten miles from Corinth and it looked as if we were close to the fault, so we spliced on to the good end and paid out new cable on that end while picking up on the faulty one. Sure enough the fault came in after about 300 fathoms, which helped to give me confidence in my testing. We carried out repairs to about five island cables on this trip and nearly killed our older Greek engineer by working long hours with much steaming.

One interesting place visited was Santorin Island in the Cyclades group. This had suffered a violent volcanic eruption about 3,000 years before. The whole centre of it became a huge crater and the sea entered it leaving the island as a ring with a central, very deep, lagoon with two entrances. At the main entrace was a zig-zag ladder of white stone steps leading up to a village. It was first seen at about 6 a.m. and looked just like a picture out of Hans Anderson's fairy tales, with the village appearing as a castle on a hill. The lagoon, a mile or so across, had steep cliffs around it with several villages with white houses and churches perched on the top. It was so deep that the island steamers could not anchor. We did so by paying out a grapnel and about 200 fathoms (1,200 feet) of wire rope, and then tying up our stern to rocks below the cliff.

After this trip we returned to Piraeus where Captain West, came out to relieve Jock Turner who reverted to chief officer. Axtell was transferred to another ship. Last who had been relieved by me in *Britannia* in 1920, arrived as chief electrician and Alfred Finnis went back to the divisional manager's office.

Soon after we went on another repair and finished up at Syra. Here orders were received to proceed to Gibraltar for a major refit in the Admiralty dockyard. Normally we would have gone to Malta but there had been a dispute over another ship, and the company decided to send us to Gibraltar.

I got permission from the captain to make a quick trip to Pireaus to see Sylvia for a day as the refit meant we should be away at least a couple of months.

The ship then went to Malta where we replenished coal and provisions. At Malta was the cableship *Amber* and Jock Turner christened her the *Ice Cream Cart* because Wilcox her chief officer, had painted her upper works blue instead of white.

On arrival at Gibraltar we went into drydock and the refit started. Head office had sent out a chief engineer, Mr Roberts to supervise our overhaul. A lot of deck planking was in bad condition and Jock wanted it renewed in teak which most of our ships had—*Levant* had pitch pine decks which were cheaper. So he engaged in a running battle with Roberts, and lost. Most of the electric wiring needed renewal as it had been put in after the ship had been built and then added to, and this had to be fought for. In the end we got most of the work done.

We had to live on shore, and Jock Turner and I stayed at the same hotel. We were up at 6 a.m. and on board just after 7 a.m. when the dockyard hands started work. While Captain West kept in touch with all the top people, we entertained all the British foremen and charge hands by standing them drinks whenever they came aboard and soon got almost anything we wanted done. This was sound business for the company. We found out that their cost estimating system only allowed the foremen 4% error either way, so they always gave a slightly higher figure to cover themselves and worked off the surplus, if any, on the

Cableship Levant in dry dock, Gibraltar.

next ship. So to get your money's worth, if you conciliated them, they would do odd jobs for you without extra charge.

Captain West was very good in backing us up in order to get a thoroughly good job done. A man called Oakley, very fat and jolly, was officer in charge of our branch office in the town, and he and his Greek wife asked us to their house.

Just as the refit was almost finished, the Gibraltar-Vigo (North Spain) cable was broken off the coast near Cape Trafalgar. Head office asked us to mend it as soon as we were ready. We had no stock cable on board as it had all been unloaded before going into drydock so a tug and lighter were sent round to our depot at Camp Bay. After loading about three miles, a south west storm came up and they had to cut it and come into the Admiralty harbour where we loaded it on board. We left next day and reached the position of the break. After grappling for some hours, the rising wind and sea stopped work and we lay to our grapnel all night. Next day the weather improved, we hooked the cable in the morning and by 10 p.m. that night completed the final splice. We were back in Gib the next day and head office sent us a congratulatory message for quick work. This is the only time we were in the North Atlantic and considering our size, only 289 tons, we had a bumpy ride. But *Levant* was what is known as a good sea boat and rode out bad weather well.

A few days later we sailed for Malta. It was a beautiful sunny morning and as we went towards Europa Point at the south end of the Rock, we saw a huge battleship with flags flying and the Marine band playing on the quarterdeck. It was HMS *Queen Elizabeth,* flagship of the Mediterranean Fleet, and flying the flag of Admiral Sir B. de B. Brock, commander-in-chief.

At Malta we loaded as much cable as we could hold from the Tanks depot and were right down to our Plimsoll loadline. Finnis went to a sale of ex-Admiralty property and bought a 10″ arc searchlight. During the refit a small upper bridge had been added in place of the previous tiny upper mount for our range-finder. We installed the searchlight on one wing of the new upper bridge. Its outer casing was brass, painted over. Jock removed the paint, and had canvas covers made for it. It proved very useful on several occasions later on as it could throw a strong beam of light.

We then returned from Syra to Athens and anchored in Phaleron Bay, and I was able to be at home again with Sylvia.

Sylvia and our dog "Towser" at No 2 Aphrodite Street, Athens.

Shortly after we moved to a second floor flat about three miles away round the bay to the east at Old Phaleron. This flat, 2 Aphrodite Street, had an open balcony with splendid views over the plain of Attica to Mount Hymettus and Athens itself with its Acropolis and church-crowned hill of Lycabetus. The landlord agreed to accept a monthly British cheque for £8 as rent for it furnished.

We had met quite a number of the British community in Athens. After the Greek army debacle in Asia Minor, there had been a revolution in Athens and about ten Cabinet Ministers had been tried and shot. The counsellor at the legation, Mr Charles Bentinck, was chargé d'affaires. The legation has a magnificent marble staircase leading up to the main reception rooms, including a ballroom, on the first floor. In addition to one or two attachés there was a consul general and two vice consuls. There was also a chaplain, the Rev Dr Wigram, who was vicar of the English Church. British prestige in Greece had always been high ever since Lord Byron died at Missolonghi in 1824, fighting for their independence from the Turks, and was especially so at this time after the defeat of Turkey and Germany in the First World War.

Mrs Bentinck was running a club for English governesses and nannies of whom there were quite a few employed by wealthy Greek families.

Sylvia was asked to help and she often went into Athens and did clerical work for it. While at the Phalere Hotel she used to hire a small rowing boat and row about the bay. Later she hired a boatman with a sailing boat and went on bathing picnics with friends.

There was a British naval mission helping the Greeks to reorganise their navy. One of their ships, a small battleship called the *Averoff*, was noticeable as having some shell holes in its funnels which were regarded as honourable scars, not to be repaired! They also had two old ex-American battleships with lattice masts, and a number of destroyers. They were contemplating buying some new ones, so Vickers, Armstrongs, Whites and other British warship builders had strong contingents of salesmen in Athens, all competing for the contracts.

Dr Wigram was an expert on Greek antiquities and took Sylvia to the museums to see them. We went up the Acropolis several times. Sylvia often went there on her own when I was away.

There was a night-club in Athens called *Caprice* which had an excellent band and a good dance floor, and we went there a good deal. One of its regular patrons was a Marconi engineer called Boome who used to get the latest music from London for the band conductor.

One afternoon I met Ebsworth of the Hollandia Milk Co on the pier at Phaleron who was going sailing with Mr Bentinck. He asked me if they could come on board afterwards? As the rule was that junior officers must ask the captain's permission to bring guests on board, I automatically said, "OK but I will have to ask the captain." The look on his face showed that he was astonished that the acting British minister might not be welcome on our ship! They came and Captain West welcomed them himself.

At the legation dances one complaint was that the Bentincks only served beer—probably he did not have much of an entertainment allowance. So on these occasions there tended to be a steady flow of men down the marble staircase and into the British Club next door for a quick one.

Mr Stevens was now the company's divisional manager in Athens as Commander Cottrell had retired. My old supervisor in Gibraltar, Mr Farrant, who had gone to Athens during World War I, was still there, in charge of the local staff department. Eventually he became divisional manager in Athens.

We also met a Mr and Mrs Webber. He had been a British engineer on the old Ottoman railway in Turkey, and was now manager of the oil

Our cutter and dinghy in Phaleron Bay, 1924.

installation of the Standard Oil Company of New York at Drapetzona near Piraeus, and we visited them there. He told me that Pierpoint Morgan's yacht, *Corsair* , came to the depot to refuel and he was astonished to observe that her hull was coated with a special compound, an inch or so thick which made it perfectly smooth. He had never seen it on any other ship. She was painted black with varnished mahogany deckhouses and had four motorboats, two small and two larger.

We met Mr and Mrs Fernie who lived near New Phaleron. He was a Scotsman who had lived in Russia for many years before the war, where he was manager of a factory. He was now working for the Save the Children Fund in Greece. Agreement had been reached between the Greeks and Turks to exchange populations in Thrace where the races were mixed. This meant uprooting many people who had lived there all their lives, and was being supervised by the League of Nations. It was very drastic but in the long run it worked, as it settled the question of the oppression of minorities and brought most Greeks into Greece and Turks into Turkey.

In the summer various yachts used to visit Piraeus or Phaleron Bay. The Mortons (jam manufacturers) came in a handsome steam yacht of 200 tons and Admiral Lord Beatty, of Jutland and Grand Fleet fame, arrived in his steam yacht. He sent over to us to enquire if we could tell him who had won the Derby. We did not know, but eventually got the answer from our Athens office.

Captain West was now relieved by Captain Gooch who had been chief officer in *Britannia* and we went off to do some cable jobs in the islands.

Levant also went to Salonika to mend our cable there. Our superintendent told us that a power cable had fallen across the aerial landline to the cablehouse and subsequently the cable was faulty. Herbert Finnis localised it at ten miles down the Gulf.

We found the fault in the cable at a joint which had a hole blown through the gutta percha insulation, evidently by the high voltage from the power line.

During the summer of 1924 Jock Turner got our shipwright and carpenters to work and build a new dinghy to replace an old one. The interior trim, thwarts, etc., were made from some of the teak we had acquired in the Dardenelles. Jock made a detachable lower keel, mast and suit of red sails which could be used for either the lifeboat or the cutter, and a red lug sail for the dinghy, so we could use two boats at a time for sailing.

Another Marconi engineer called Benning arrived from England and Boome brought him to see us. Benning told me about the experiments with short wave-length wireless waves then being carried out by Senator Marconi in his yacht *Elettra* and said he thought it would revolutionise long distance wireless telegraphy. As since the invention of wireless at the turn of the century, it had been predicted that Marconi would put the cable companies out of business, Benning's news did not seem very important. But it was, and five years later led to the merger out of which Cable and Wireless Ltd, was born. What I did not know at this time was that a team of experimenters in our head office led by K. L. Wood and including Jacob and Higgett, had in this same year perfected a method of relaying cable signals which would also cause a revolution and lead to automatic working of long cable circuits. It caused about 2,000 of the cable men to lose their jobs with economies in operation. It was even adapted for use on wireless circuits.

Captain Gooch was relieved by Captain Llewellyn Jones and Jock Turner by Wilcox who had been in *Transmitter* with me. The ship went to Syra to get some more cable from the depot and Mrs Jones and Mrs Wilcox came by island steamer, and stayed until the ship left for a repair.

The assistant superintendent in Syra was F. G. Hamilton Spratt, the brother of my old chief, Bob Spratt. He was married to a South African widow who had a daughter of nineteen years of age, a pretty girl called Miss Maclear.

One of the supervisors at Syra was Stark who had an attractive French wife. I well remember her chattering away in French with our superintendent at a party and he replying in the same language, very fluently but with an Anglo-Saxon accent, the contrast was rather odd. Many years later Stark became divisional manager in Greece but had to leave Athens when the Germans invaded in 1941. He and McTaggart went to Crete and then had to get out again when that island was invaded. They fled across the mountains to a southern port where they were picked up by a British warship and taken to Egypt.

The *Levant* was ordered to go to Messina to mend one of the Italian cables across the straits. I had been there in 1919 but this time had to land at Torre Bianca cablehouse from the sea. It was rough and by the time I reached shore with the end of our testing lead and telephone, I was soaked to the waist. When we had finished this job we went to Malta for coal, etc. While there Bob Spratt came on board. He was now working in our office in Malta.

The superintendent at Malta came on board with a couple of army officers who wanted us to repair their cable to the island of Gozo. They had been told by Head Office that the charge would be £150 a day plus cost of new cable expended. These were the usual charter terms for cableships, the amount varying with the size of the ship. They said they only had about £250 available and if it would cost more they would have to defer it. So the captain said we would do our best. We chose a fine day and managed to do the job within their limit.

Coming on board one morning I was just in time to rescue the ship's cat which had gone ashore for the night by jumping on to a lighter near us. On its way back, it lost its foothold and fell into the harbour. We dried it out in the galley and gave it some warm milk and it soon recovered. Unfortunately we lost it overboard about three months later.

It was a rough sea just as we slipped a final splice and as the ship turned rapidly, she shipped water over the quarter deck. Later we noticed the cat was not around; it must have been washed overboard.

We had one or two near accidents in *Levant*. The ship was sheltering one evening in a bay on the south east side of Tinos island owing to a northwesterly gale. About 1 a.m. in the morning the wind went round to the south east and blew right into the bay, putting us on a lee shore. We started to heave up the anchor to get out to sea, when all the bridge lights went out. We had no hand electric torches in those days so the captain steered into the wind as he could not see the compass. We got the lights on quickly and only just in time as the wind had veered about eight points and we were steering for one shore of the bay instead of the entrance. On another occasion we had a bad fog and reduced speed while sounding the siren. Suddenly we heard another siren on the port bow and the ship was stopped. Sure enough, an island steamer loomed up to port and just passed across our bows before disappearing into the fog—a near miss.

Soon after Christmas 1924 we were sent to mend one of our cables off the north coast of Crete. This island, about 150 miles long, has a large harbour, Suda Bay, near the west end with the town of Canea nearby. As the weather turned bad we had to shelter there for several days. As one entered, the wreck of a large Atlantic Transport Lines ship, the *Minnetonka* about 15,000 tons came in sight. She had been torpedoed during the war, had just managed to reach the bay and was now a complete wreck, lying on her side just inside the entrance; a sad sight.

As one proceeds eastward from Suda Bay along the north coast of Crete, the backbone ridge of mountains is clearly visible from the sea and culminates in the beautiful rounded peak of Mount Ida, over 8,000 feet high and usually snow covered. It is a magnificent sight, being over twice the height of Table Mountain. Towards the eastern end of the island is the town of Candia which has a small harbour protected by the old walls of the town, originally fortified.

On returning to Piraeus in February 1925 I found that my relief had arrived. The company had recently notified their ships that as from the 1st January leave would only be given after two and a half years service, instead of two years, except the West African ship where it was one year. This did not apply to me as I was due for leave before January 1925.

So Sylvia and I left Piraeus by sea for Brindisi in Italy to go by train from there to the English Channel. There had been a landslide in the Corinth Canal which was blocked, so our ship had to go via Cape Matapan, round the south end of Greece.

We got to Rome and put up at the Continental Hotel near the railway station where we stayed for a few days to see the city as we might not have another opportunity. We even went to a night club which had a good orchestra and dance floor, and where a man showed how one could play tunes on a handsaw.

We left by the famous Rome Express. This runs along the north west coast for some distance with splendid views of the sea, towns and hills inland. Even the Leaning Tower of Pisa was clearly seen from the train. We crossed the French frontier at Mt Cenis in the middle of the night. The main part of the train stopped in Paris but our Wagon Lit coach was whisked round Paris and attached to the train for Boulogne at the Gard du Nord.

When we got to Boulogne in the late afternoon the weather in the channel was very rough. We eventually arrived at Folkestone and into the train to Victoria where we stayed the night at the Grosvenor Hotel. It took Sylvia about two days to recover from this sea voyage. Actually she is a better sailor than I am but I had just had two years in *Levant* and though seasick, recovered quickly.

On reporting to head office Mr Lynn Robinson, the staff superintendent, told me he had received a bad report on me from Captain Jones. He said I would not be returning to the ships but would be appointed to Suez station. On reflection it is obvious that, having extended ships' tours by six months, there would be no vacancy on any ship until July at the earliest and this was probably the real reason for sending me ashore. I was rather annoyed at the time but it was the best thing that could have happened to me as will be seen later.

After visiting Warkworth, we rented a flat in a block almost opposite St Thomas Hospital at the south end of Westminster Bridge and in due course received orders to go to Suez. Sylvia decided to remain in London until I was certain of a house in Suez. All the company's married quarters there were full up.

So I sailed in the P & O *Malwa* for Port Said. One of the passengers was Prince George, the late Duke of Kent, then in the navy who was going to join his ship at Hong Kong.

CHAPTER SEVEN

Suez

The voyage to Port Said was uneventful and from there I caught the train to Suez. The railway ran to Ismailia half way down the canal and there divided, one line going to Cairo and the other to Suez.

The town of Suez is over a mile from the ship canal, and about two miles from the southern entrance which is at Port Tewfik, a small town itself. All the land around is desert, very flat, but to the west about six miles away is a range of hills called Gebel Ataqa, while there is another low ridge about twenty miles to the east in the Sinai Desert. The road to Cairo, eighty miles to the west, skirts the north end of Gebel Ataqa.

The cable station was almost in the centre of Suez in Shari (i.e., street) Halim facing the railway line to the south west. It consisted of a rectangular compound with a garden and pond in the centre. On the Halim Street side were the mess and administration offices, with a two storeyed block of bachelor quarters and house for the superintendent on the opposite side. This block was known as the 1915 Quarters. The main instrument room and workshop were on the side facing the road and railway. Where Halim Street intersected the railway, there was a level crossing, and over this was the Bel Air Hotel, at that time the only good hotel, and where I stayed on arrival.

There was also a two storeyed block of bachelor quarters on the opposite side of Halim Street called the Old Quarters. It contained a sitting room for seniors on the first floor. Over the railway level crossing and opposite the Bel Air Hotel, the company was building a large block of bachelors' quarters known as the 1925 Quarters. This was finished in 1926 but was hardly used. It is the only case I know of where the left hand did not know what the right hand was doing, as the new method of working cables, approved about 1924, meant that the building was redundant before it was finished.

Halim Street then continued towards the bay and this stretch was known colloquially as Cable Walk as originally the submarine cables landed near the bay end. The road then turned west and went to the refinery a mile from the town. It belonged to the Anglo Egyptian Oilfields Co, which had oil wells down the Gulf of Suez. Later the company was renamed The Shell Co of Egypt. Beyond this was a small government refinery.

Between the town and the Shell refinery was a nine-hole golf course and clubhouse, a sports ground and two tennis courts leased to us. There was also a private tennis club and some blocks of flats, two of which were rented to us for married quarters. There were a few other houses and flats in the town for the assistant superintendent, chief electrician and other married men. We had a staff of about a hundred British Europeans of whom about sixty lived in the mess, the rest being married men in the flats, etc. So we were the largest foreign community in Suez. The Shell refinery had about twenty-four British staff.

The railway ran through the town and then along a two mile causeway to Port Tewfik. A narrow road ran alongside the railway. Later a second road was made on the other side of the line. At Port Tewfik were all the shipping agents, consulates and the canal offices and workshops, etc. There was also a harbour called Port Ibrahim with quays and where we had a cable tanks depot and the refinery had fuel oil tanks for shipping. Port Tewfik's streets had been laid out by the Canal Company and had some pleasant avenues of trees and an excellent club, known colloquially as the French Club, but officially Le Circle Internationale.

When the ship canal was being built in 1869 fresh water was essential. So a narrow canal was made which ran from the river Nile in Cairo to Ismailia, half way down the ship canal. Here this so-called Sweetwater Canal divided, one branch running north to Port Said and the other south to Suez. All along it date palms and market gardens had proliferated, but it is infested with the snails which propagate the disease of bilharzia and Europeans are warned on no account to wash or bathe in it. At Port Said, Ismailia and Suez were waterworks which purified and disinfected this canal water and distributed it in pipes in the usual way.

The cable station was similar to that at Gibraltar and the main instrument room was laid out in the same way. All through messages were received as perforated tape which was put into automatic transmitters for sending onwards. There were five cables down the Red

Sea to Aden, four of which landed at Port Sudan (about half way) where the signals were relayed automatically. To the north there were two or three aerial landlines to Alexandria where the Mediterranean cables terminated. Copies of all messages in the form of gummed tape on forms were made at Suez as it was what was known as a control station on the Indian and Far East route. That is repetitions of faulty messages could be obtained here by stations to the west and east.

So now I was back to being an operator again and after six years absence had to take my turn with all the juniors at first. Later I was put on more senior jobs. We did shifts round the clock with a 39-hour week plus three Sunday duties a month. I found I could rent a flat on the first floor of a house on the Sweetwater Canal. It was called Makhzangis and was about a mile from the town. So Sylvia's passage from England was arranged on the P & O mailboat *Narkunda* and she sailed in June for Port Said and duly arrived by train.

The golf course had hardly a blade of grass on it, as it was stony and sandy and the greens (known as Browns) were circular level patches covered with sand mixed with fuel oil from the refinery and swept circularly so that any slight ridges were at right angles to the line to the hole. The fairways were just rock and sand. This meant that a topped ball would usually run well and it was difficult to get under a ball to loft it for a dead approach, but the skilful could do it. The sports ground was similar, and for football it was essential to wear kneecaps of elastic material with padding, otherwise one ended up in hospital with a septic leg. The cricket wicket was matting laid on hard soil and quite true, but with the ball bouncing on uneven ground, some experience was needed for fielding.

W. H. (Bill) Andrews was our superintendent, a cheerful man and he and his wife were popular. Swanson was assistant superintendent, a reserved bachelor. Davey was the chief electrician and he had a wife and two teenage daughters and a younger son. Some of the staff had wives, like Sylvia, born in South Africa, i.e. John Mills, Chitty and Hocken. "Agony" Payne whom I had known in Gibraltar was also there, now married. The secretary of the golf club was F. E. Andrews who used to make golf clubs in his spare time and we bought some from him. Rodney Holden, about two years senior to me, a tall, dark, well-built man, who also had a sarcastic tongue, was mess president and did the job very well. He now (1977) lives in Bournemouth.

At Port Tewfik was the Sinai Hotel which was kept by Captain and

Mrs Carew. They were the parents of Captain Goodland's wife and her sister whom we had met in Greece at Phaleron.

The Egyptian government had a ship of 1,000 tons called *Aida* belonging to the Ports and Lights Department which had the job of servicing the various lighthouses and buoys in the Red Sea. The ship had two British officers called Dent and Blake. The first was tall and dark, and the second short and fair and they were a cheerful couple who often came to the mess and our parties.

The Canal Company had a bathing place on the other side of the ship canal opposite Port Tewfik. It was on stilts in the water, and we were often invited by the Carews to join them there for a swim.

The cableship *Mirror* was stationed at Suez then and Captain Smythe was in command. He came to see us in our flat on the Sweetwater Canal and said to me, "Swallowed the anchor, eh? Has it given you indigestion yet?" Foy was chief officer, and his wife came to Suez. She was a South African from Malmesbury in the Cape and a very good tennis player who could hold her own in a men's four.

We also met the assistant manager of the refinery and his wife, Mr and Mrs Taylor, with whom we exchanged dinners.

The Carews introduced us to two young Frenchmen in the Canal Company. One, very dark and good looking was known as Paul. The other Domergue was always known as Cash. He was the accountant, and had a large launch to take him up the canal to pay the staff at the stations. He invited us and the Carew girls to come with him and we took lunch and tea, and were able to tie up and bathe, and it made a good day's outing.

At Christmas the mess had their own dinner party and when they got a bit lit up, they invaded the town and removed a large number of advertising signs from shops, and decorated the patio with them. The Egyptian police sergeant arrived next morning and arranged to return the signs to their owners, with monetary compensation if damaged, and all was forgiven. We were, after all, their best customers.

The mess also gave a New Year's dinner and dance to which the European community were invited.

The climate in Egypt in winter is one of the best in the world, being dry and sunny with cool nights. In the summer it is very hot but only a trifle humid in September. The rainfall is small but we did have a severe storm once.

Mr and Mrs Hadwen, whom we had known in Greece, arrived as he had been appointed British Vice Consul, and they took a flat in Cable Walk until they could get into their proper one over his office at Port Tewfik.

In February Sylvia decided she wanted to visit her own country again, so her passage was arranged in the Union Castle steamer *Gloucester Castle* to Port Elizabeth.

D. K. Smith, my old shipmate from *Transmitter* days was now in *Mirror* at Port Tewfik, and one of the engineers called Parker had invented a one man band, in which he played several instruments at once or in succession.

About two years earlier, teams at soccer, rugby, cricket and tennis from the cable stations at Alexandria and Suez had begun to play against each other. Alexandria was a large station like Suez, and these were the only two in the cable service close enough to be able to do this. The new managing director, Admiral H. W. Grant, had given a cup to be held by the winners each year, the contests being at each station in alternate years. The winter games were in March, and the summer in September. The away teams left on Friday and returned on Monday or Tuesday, and only twenty men could go as the cable stations worked day and night every day. Men going away had their duties worked for them by volunteers from the rest of the staff, to be returned later.

Mr Swanson went on leave and Mr Mann relieved him. His wife and stepdaughter, Peggy Robinson, came with him. She was a pretty and charming girl and there was much competition from men in the mess to play golf and tennis with her and take her out. Later she married "Tickey" Eastwood who had relieved me in *Britannia*.

In April the company advised us that a new system for taking the exams which made one eligible for promotion to the fourth grade (supervisor) would be introduced on 1st July.

I had been studying for the two exams since Sylvia left so I decided to take them before the 1st July deadline. Having done electrical work for five years on the ships, the preliminary electrical did not present any problem, but the general exam covered the whole of administration at company's stations, and international telegraph law and regulations, and meant a great deal of swotting. An accounts paper on the monthly accounts of a station was part of the exam. This took a whole day to answer, and failure in it meant failure in the exam.

The company had instituted what was known as station leave. This was a week's local leave every six months but there was a snag. It could only be taken *if one could be spared*. In practice one rarely could and I only got about six weeks in 30 years. However, in May a week's leave was granted, but I could not afford to go away anywhere—even if there was anywhere to go, except perhaps Cairo which I never visited. So I spent it swotting for my exam and playing golf and bridge after tea.

At Abu Sueir near Ismailia, the RAF had their Flying Training School, with about fifty pilots. We used to play them at games and in May they sent a team to play us at cricket on a Saturday and Sunday. We accommodated them in the mess and had a dinner on the Saturday night. They were a very cheery crowd.

Also in May, Lord and Lady Lloyd came to Port Tewfik to unveil the war memorial which had been erected on the left of the entrance to the ship canal to commemorate those of the Indian Army who had come to fight in Europe and the Middle East during the 1914/18 war. Lord Lloyd was the British High Commissioner in Egypt. They came from Cairo by car, a Rolls Royce with Union Jacks about a foot long on small staffs on each wing. It was preceded by two police outriders on motor cycles. There was a guard of honour of British and Indian troops, and a couple of Indian rajahs in their ceremonial native dress. It was very impressive.

In June the holy carpet arrived by train from Cairo. It was made each year and taken to Mecca during the pilgrim season where it was draped over the tomb of Mohammed. We watched the train pass the office. It was festooned with wildly shouting Egyptians on the roof and hanging out of the windows and clinging to the running boards outside. They love making a noise. When there is an eclipse of the moon everyone bangs petrol cans, dustbin lids or anything handy, and the resulting din is fantastic. They have a custom that cats are sacred and must on no account be killed, so there are dozens about and they sing their love songs at night and keep everyone awake.

The other pests in Egypt are flies which settle on anything in the hot weather and appear to breed in millions. Fly whisks come in useful.

The last week in June I sat for my exams finishing exactly on 30th June, the last day before the new regulations came into force.

Two days later I went with our cricket team to Port Said to play against their club. We left on Friday evening and stayed at the Eastern Exchange Hotel. We played cricket from 11.30 a.m. to 6.00 p.m. on the Saturday and Sunday, and were given a dinner and dance by the Port Said Club at the Casino Palace Hotel on the Saturday night which went on until about 2 a.m.

A week later my brother, Miles, passed through the canal, going on leave from India to England. I went on board for an hour while the ship waited to enter the canal. We had not seen each other since 1916.

In August I went by train to Port Said to meet Miles again as he returned to India in the *Rawalpindi*. Before going I called on the general manager of the Canal Company at Port Tewfik and asked him if I came down the canal in *Rawalpindi* could I came ashore with the pilot as the mailboats arrived about 1 a.m. in the morning and did not stop except to drop the pilot? He said, "Yes, Certainly tell the pilot you have my permission."

Miles was travelling second class as Indian Army officers were given passage money every so often. As they could easily get extra leave, they often, when young, went second class so that they could come to England more frequently. In *Rawalpindi* there were about a dozen subalterns like Miles. After dinner we played bridge—at which I lost steadily—until about 1 a.m. when a quartermaster came and said we were near Port Tewfik and the pilot was ready to go ashore. I said goodbye to Miles and climbed down with the pilot into his launch and the ship went off down the Gulf.

A Mr Carter arrived from head office to install a new system on the cable circuit working to Bombay via Aden. This was the revolutionary method of relaying between submarine cables developed in 1924 by Mr K. L. Wood and his co-workers in London and mentioned in chapter six. It was christened *The Regenerator* and worked like this.

Signals passing through a submarine cable are distorted, some more than others. If the ordinary magnetic relay were used to re-transmit them into another cable, the distortions were sent on as received. With more than one relay station cumulative distortions made a cable unworkable unless the speed, i.e., the carrying capacity, were drastically reduced. The regenerator obviated this by regenerating the signals at each relay station and sending them on in undistorted form no matter what distortions were received. The directors had decided to introduce it throughout the whole cable system at a cost of about a million pounds—a lot of money in those days. It worked splendidly for many years and was not superseded until the 1960s when co-axial telephone cables with submerged repeaters were introduced.

I used to visit Hadwen a good deal as his wife had gone to England, and he dined in the mess with me several times. He told me that Lord

Lloyd the High Commissioner in Cairo had instructed him to try and restart a Rifle Club in Suez. There had been one there before the war. The political situation was that in 1925 the British government had set up a parliamentary system in Egypt and handed over the internal administration of the country to the Egyptians except for the responsibility for the protection of foreigners.

There were at that time 11,000 British troops in Egypt, mostly stationed near Cairo and Alexandria, except for one brigade at Ismailia called the canal brigade. There were a good many British officials in Egyptian government service including the chiefs of police in Cairo, Alexandria, Port Said and Suez. As there were no British troops at Port Said and Suez, Lord Lloyd had decided there ought to be some form of civil defence against local riots so that the British community could defend itself for a few hours pending the arrival of troops. Hence the proposal to form Rifle Clubs at these places.

Hadwen called a meeting of the British community in the church hall, and a committee was elected to run the club. Taylor of the refinery was made captain and I was elected secretary.

The day before the news had arrived I had passed my two examinations, so I asked the superintendent if I could now have a job

Rifle range, desert and Attaka Mountains, Suez.

on the electrical staff. I was put on electrical maintenance work, and later on what was called the rounds, that is as watch electrician in the main office.

The electrical staff at that time consisted of the chief electrician and his deputy, four watchkeeping electricians, and a couple of men on maintenance of apparatus. In the workshop there was a British mechanic called Harper who had one or two local staff assistants. Most of the large stations had British mechanics, the majority of whom had joined after training in a telegraph instrument maker's factory. Messrs Creeds trained a good many of our mechanics. One or two of the watch and maintenance electricians were young men who had been trained on the two year courses at the company's Hampstead school started in 1920/21 and already mentioned. They were irreverently referred to as plumbers by the operating staff. There was a generic name by which all British foreign staff of whatever rank were known. This was TC which stands for telegraph clerk. This was what operators had been called when cables were first laid. Another odd word was phundie (or fundi) applied to anyone who specialised in a particular piece of equipment, e.g. "He is a phundie on relays."

I set to work to organise the Rifle Club with the help of Taylor and the committee and several of our men who volunteered. During the war one room in the 1915 staff quarters had been made into an armoury and it contained fifty sniper rifles. Hadwen advised us the army in Cairo would send us fifty Short Lee Enfield rifles and ammunition and withdraw the sniper rifles.

Mr Swanson, who had returned as superintendent, told me his predecessor had not approved of the Rifle Club. He did not say he disapproved but it looked as if he was trying to induce me not to take on the job of running it. I was not amused about this and repeated it to Hadwen.

Soon after this the mess president told me we would no longer be able to use the armoury. Mr Swanson said we could keep the rifles in his own office—a quite unworkable suggestion—as I needed access to them at any time for cleaning and maintenance.

There was a firm of shipping agents called Beyts & Co and the manager, Mr Innes, was a Golf Club and Rifle Club committee member. He offered to let us keep a dozen rifles there where he had an enclosed rack for rifles. Taylor arranged for about twenty rifles to be kept at the refinery where he was now manager. A few were kept in

Swanson's office, and the rest at the British Consulate at Port Tewfik. Hadwen said the RAF would fly the new rifles to Suez.

So on December 31st, 1926 we hired a lorry, put all the sniper rifles in it, and went to the airstrip. It had been a regular RAF station during the war but was now only an emergency landing ground.

While waiting for the aircraft to arrive from Cairo, a Bristol fighter suddenly approached the airstrip. As it landed long streaks of fluid were observed coming out of it underneath. On inspection the pilot said it was petrol. His rear gunner got out and removed the engine cowling to reveal a broken petrol pipe. They were extremely lucky it had not caught fire.

Then two large Vickers Vimy transport aircraft were seen coming over the Ataqa hills to the west. They landed and began unloading our fifty Lee Enfield rifles, and loading up the old sniper rifles.

Soon after another Bristol fighter arrived from Moascar with a new petrol pipe which was rapidly fitted. Then they departed and the Vickers Vimys took off to return to Cairo. Hadwen and I took the rifles back to the mess with two field telephones and some wire which had been sent to us.

During January and February 1927 we got the Rifle Club going. Just beyond the airstrip there had been a rifle range during the war. We only had to clear the sand out of the butts, fit them with targets and lay our telephone wire down the range, 600 yards with firing points at 100 yard intervals.

Taylor had target frames and posts made at the refinery workshops and a flagpole for a red flag. Some warning notices in English and Arabic were erected some way behind the butts in the desert. The committee decided to have two shoots a week, Sunday mornings and Thursday afternoons, with a small bus to take people to the range. Mr Hall, the Padre, at the English church said he supported the club and would come himself if we ran a special bus after his Sunday morning service and this was agreed. One of our men, Sealy, had a four cylinder motor bike and sidecar, and was very helpful in taking us to the range to get everything in order.

There was an old RAF mess building and for a nominal pound a year they rented it to us. After a shoot we went there to clean rifles and have a glass of beer. We only operated for the six winter months. It was too hot in the summer. In the cool and sunny winter of Egypt, it was very pleasant out on the range surrounded by nothing but desert. We organised teams to shoot against each other, and the club was quite popular.

Some books and pamphlets on rifles and their maintenance were obtained from the BSA Company and we all learned how to shoot and look after our arms, which no doubt was what Lord Lloyd intended. Many of our men had been in school OTC's and already knew something about rifles.

During the summer of 1927 I played cricket regularly and we had the usual matches against fourth FTS and 208 Squadron, RAF and Port Said. In winter there were soccer and rugger games amongst ourselves.

Going one morning to see Hadwen, I found a lady in his office and was introduced to Mrs Elliott-Lynn, who was famous for her long solo aircraft flights. She was a tall handsome woman of about thirty. She had been staying at the residency in Cairo with Lord and Lady Lloyd and had been invited by the commanding officer to visit 208 Squadron at Moascar.

The old Aga Khan arrived by sea and went on to Cairo. Hadwen told me he went to meet him and the chief of police laid on a guard of honour. Hadwen said one of the Aga Khan's secretaries pulled out a pocket case stuffed with banknotes and asked him if it was all right to give each policeman a pound. He was told on no account to do so. Hadwen remarked that as an impecunious young vice consul, he could have done with a tip too!

It was at this time the Empire Beam short wave wireless service commenced. After Marconi had experimented with short waves in his yacht in 1924, the government had decided to scrap the original scheme to use long waves and adopt the much cheaper short waves system. The Marconi Company contracted to construct the equipment and install it, and Marconi's two principal assistants worked on this. Mr Franklyn designed the transmitters and aerials, and Mr Mathieu the receivers. It had to be done very quickly and the company made hardly any profit out of the deal.

When the wireless circuits opened for traffic to Canada, India, Australia and South Africa, the rates charged were three quarters of the cable rates. They worked fairly well from the start, and immediately captured a great deal of the cable companies' traffic. In Suez it was observed that the number of through messages to Bombay, Calcutta and Rangoon was more than halved.

Mr Davey, the chief electrician, went on leave and was relieved by Mr

Broadbent who had looked after Hancock and me in Luanda when we called there in *Britannia* in 1920. He did not know much about the electrical side of the business but was a good administrator. So we did our best to keep him from trying to monkey with the apparatus in the main office.

My old friend (or enemy) Captain Llewellyn Jones passed through Suez but I did not meet him. Mr Mann was relieved by Mr Sturrock as assistant superintendent and one day he told me that Swanson had said that he had received from head office a copy of a bad report that Llewellyn Jones had made about me. Sturrock said Swanson had thrown it into the waste paper basket, saying it was a lot of rubbish, and he considered me one of the best men he had on the staff. This astonished me as I had thought he did not love me over the starting of the Rifle Club. When I told Sturrock this he said Swanson had remarked that I had managed it very well.

I think that Hadwen had told Lord Lloyd that Swanson was obstructing the club and this had reached the Foreign Office who told our head office to tell Swanson to co-operate. So he was not sorry the club was successful.

In the winter Mr A. W. Keown-Boyd, the director general of the European Department of the Ministry of the Interior, came to Suez and after inspecting the club's arrangements, invited me to lunch at the Sinai Hotel with Hadwen and Chetwynd Bey, the OC of the camel corps. He discussed the Rifle Club and all its implications as a civil defence aid and seemed pleased with what we had done.

Mr Keown-Boyd also saw Swanson and the new manager of the refinery (Taylor had gone on leave) and told them what should be done in an emergency. In Suez town the Europeans were to gather in the cable office compound. It had a strong iron fence where there were no building walls. At Port Tewfik they would go to the British vice-consulate, while the refinery could look after itself. We were provided with strips of bright material to signal to aircraft. Troops would be sent at once and should arrive in about two or three hours.

Chetwynd Bey was a most cheery soul, of the Glubb Pasha type of officer. The main job of his camel corps was to prevent drug smuggling across the Sinai desert, and his men and camels were a fine lot. They spent most of their time patrolling in the desert and only occasionally visited Suez.

An armourer sergeant came down from Cairo and inspected our

rifles and said they were in good order. He took away one or two which we had found inaccurate or were nickeled up, i.e., had a fine coating of nickel from the bullets fired. We had some special cleaning powder from BSA to prevent this.

Padre Hall came on to the mess patio one morning (he had been made an honorary member) and said he wanted eight men to help him. He told us that a young man travelling out to Kenya had been landed from a ship at Port Tewfik with acute appendicitis. He had died of peritonitis after an emergency operation and had to be buried that afternoon. He had no friends or relations there. So eight of us volunteered as coffin bearers, the only time I have ever helped with such an office. The padre afterwards wrote to his relatives.

Padre Hall was about thirty and a good sort. He came to shoot with the Rifle Club and was a first class shot, though he had only one good eye, the other having been damaged during the war. He had joined up early in 1916 and after training was sent to Dublin where his regiment had been fired on by the IRA while marching through the streets of the city. He used to entertain us by singing the doleful ditty, *Just before the battle, Mother* while we were cleaning rifles after a shoot and, at a mess concert, did a humorous monologue entitled *Being bright at Breakfast Time*.

There was a cloud burst one evening over the Ataqa mountains to the west. Only a few drops of rain fell in Suez but water poured down from the hills and flooded the refinery which had to douse its furnaces. The Cairo road which ran north west on an embankment about 15 or 20 feet high was cut through in half a dozen places a few miles outside the town. I went to have a look next morning but most of the water had run off into the bay. It had been up to six foot deep in some wadis near the road, as could be seen by the marks on them. We usually had little rain and this event was most unusual.

Sand storms were much commoner, and a good one with a whirling pillar of sand like a waterspout, could cause a blackout besides filling eyes, ears and nose with grit, and covering everything even inside a house with dust. The landlines to Alexandria got blown down once or twice and once were sabotaged by some Egyptians. Usually they were repaired in hours but once they were interrupted for a few days. The RAF laid on flights to carry messages, as reels of perforated tape, in both directions. Urgent messages could be sent by Capetown but there were traffic jams.

A lot of apparatus for the new regenerator system arrived and I got the job of helping to install it.

There was a local epidemic of pneumonic plague which caused many deaths amongst the Egyptian population, and we all had to be innoculated. In the native quarter of Arbiin they were throwing the corpses out into the street.

One of our juniors, Basil Biron, took over the secretaryship of the Rifle Club as I was busy all day working on the new installations in the office. Mr Broadbent asked if I would stay on a few extra months before going on leave. But if I did so it would delay my taking the final electrical examination. When passed, one got a three year jump into the next grade, and I did not want to miss this. He agreed and said I should go when due.

Bishop Gwynne paid us a visit and a dinner in the mess on Sunday night was held in his honour. Next day about thirty men were ill with "Gyppy tummy". This included me, but I managed to stagger through afternoon duty. Djubreel, the head boy, got me two bottles of milk and some ice and I retired to my room and had recovered by next morning. It was traced to some prawns not being properly cleaned and cooked. The bishop was unharmed!

The president of the golf club was Mr Macdonald, the Port Tewfik manager of Messrs Worms Ltd, the big firm of coaling and shipping agents. He was a charming man and he, Innes, one of our men called Lear and I had a regular golf foursome on Sunday afternoons, followed by bridge at the clubhouse.

Mrs Macdonald was the elder daughter of Sir Hubert von Herkomer, the famous portrait painter and one time president of the Royal Academy. Sir Hubert had built a sort of German Schloss (castle) at Bushey where we lived when I was a boy. He also ran a school for art students. I once sat for him in his castle when a very small boy as he wanted one with fair hair for a picture. Mrs Macdonald was a tall imperious woman—someone christened her the Duchess of Port Tewfik— but she was very friendly to me when she found I had lived in Bushey, and knew her father. Sir Hubert had died in 1914.

Towards the end of April my passage on the Ellerman liner *City of Paris* was booked from Port Tewfik. The Macdonalds invited me to have breakfast with them, and his launch put me on board afterwards.

My cabin on board was shared with an elderly man who said to me: "The only person with your name I have met was a schoolmaster many

Christmas day celebrations, members of our mess at the railway level crossing close to our office, Suez.

years ago." I told him it was my father who had been one before he got married.

The voyage home was uneventful. I was invited to join a bridge four and, being lucky this time, won enough to cover all my tips to the stewards.

The ship berthed at Tilbury and I remember talking to a policeman while waiting for the train to Liverpool Street. A few days before a policeman, who had stopped a motorist near London, had been shot and killed. This bobby said: "We will get the murderer, sir, if we have to search for years." They did, and he was hanged. Men who kill policeman are for it. It is a pity they do not hang them any more.

At Liverpool Street station I was met by Miles and Mother who had come up to London from Warkworth. Miles had bought a car, an Austin 12 Tourer. I reported to head office and saw the staff superintendent and the doctor. We went up the Great North Road to Warkworth the next day.

CHAPTER EIGHT

England

The summer of 1928 was spent at my parents' home at Warkworth. Most of the time my brother Miles was there and we played golf, tennis, cricket, bowls and attended meets of the local otter hounds. Generally the weather was good and we had a pleasant time.

An historical pageant was performed in the courtyard of the partly ruined Warkworth Castle. In one scene the Duke of Northumberland and Hotspur, his son, were seen studying a map before the latter left Warkworth to fight the battle of Shrewsbury where he was killed—a solemn moment. Macnab, our local doctor, who was sitting next to us remarked, "He is making a list of the pubs on the road to Shrewsbury," which convulsed those nearby with laughter.

Head office advised that I was posted to the London cable station when my leave finished at the end of August, and then on 1st October to the Training School at Hampstead for the six months course, prior to taking the final electrical exam.

I went to London to find some digs. At 124 King Henry's Road, not far from Chalk Farm Underground station I saw the landlady, Mrs Batt. She said she could put me up for thirty shillings a week inclusive of meals, except lunches and teas Monday to Friday. The house was one of those large terrace houses with a basement and three floors, which were built in Victorian times. We had meals in the basement in a room which no doubt had been the servants hall. There were five men staying there including me. Two of them worked for the Burmah Oil Co and another was a young chartered accountant. I had a small room on the top floor, originally intended for servants, but it was quite comfortable. No house or other allowances were paid while in London station or the school so I had to be very economical. Mrs Batt was a good cook and fed us very well, so there was nothing to complain about.

London cable station was on the second floor of Electra House but it took in a narrow adjacent building called Tower Chambers which had an entrance of its own always open, as we worked shifts, day and night. The entrance lobby appeared to act as an unofficial police station as the local city bobbies used to hang their capes in it and were in and out at all hours—a useful security arrangement for a cable station.

The circuits were in two long rooms connected at one end and in the centre by a sort of glass enclosed passsage which ran across the central open well of the main building. The duties were on a spreadover basis. As the operators had to catch trains, night duty lasted 9 hours, from 11 p.m. to 8 a.m. but one got a short morning duty from 8 a.m. to 1 p.m. The official "day" was 8 hours, with half an hour off for a meal, i.e., a 45 hour working week. There was occasional Sunday duty, paid extra.

The regenerator had now been installed at intermediate stations abroad and the main cable circuits worked direct to Alexandria, Bombay, Singapore, Capetown, Carcavellos (for Lisbon), Rio and Buenos Aires. All messages were received as perforated tape which was fed into Creed printers which translated the morse signals into letters, figures, etc., on paper tape which was gummed by the operator straight on to delivery forms. Copying ink was used so that a "wet" tissue copy of each message could be made before delivery. The company now had too many operators, many from abroad, and as a first step had introduced what was known as extended furlough. Older men over fifty were given extended leave on basic pay until they reached the normal retiring age of fifty-five when they went on pension. Meanwhile the surplus younger men were sent to London station which was becoming overstaffed. I did ordinary operating duties. I found this interesting for a short period as it enabled me to learn how this large station was run.

I started my six months course at the school in Hampstead on 1st October. The main building was on the north side of a cul-de-sac with, on the other side, a large hall with two small ante rooms, and another single storey building used as a wireless school for ship staff. The hall was occupied by the examiner for the final electrical exams.

My digs were within walking distance, and lunch, Monday to Friday, was provided at the school for a shilling, and tea was brought round in the afternoon. In addition to those like myself, there were some senior men on the same course. They had passed their exams before it was introduced. The school had juniors doing the two year course, and there was a section for training operators to touch-type on machines which produced morse perforated tape from a typewriter keyboard.

Our course was divided into five sections. First we had a month in the workshop learning to repair instruments, and make parts for them. Then the maintenance of instruments, instruction in suspending relay and recorder coils, etc., location of faulty or broken cables and finally signal shaping and cable balancing. The wireless school for ship staff was run by Mr Marchant who was a wireless engineer. Mr Stephens who had been assistant superintendent in 1916 was superintendent, and Mr Schaefer was still there but now did administration work. As well as practical work in each section there were lectures on aspects of our job.

Izard who had been second electrician in *Transmitter* when I met him in Capetown in 1920 was doing the course, and A. W. Browne who had been in Gib with me during the war was also there.

I became friendly with H. G. Wellingham who joined the company originally as workshop instructor at the Western Telegraph Company's school at Madeira and had recently come to the Hampstead school. There was no doubt about his ability. He had re-organised the workshop and made it a model of efficiency.

At Christmas the school was closed for four days and I went to Warkworth by train. On Boxing Day the Percy Hunt, led by the master, the Duke of Northumberland, met at the village bridge and was entertained by Mr Taylor of Bridge House. The Duchess and their children (including the present Duke) were also there, and it was a colourful scene.

During that spring there was a cold frosty spell lasting over a week, and all the ponds and lakes were frozen. I bought a cheap pair of skates and went on the Regents Park lakes where I fell down a lot before becoming moderately safe. One Saturday three of us from Mrs Batt's went to the Welsh Harp at Hendon and skated, and on the Sunday the three Harcourt girls from Bushey, whose brother had been at school with me, invited me to join them at Elstree for an all day picnic to skate on the large reservoir.

I became friendly with a man called Lyndsay who lived in digs near mine. He was a naval architect and personal assistant to Sir John Biles who ran a naval architectural consultancy. He told me a story against himself. A tall elderly gentleman called at his office and asked to see the boss, who was out at the time but expected back shortly. Lyndsay asked the visitor to wait but forgot to ask his name. Thinking he might like something to read, he found a copy of a magazine called *The Motor Ship* which he handed to him. When Sir John returned he found his guest was Sir Charles Parsons, the famous inventor of the steam turbine, who would not be interested in motor ships!

At the end of March 1929 I took my final electrical examination. Mr Elms was the examiner and most of it was practical work, but there was a *viva voce* with questions on anything about our work. The cable testing came last and I finished this just before tea, so Mr Elms sent for our tea and we chatted. He asked me where I had served, and when he heard I had been in the ships for about five years a gleam came in his eye. I think he thought if he had known that he would have given me a much tougher problem in testing.

I then returned to London station and early in May I was informed that I had passed. Shortly afterwards I was on night duty and working next to me was George Eastwood, the younger brother of "Tickey" Eastwood of the cableships. He told me he had recently taken his preliminary electrical exam which he had passed and was under orders to sail for Durban. I returned to my digs and went to bed, but was phoned about 10 a.m. by someone in the office who wanted to know if I had any special commitments in London as staff department had mentioned something about sending me to Durban. I said: "I can leave for Durban tomorrow if necessary."

I guessed I was to go instead of Eastwood, so I sent a cable to Sylvia saying that I expected to come to Durban shortly. She was then staying in Windhoek, South West Africa, where her brother Douglas and his wife were now living as he worked in the government survey department there.

On duty that night, George Eastwood said, "My appointment to Durban is cancelled and I am going to the Hampstead school for the six months course." I said, "Yes, I know. I am going to Durban instead of you." My official appointment came the next day.

I was given three weeks leave before sailing, which I spent at Warkworth.

My ship was the *Gloucester Castle* sailing from London, and Hammond of the Burmah Oil Co from my digs, gave me a note of introduction to a friend, who was the Union Castle manager in London. I called on him and he kindly said he would tell the purser to welcome me on board.

I met the purser, a charming Irishman called O'Hara who said he had arranged for me to sit at his table in the saloon. There was another TC a couple of years junior to me, called Selfe, also going to Durban. The purser sat at the head of his table and he had a lady on his right and me on his left. He told me she was the young wife of a naval commander who had gone to Capetown on their previous voyage and had asked him to look after her when she came out. O'Hara said she had led a sheltered life in an English village and she might be in for some shocks when she got abroad. So he proposed to shock her gently en route.

There was a well heeled Rhodesian and his wife returning via Beira to Salisbury. He had a car stowed on board and whenever they took cargo out of it we used to come and tell him they were bashing his car as they unloaded long iron bars!

We arrived at Durban and I reported to the Superintendent, Mr S. H. Davis. It had been arranged that as soon as I learned about a house, Sylvia would come by train from Windhoek.

While I had been on leave and during my school course, the Eastern and Associated Telegraph Companies had been considering the question of the Beam wireless competition. Through the intermediary of their auditors represented by Sir William Plender of Deloites and the Marconi Company's auditors, Sir William McLintock, it was proposed that a merger be arranged. The Pacific Cable board (set up by the governments of England, Canada, Australia and New Zealand in 1901)

Married staff flats, Essenwood Road, Durban.

who owned the British Pacific cables had also been heavily hit by the wireless competition. The upshot was that an Imperial wireless and cable conference held in 1928, had recommended that all the empire wireless and cable services should be amalgamated. This was approved as from September 1929. The details are given in Mr K. C. Baglehole's book *A Century of Service* published in 1969 by the Company. The operating company for the amalgamation was called Imperial & International Communication Ltd, later changed to Cable and Wireless Limited.

CHAPTER NINE

Durban and Lourenço Marques

When en route to South Africa one is given a large form to be filled in for the immigration authorities. In this one has to state, amongst other things, whether one has ever been in jail before and your means of support. South Africans sometimes got a bit restive about this and just before my arrival in Durban, a barrister who lived there, refused to fill in the form. They put a guard on the ship to stop him going ashore, but he left on a friend's yacht from the seaward side and went to his house. When this was discovered they tried to persuade him to fill it in but he refused and they could not do much about it. However, he had made his point, as now only foreigners have to complete the long form. There is a short one for South African nationals.

Durban is a town of varied characteristics. Foremost is its fine harbour and excellent port facilities. It handles a great deal of the shipping and trade of this part of Africa. It is also a seaside resort having a beach and many good hotels. The town has excellent shops and general facilities, and finally it has a splendid residential area on the low line of hills behind it called the Berea. Between the town and the Berea is a golf course and racecourse. On the promontory of land on the outer side of the harbour, called the Bluff, is a whaling station, and the South African navy has a base on Salisbury Island inside the harbour.

The climate in winter is similar to that of the South of France. In summer it is semi tropical but humidity is never high. Many streets are lined with jacaranda and flamboyant trees and flowers, especially canna, grow profusely in public and private gardens.

About this time, probably because of the merger of the cable and wireless interests, the titles of superintendent and electrician were abolished, and manager and engineer substituted. The young plumbers were called assistant engineers. Only in cableships was the title electrician retained for some years, but they are now called cable engineers. As already mentioned, Mr S. H. Davis was manager, a nice man with a charming wife. Mr Stevens was his assistant and Mr Relle was engineer, with two young assistant engineers on his staff. There were four supervisors on the rounds.

The station was smaller than Suez but quite important as apart from the considerable local business traffic, most of the UK/Australian cablegrams were routed this way. There were about thirty-six English foreign service staff of whom about twenty were bachelors. There were also about twenty white South African local staff and the usual native messengers and servants.

There were three submarine cables and a landline to Capetown. One cable was worked direct to Adelaide in South Australia, via relays at Mauritius, Rodriguez, Cocos Island and Perth. Another was to Zanzibar with a relay at Mozambique and the third to Lourenço Marques.

Sylvia came by train and brought with her an Irish terrier called Paddy, to which she was much attached. We got accommodation for three weeks at the Coogee Hotel, not far from the sea front, and then went into a company flat on the ground floor in Essenwood Road on the Berea. We had a Zulu as a servant and a small boy as his assistant. There was a tram service from the town which ran along Musgrave Road (parallel but lower than Essenwood Road) for the whole length of the Berea. This was a circular route, going up the hill at one end, and coming down the other. The company's married quarters were provided with all the heavy furniture but one had to have one's own oil stove, cutlery, crockery and linen. These flats had five rooms with lounge and dining room with an archway between, and a verandah in front. There were servant quarters at the back. Managers and their assistants got fully furnished quarters, and the former had a servant allowance.

The small cable stations at Beira and Quelimane up the east coast were staffed from Durban by sending men there for a year, including officers-in-charge recruited from the supervisors. Not long after my arrival one was sent up to Quelimane. As I was fully qualified, I applied for his job in Durban and was now in charge of a shift which was more interesting and I earned extra pay.

One really needed a car in Durban as it is rather spread out, but we could not afford one and hardly any of our men had one. The tram service, however, was good. One bought books of twopenny tickets beforehand, otherwise stage fares were threepence. There was also five per cent discount on electricity bills for prompt payment. It is a pity these ideas are not more widely adopted these days. The municipal authorities were good managers. We got our first broadcast radio receiver as there was a local broadcasting station. There was also a good municipal orchestra conducted by Mr Dan Godfrey, the son of the late Sir Dan Godfrey of Bournemouth fame.

All the staff was now called on to sign agreements of service with the new company produced by the mergers. This guaranteed a minimum of five years service, unless due to retire before then, and half pay free of income tax on retirement together with half average foreign service allowance.

In the new year orders were received from head office for me to go to Lourenço Marques. So Sylvia and I packed all our belongings and embarked on a Union Castle steamer for the journey which took just over a day, about 300 miles.

Our Lourenço Marques station had only two foreign service staff, the manager and his assistant. We were met by Wallace Donaldson, the assistant whom I was to relieve, and his wife Nellie.

Lourenço Marques (now known as Maputu) is situated in Delagoa Bay, on the north side of the estuary of the river Esperito Santo. It was then the capital of Portuguese East Africa (the colony of Mozambique) and was the main port for both that colony and the Transvaal, being connected by railway to Pretoria and Johannesburg about 365 miles away.

The climate in the winter months, May to September, is mild and quite pleasant. It is hot in summer, average about 80°F but there are regular sea breezes.

The business part of the town is about one and a half miles from the mouth of the estuary and low lying. Towards the sea there is a plateau about 100 feet high, and this is the main residential area. The cable station was situated in the Avenida Miguel Bombarda, the main road leading from the town to this plateau and was about a mile from the business centre. But all cablegrams were taken in and delivered by the government telegraph office in the town to which there was a landline.

Owing to the opening of wireless telegraph circuits to Lisbon and places in Portuguese East Africa, we did not handle much traffic. The two storied building for bachelor staff in the middle of a compound 150 yards square, had been divided and turned into two houses for the manager and his assistant. There were numerous trees, bushes and an old gun on its wooden carriage, used in the past to give time signals to the town and shipping.

Our half of the old quarters had four bedrooms upstairs and a large lounge cum dining room downstairs. Next to this was a billiard room with its table in fair condition, and a very wide verandah all round. It was all netted in with wire mosquito guaze. The kitchen and servants quarters were in a separate building. At the back, via a covered way, was a building containing bathrooms, etc.

As there was plenty of room we shared the house with the Donaldsons and their two children for the fortnight which we overlapped. The manager, Mr Fletcher, was being relieved by F. R. Spray who arrived within a few days of us, his wife coming later.

The cable station was rather antiquated and we were back in the early days of cable telegraphy. There were two cables, one to Durban, and the other to Beira, an important port for Rhodesia and Nyasaland, 475 miles north of us. Then it went on to Quelimane another 140 miles further north, and on from there to the town called Mozambique.

Though we had mains electricity for lighting, there were no power supplies in the office for working the cables. What are known as primary (chemical) batteries were used both for driving small motors for pulling the telegraph tapes, and for signalling currents in the cables. For the former there were tray batteries, so called because they were built up in lead lined wooden troughs, or trays about twenty inches square; and for the latter Leclanche batteries already mentioned. The office closed at 9 p.m. There was an electric bell to our house in case of trouble after 4 p.m. I found it was being rung far too frequently, usually for a demand for a change of batteries; so it was soon arranged that this could be done by the Goanese operators on duty.

At that time Britain, South Africa and Portuguese East Africa were on the gold standard and one could draw golden sovereigns from the banks in Lourenço Marques. The local escudos were just over 100 to the pound sterling. Our house servants asked for and received their wages in sovereigns. What they did with them I have no idea—probably saved some for a rainy day.

I soon found we were a land sales office as well as a cable station. When the company first went there in 1880, the plateau to the east of the town was entirely unoccupied, and when the cable station was built it was given a large area around it of almost a square mile to the north of the Avenida Miguel Bombarda. Early in the century it was realised that this plateau was the ideal place for a residential suburb and the company was called on to develop it. At that time the cable station was doing well financially and it was reluctant to take on this work, so an agreement was made with the government. The latter undertook to survey the area and make roads. It was divided into large building plots of which there were 404, each numbered. In those days of cheap labour a large garden was considered necessary for each house. The government and the company then solemnly drew odds and evens out of a hat and each became the owner of half the plots.

Now the roads were all made but only about thirty or forty plots had been sold, and the price for the best had reached 15 shillings per square metre, making each plot worth about £1,500, i.e. for almost 2,000 square metres. After some people had bought plots and divided them into three, Spray suggested to head office that we divide them if requested, each plot being charged the survey fee of £15. So I set up a drawing office on a large table in the instrument room to prepare plans of sub-divided plots, and we produced various kinds of sub-division to suit the sizes and shapes. All this was interesting and a change from my usual duties.

We soon joined in the social life of the British and South African community. Sylvia met a young S African called Gil Williams and his wife whom she had known in Capetown. They were a cheerful couple and good company.

At the eastern end of the residential area, and facing out into the bay, was the Polana Hotel, a tourist resort built by the S African entrepreneur, Mr Schlessinger. Below the hotel was a bathing enclosure and pavilion and we went there regularly. We used to walk the half mile to the cliff top and down a sloping path to the pavilion. The enclosure was fenced with steel nets to keep out sharks and had a roofed platform on piles in the centre with diving boards. We taught Paddy, our Irish terrier, who was a good swimmer, to dive from a springboard and retrieve a tennis ball in the water. He used to jump off the board with all his legs stretched out below him to break the water and really seemed to enjoy it.

Sylvia's mother, Mrs Cairncross, came to visit us by train from Johannesburg and stayed about two months. She was seventy-five years of age but full of life and energy.

About this time the South African government arranged with the Portuguese government for the establishment of a S African consulate general in Lourenço Marques, and the new consul general arrived.

He was a pleasant and genial man and Mr Pike, the British CG helped to introduce him to everbody. But when he put a notice in the local English language newspaper saying S African nationals should register with him, there was much discussion among the British community as to who was, and was not, a S African national. Some Englishmen there had lived in S Africa for years but did not really regard themselves as S African nationals, though legally they probably were. In foreign countries consulates urge their nationals to register so that in case of trouble they can advise and assist them.

Owing to the general world slump in trade which followed the financial crash at the end of 1929, telegraph traffic, which depends on business activity, had decreased and our company had to institute severe economies, especially in the reduction of overtime. This meant take-home pay decreased, and we had to economise ourselves.

We gave dinner parties to various friends and led a cheerful and pleasant life, in spite of being hard up. Tennis parties with the Sprays were held on the court at the back of the building. The billiard table was useful for play after dinner.

We were invited by our local Goanese staff to a party at the Goanese Club. This was well appointed as their community was large.

Sylvia did a great deal improving the garden round our house. She made a sunken paved garden and grew some magnificent sunflowers about six feet tall. Spray had a new wooden carriage made for our gun which was mounted under a flagstaff, which gave us a naval appearance.

The cable from Durban to Mozambique broke, cutting off direct communication between S Africa and Tanganyika, Kenya, etc. So we were called on to relay messages on the coast route. This involved what was known as hand translation which is a human relay where the operator sends on by hand key the signals received on tape. Before automatic relays this method was used for many years in cable stations and demanded much skill and concentration to do it for hours on end. We were suddenly informed the cable station was to close down as were the others at Beira and Quelimane. Spray was to remain on until the end, but we were to return to Durban.

These stations were no longer remunerative. In addition, the wireless telegraph service to Europe via Lisbon was operated by a Portuguese subsidiary of the Marconi Company which had been transferred to

Cable & Wireless Ltd, so we were competing with our own wireless circuit. The Portuguese colonial government wireless stations had been taking most of the local traffic between the east coast ports for some time.

We sailed for Durban early in 1931 on a Dutch ship, and Sylvia was sick all the way due to an attack of malaria, from which she soon recovered. We stayed at an hotel on the Berea for about a week and then went into a first floor company flat in Sydenham Road.

We had a problem with our household goods. When I brought them out from England customs duty was avoided by arriving as a settler, allowing household goods up to a certain value free of duty. Naturally this is only supposed to happen once. However, after explaining our position to the chief of Customs at Durban, he agreed as they were the same goods, he would let them back without duty.

With the return to Durban of staff from the closed stations we were over-manned and about ten of the more junior men were sent home to England.

There was no vacancy for me as a supervisor so I was made assistant to the engineer, Mr Relle; new supervisors included Rice my old instructor from Porthcurnow, now married, and Snook, the younger brother of the Snook in the London Training school whom we had christened the Admiral.

We only stayed about three months in Durban and were then ordered to return to England, together with about a dozen others.

As soon as our passages were booked in the Bullard & King cargo liner *Umvuma,* I went to see the agents who said she sailed from Beira calling at Lourenço Marques where we had left our dog and could pick him up and bring him on to Durban. So we wrote at once to the Ministry of Agriculture and Fisheries in London for an import licence, and to Spratts for accommodation in their quarantine kennels. Then the agents told us that the *Umvuma* was not calling at LM on the homeward voyage but only on the outward one to Beira. But they said Paddy could join the ship on her way to Beira and then return in her to Durban without extra charge.

She arrived at Durban but had to load sugar and would not sail for England for four days. So we went down to the ship to see Paddy. On arrival we asked the quartermaster on the gangway and he said the only dog belonged to the captain and we had better go up and see him. When we got to his cabin door, out popped Paddy and greeted us enthusiastically. The captain said his kennel had been put on the boat deck aft of his cabin; the first night at sea he had squeaked, so he had let him out and into his cabin where he had been living ever since. He had obviously become fond of Paddy. We learned later from the stewards that he followed the captain about wherever he went.

On embarking we found we had a cabin opening on to the promenade deck and the captain said we could keep Paddy there. He looked a bit doubtful about this but soon settled down. Next morning at 8 a.m. he was missing. He had gone up on to the bridge to see the captain and throughout the voyage he went up there at the same time every morning.

We disembarked at London Docks and after handing over our heavy baggage for forwarding, and our household goods for storage to Thos Cooks, we caught the train to Newcastle and on to Warkworth where we were welcomed by my mother and stepfather. Paddy had been handed over to Spratt's representative who took him in a van to their quarantine kennels.

We had been advised that it would be better not to go and see him at once but give him a few weeks to settle down. This was a mistake, as we heard by letter that he was not settling down and was difficult to handle.

After a month at Warkworth we came to London and stayed at the Exiles Club at Twickenham and went to see Paddy. He greeted us warmly. Mr Ashthorpe, the head kennelman, said the girls had found him difficult but that after our visit had no further trouble.

I had been told to attend the Training School at Hampstead for a week's special course in new apparatus, so I telephoned Mrs Batt at my old "digs" in King Henry's Road. She had a double room vacant but did not take women lodgers. I said it was only for a couple of weeks, and I would bring my wife over to see her. When she met Sylvia she agreed to take us.

Mr Stephens, the previous manager of the school had retired, and Mr Freathy was now in charge. The course was about the introduction of thermionic valves into cable receiving equipment.

Head office appointed me to Malta, sailing from Liverpool in the Ellerman cargo liner *Malatian* and we arranged for Spratts to send Paddy to join us. So in August 1931 we went by train to Liverpool and embarked for Malta.

CHAPTER TEN

Malta

We had a good voyage on the *Malatian* which carried twelve passengers. Paddy was accommodated in his kennel on the poop but we could go and see him at any time and walk him about the after deck.

On arrival the ship berthed in the Grand Harbour and we were met by Wallace Donaldson. He had booked us at the Meadowbank Hotel at Sliema.

Malta cable station had changed since 1919. Gone was the large staff of English operators as the cables were worked automatically by the new regenerator system. The foreign service staff consisted of only twelve men instead of a hundred. Maltese operators and workshop staff still numbered about forty with a few running the branch office in Valletta.

As mentioned before, the cable office was at St. Georges, beyond Sliema. It consisted of a handsome pillared portico at the top of a flight of stone steps with windows on either side. A large flat for the manager was on the first floor with administrative offices below. Behind this was a courtyard with rooms on either side. On the left were a small rest room and bar, and traffic accounts offices; and on the right workshops, engine, motor-generator, and battery rooms with more batteries in a cellar below. In the middle of the courtyard and stretching back for 150 feet was the very large main instrument room. Right at the back was the wireless room with a 100 foot steel tubular mast supporting the aerials used for working to ships.

Apart from the manager's flat, there were only three houses owned by the company, and other married men rented furnished houses for which they got £5 a month house allowance. We went to see a Mr Azzopardi who kept a furniture shop in Prince of Wales Road and rented houses. He was obliging and we agreed to rent a two storey house in Victoria Terrace about a mile from the office for £5.10.0d. a month.

Cable Office at St Georges, Malta, manager's flat on upper floor.

At an interview with the Maltese director of the department which dealt with imported animals, he solemnly informed us that Paddy could be released from quarantine when he was satisfied that our house was suitable for him!

So we were soon installed, with two girls to cook and do housework. Most Maltese houses are built of a local cream coloured stone which is soft at first and can be sawn and planed like wood. It hardens when exposed to the air. There is a harder but more expensive variety which was used to build important buildings such as the famous auberges, or inns, of the Knights of Malta in Valletta, and the town's defensive walls. Our house, like most in the island, had a flat roof with a stairway to it, and on it was a room for the servants.

Malta is a flat stony island sixteen miles long by seven miles wide, with twenty or so scattered towns and villages. Valletta, the capital, is on the east side, with its natural deep water harbours on both sides of the town. The old capital, Notabile, or Civita Vecchia as it is usually called, lies towards the western side and is perched on what is the only hill. At a village called Musta there is a church with a large unsupported dome, alleged to be the second largest in the world. Practically all the inhabitants are Roman Catholics and each town or village has its church—with church bells! The Maltese language derives from Arabic but has many Italian and English words. Maltese, Italian and English were all allowed as the languages of the courts of law.

The island is poor and depended a great deal on the British fleet and garrison. There were barracks beyond our office at St Georges and St Andrews, and also on a low flat hill called Imtarfa, near Notabile. The naval dockyard was grouped round two narrow creeks, Dockyard Creek and French Creek, which ran out of Grand Harbour on the opposite side to Valletta. The shore headquarters of the Mediterranean fleet was in a handsome stone building built by the Knights of Castile known as the Castile. The point of rocky land opposite to Valletta next to Dockyard Creek was crowned by an old stone fort called Fort St Angelo. This was used by the navy as a shore barracks for ships being refitted. During the last war it became known as HMS St Angelo.

In the main street of Valletta was the handsome opera house which gave performances of Italian opera, and further down fronting a small square, was the governor's palace, another auberge of the knights.

Our assistant manager, Mr Haines, was going on leave without a relief as, owing to the small staff, his job was redundant, the chief engineer now becoming the second in command. Mr Haines had a short wave wireless receiver which we bought and used to receive the BBC transmissions from England. The chief engineer was Mr Joe Broadbent already known from *Britannia* and Suez days. Hopecraft was deputy engineer and had my boyhood friend, Phil Alfieri as his assistant. Phil had left cableships, got married and lived in a company house in Strada Reale, Sliema.

While Sylvia was coping with the complexities of setting up house in a new environment, I was busy getting acquainted with my job in the office which was very different from Lourenço Marques. There were two supervisors who did 7 a.m. to 1 p.m. and 1 p.m. to 7 p.m. alternate weeks, and four assistant engineers who went round the clock, being also supervisors from 7 p.m. to 7 a.m. I was one of these four.

Malta cable station was then one of the largest in the world, having sixteen submarine cables. There were six to Alexandria, five to Gibraltar, one to Bona in North Africa with extension to Marseilles, two to Sicily, one to Tripoli in Libya, and one to Syra in Greece. The first twelve of these were through circuits with automatic operation. The Sicily, Tripoli and Syra cables were operated by local staff who also worked the wireless coast station. The complexity of the automatic equipment with its relays, mechanical repeaters, tape records, switchboards, alarm lamps, and indicators was comparable to, say, a large modern aircraft's control deck, like Concord. So a new watchkeeping engineer, though fully trained, had to spend his first three weeks on duty with the man he was relieving before he was fit to be left alone to run the office on evening and night duty. Head office recorded on a weekly graph the times and details of all stoppages on the main line circuits to pinpoint the cause of faults, and woe-betide an assistant engineer who failed to remedy any promptly! There was plenty of spare equipment, and all machines were regularly maintained by four Maltese mechanics under the supervision of the chief mechanic, Frank Bonnici.

The Manager was Mr Lee Lander, and he had as his clerk Huggins who had been a noted soccer and tennis player when I was there earlier in *Levant II.*

Bathing in Malta was good, but only off the rocks in Sliema along the sea front. One could put on a bath robe over a costume and walk down to where the rocks were flat next to the road. We usually went to a place in front of Sunstroke Terrace already mentioned in Chapter 3, where there was a springboard for diving.

To go shopping in Valletta we could either take the ferry or a dghaisa (hire boat) with two rowers, across Marsamuscetto harbour, or go by bus right round the harbour, a journey of about three and a half miles. Malta being the home of the Mediterranean fleet, destroyers, submarines and depot ships were moored in Marsamuscetto harbour, while battleships, aircraft carriers and cruisers were in Grand Harbour, the other side of Valletta.

The cable to Tripoli went faulty and the trouble was believed to be near the beach there. As no cableship was available, head office told the manager to send Phil Alfieri to Tripoli to see if he could repair the fault. So a service telegram was sent to the Italian Administration to advise he was coming. As was customary, it was translated into Italian by one of our Maltese operators. When he arrived and only spoke a few words of Italian, they were naturally astonished. During World War I the Italian Chief of Staff was a General Alfieri and one of Phil's cousins produced a photo of the general one day and said Phil looked just like him—especially his long nose.

With the reductions in staff at all stations there were too many men on the foreign service staff. This was accentuated by the slump in world trade after 1929 and the amalgamation with the wireless companies. So a redundancy scheme had to be introduced. Under this the company chose the men who were to lose their jobs and they were given two years basic salary and a pension proportionate to their number of years service. It was hard on men of middle age, many of whom had families, but the terms were generous.

Economies of every kind were introduced, one of them being that men with supervisor's certificates were used only as acting supervisors, and thus getting less pay. Overtime was cut to the minimum. We were also asked to accept a reduction in gross salary—5% for those on less than £250 a year, 10% from £250 to £750, and 15% for those over £750. Though nominally voluntary, in effect it was compulsory as no one wanted to be made redundant.

Barraca Lift,
Valletta Grand Harbour.

Not long afterwards Mr Lander was relieved by a tall handsome man in his late forties. When a man was axed, the dread news usually arrived in the late afternoon by service message from head office. After its own reference, it would say "RE OUR D/N... etc." the rest being in the company's private code. These words: re our D/N, indicated that someone was for the high jump but we would not know who until the manager sent for him the next morning. One evening one of these messages arrived and was duly sent to the manager's flat. Next day no one was sent for, and we could not make it out. It eventually turned out that it was the manager himself who was being retired. He was relieved by Mr Camozzi who remained there for many years, right through World War II.

Captain Port came to see us when the *Malatian* was next in Malta and asked us to visit a wireless operator from his ship in our local hospital called The Blue Sisters, after the nuns who ran it; We visited him until he got better and left. A few weeks later a clergyman called; he said his name was Clayton, had heard that we had been visiting a sick man in hospital. Would we go and see an American sailor who knew no one there having been put ashore from his ship? The clergyman was the famous Tubby Clayton who founded Toc H. We went to see the American who turned out to be a nice young man from the Middle West.

We met J. H. Clark who was a commissioned gunner (T) in HMS *Blanche,* one of the destroyers in Marsamuscetto harbour. Clark had joined the navy as a boy seaman and had been present at the battle of Coronel in HMS *Glasgow* the only British ship which was not sunk. He was now a senior warrant officer and he came to our house several times. He invited us to dine with him on board but as ladies could not be entertained in the wardroom, he borrowed his captain's day cabin and gave us an excellent dinner.

He invited me to go to sea for the day in his ship which was to take part in a gunnery and torpedo practice. So at 7 a.m. I took a dghaisa at the Sliema Marina and was soon on board. HMS *Blanche* in company with the other eight destroyers of the fourth flotilla left the harbour and steamed out to sea. All their names began with the letter B (except the flotilla leader *Keith*), *Basilisk, Beagle, Boadicea, Boreas, Brazen, Brilliant* and *Bulldog.*

After breakfast in the wardroom I was taken on to the bridge and introduced to the captain, Commander Glennie, who was most charming. A flotilla at that time consisted of a leader and eight destroyers, two of which were known as half leaders. The leader had a post captain in command and was a slightly larger ship. The half leaders were captained by commanders and the rest by lieut commanders.

We steamed in line ahead until we were out of sight of Malta and then saw in the far distance HMS *Chrysanthemum*, the fleet target ship, towing a target.

Each ship in succession was to fire so many rounds from its four guns and then fire one torpedo. As each reached the firing area, it turned sharply to starboard, increased to full speed and after a short interval fired all its guns several times in rapid succession. This was a most exciting sight and sound. An officer stood next to each gun with a stopwatch to time each round fired. HMS *Chrysanthemum* had a cine camera trained on the target with a synchronised stopwatch shown on the film. Thus by examining it, it was possible to identify the splash of each shot from all of the guns. *Blanche* then fired a torpedo from one of her quadruple sets of tubes on deck.

The ship then turned in a large circle towards the target area and came to a position to recover the torpedo. It had been set to run so many thousand yards, surface and release a small coloured buoy.

When all nine destroyers had fired and recovered their torpedoes, the flotilla reformed in line ahead and returned to Malta.

I asked Commander Glennie if he would care to see the cable office. He accepted and a few days later I showed him over it, and he came to tea at our house. He had a distinguished career, becoming Vice Admiral Sir Irvine Glennie before retirement. He performed particularly brilliantly when in command of a cruiser squadron during the Cretan fighting in 1940. We met a Lieut West who was a gunner officer and lived at Tigni barracks near the Sliema Marina. He presented Sylvia with a small dog, called a Maltese pomeranian. We were doubtful at first how our dog Paddy would react to this, but after being stand-offish for a few days he quite adopted Terry, as we called the new dog, and they soon were firm friends. Terry had an interesting characteristic. If we had been out without the dogs and returned home, he would greet us with a smile of evident satisfaction, showing all his teeth in a grin.

The commander-in-chief of the fleet was Sir W. W. Fisher who went to see an exercise in an aircraft which had engine failure and came down in the sea. *Blanche* was the nearest ship and picked him up.

Lord Louis Mountbatten was fleet wireless officer in Malta and he and his wife had a house at Gardamangia, near Sliema. Noel Coward came to stay with them and amused us by sending streams of cablegrams to his friends, more like letters than telegrams.

The Prince of Wales came to Malta to visit the fleet and caused quite a crisis one day. He went up in an aircraft from one of the carriers and it became foggy and it was only with difficulty that his pilot got back to the ship. Several of her aircraft had to land in Sicily.

Phil Alfieri and his wife went on leave and D. K. Smith who had been with me in *Transmitter* arrived. He was now married and had left cableships. I managed to get a few days station leave and we went to stay at a small hotel at Marfa near the north west end of the island, and opposite to the sister island of Gozo.

The climate of Malta is hot in the summer and at times humid; and the hot sirocco wind blowing from North Africa brings dust which settles on everything. The sea is generally calm then, but violent gales occur in the winter, and once the sea breached the high stone wall flanking the Sliema sea front, and washed half the road away as well.

In 1933 the cableship *Retriever* arrived from the west coast of South America. She was of 674 tons and had been built in 1909. Her Peruvian officers and crew went home by sea and she was taken over by Captain Gammon with British officers and a Maltese crew was recruited. D. K. Smith was appointed chief electrician with Drayton as second. She was refitted in the dockyard and thereafter stationed at Malta.

Head office instructed us to make a complete check and inventory of all the ships stores in the cable tanks. As the only ex-cableship man, the job was given to me, and I spent two or three weeks at the tanks depot. My old ship *Levant II* had been laid up in a creek at the far end of Grand Harbour in 1930 and all her stores were in the depot.

While I was on this job Trudgian was transferred to Alexandria station and O. L. Hart relieved him. He was a tall benevolent looking man and his looks did not belie him as he was one of the nicest men I have met. After doing the tanks check I set to work to enter all the details in a large stores inventory book sent out from London. While I was doing this, Messrs Edmonds, Knight & Simpson arrived to inspect the branch. Edmonds was a very senior Western Telegraph Co man, appointed inspector of branches, W. J. Knight was his engineering assistant, and Simpson acted as secretary to the team. They were making a world tour of stations. Members of the staff, including ourselves, entertained them to cocktail and dinner parties. We also took

Cableship Retriever, Malta, 1933. Sunk by German dive bombers off Piraeus in 1941

Knight to a dance at the Boschetto Palace Hotel about six miles away, and Sylvia said he had "very intelligent feet"—her discription of anyone who danced well.

One evening we went to a party at Mary Cooper's house. As I was on night duty at 1 a.m. I went home about 10 o'clock to get some sleep. Our two dogs were asleep under my bed. Sylvia returned home with friends about 1.30 a.m. and found a policeman who said the neighbours complained that the dogs were barking. She said she was sorry and went to bed. Next day I went to the police station in Prince of Wales Road and saw the Maltese assistant superintendent, explaining that the dogs could only have been barking a short time as I was in the house myself till twenty minutes to one. Nothing happened for two months, then I received a summons, this seemed rather a long time for the police to make up their minds to prosecute.

On going to the court in Valletta with Mary Cooper and Sylvia, I found the magistrate was a Mr Scerri, the uncle of one of the local clerks in our office. The superintendent was there with some witnesses. I pleaded guilty to the charge and explained to the magistrate about being on night duty. He said to the superintendent: "This seems a very minor matter"; and to me he gave an absolute discharge. As I was leaving the court, the magistrate's clerk came over and wanted to know my father's name and where he was born. I said he had been dead over twenty years, but he said his name must be in the court records!

This is the only time that I have been the defendant in a police court.

Like most branches the company retained a local doctor as their medical officer, and staff who went sick, including the local men, were expected to get a sick certificate from him if they were off duty more than a day or two. About this time the manager was concerned about the amount of sickness amongst the Maltese staff and suspected some were swinging the lead, and the Maltese doctor was not being strict enough with them. So he consulted head office who told him to write to the offenders and tell them their medical record appeared to show they were not suitable for the company's service. Needless to say, this had the desired effect.

With a few days station leave, we went to St Paul's Bay, about seven miles from Sliema, stayed at an hotel there, and had a very pleasant holiday. This is the place where St Paul is said to have been shipwrecked on his way to Rome, and in the middle of the bay is a tiny rocky island with a large statue of him on it. We hired a boat and rowed out and had a look at it and took some photographs.

M. C. Clarke, our deputy engineer was due for leave and his relief had left England in a P & O liner, when Head Office wired out that, owing to sickness, he was being told not to get off the ship at Malta but to go on to Colombo. They added that Clarke was to go on leave without a relief who would be sent later.

Owing to promotion restrictions, the situation was anomalous. Histed and another man, Morgan, both about two years senior to me and both with tickets were acting supervisors in the office and drawing the minimum salary of that rank. The deputy engineer's job was normally held by a man in the third grade, one higher, but there was no rule about anyone getting acting pay for doing it. Histed was next senior to Clarke, but if he did the job he would lose his present acting pay and I would get it and his job.

I was just finishing the tanks depot inventory at the time, and it was decided that I should relieve Clarke but be listed on the duty sheet only as assistant to the engineer instead of deputy. This left the other two drawing their acting pay as before but no extra pay for me. However, this did not worry me as the job was interesting and instructive. Hart was a splendid man to work with, and the experience was invaluable. The work also involved a weekly visit to the cable tanks and to the cableship *Levant* in Grand Harbour.

At the tanks there was a foreman and a gang of labourers to strip the sheathing wires off scrap cable landed by ships. The cable core recovered was reeled and sent to the factory in England to be repaired and re-used. The steel wires were sold locally and often used for nail making. While compiling the inventory I had got to know the tankman who was an ex British soldier who had married a Maltese. Whenever I went there at odd times I found the new man always working busily and it was clear he was honest and conscientious. He asked whether there was any chance of getting a rise in his wages which were £8 a month.

I thought this was scandalously low and told Mr Hart, asking him what he thought a judge would say if a tankman in charge of hundreds of thousands of pounds of cable and equipment should pinch something and the amount of his wages should come out. He agreed and said he would speak to Mr Camozzi about it. The latter wrote to head office who increased his wages at once to £12 with promise of further increases. In general, it was always the company's policy to ensure the integrity of their employees by giving them regular increases of pay, especially in positions of responsibility.

Hart and I had a very busy time one week. After a repair to one of the Gibraltar cables we had to do what is known as restoring the duplex balance. This demanded careful adjustments, so that alterations made by the repair ship were allowed for. It has to be done by trial and error, plus experience. This one took us about three days of almost continuous work day and night, each of us doing about four or five hours work and then going home for a rest and then back again. The engineer of a large station received, like the manager, a charge allowance, for having to be on call at any time. Normally the deputy engineer would get overtime payments for extra hours worked, but owing to the slump economies, head office had laid it down that wherever possible staff were to have time off in lieu of overtime. This applied to me but I did get some overtime and Mr Camozzi recommended that I should get acting fourth grade pay while assistant to the engineer to which head office agreed.

Some time after that Histed, Morgan and I were officially promoted to the fourth grade.

The company decided to sell the old sports ground and tennis courts a few hundred yards down the road from the office, and there was competition between two sets of people who wanted to buy. During the negotiations head office sent a service telegram to the manager about one offer. The next day the other party arrived on the doorstep and made a fresh offer which made it seem likely that some clerk in our office had disclosed the head office telegram to them. Camozzi was angry but could not detect the culprit. He asked head office to telegraph in code in future. Leaks of information in our stations were rare, and this is the only one known to me.

The sports ground and tennis courts were sold to a syndicate of Maltese businessmen. The company stipulated as part of the price that two new tennis courts should be constructed on land they owned next to the office, and the pavilion, a stone building with three rooms, should be re-erected next to the new courts. One afternoon after finishing a game of tennis, three or four Maltese arrived and spoke to Mr Camozzi who called after me and asked me to stay. These were the men who had bought the land and they now tried to get Mr Camozzi's to agree that the pavilion to be re-erected was a small shelter with seats next to the old courts. After much argument, we all went to Mr Camozzi's office and he produced the legal agreement which showed clearly that their contention was wrong. It was just a try-on to see if they could get him to make an admission before their witnesses.

Our cable to Tripoli landed at Birzebuggia (pronounced Birzi-boojia) in the Marsa Scirocco Bay at the south end of the island. It was not a important link and was connected to the office by an overhead landline. Our records of the line were incomplete so I did a survey of it on foot with the help of the tankman. Some of it was on brackets attached to houses in villages, and people used to hang their clothes on it from upstairs windows, but it usually worked all right.

In September 1934 M. A. Barnes arrived to relieve me. We arranged to leave Terry with Mrs Mary Cooper and wrote to the Ministry of Agriculture and Spratts to arrange for Paddy's entrance to the UK. Passages were booked in the *Jervis Bay* of the Commonwealth Line, a one class vessel of 14,000 tons, carrying 700 passengers. Fares were cheaper than first class on the P & O, so we had a good cabin on the upper deck.

This ship was famous in World War II as an armed merchant cruiser. She engaged at impossible odds, a German pocket battleship and was sunk with heavy loss of life. But she enabled the convoy she was guarding to scatter and saved many of the ships from being lost.

We sailed on 18th September 1934 and arrived at Tilbury about ten days later. I had written to Mrs Batt in King Henry's Road and she replied that she could put us up. Paddy went, as before, to the quarantine kennels in Beddington Lane; we went to see him next day and renewed acquaintance with Mr Ashthorpe.

The company was sending some engineers to the Marconi School at Chelmsford followed by a period at one of the large wireless stations in the UK. Being keen to learn about modern wireless apparatus, I had borrowed from E. Bailey in Malta the notes he made when taking the course. I asked Mr Frost, the staff manager, if I could take it, but he replied that only younger men were being sent. So I asked if I could go in my own time during my leave to a transmitting and receiving station for a month or so to learn how they worked and it was arranged that I should visit Ongar and Brentwood stations. In the meantime Sylvia and I went to Warkworth to see my family.

On our return we went to North Weald (where Ongar wireless station was sited) and were able to get some good digs with a Mrs Gow, a doctor's widow. Mr Hill the manager at Ongar was very pleasant and invited us to his house for dinner.

Ongar station had one 100 kilowatt (133 horse power) long wave transmitter for the north American service, and two or three medium wave ones of 20Kw operating to Europe. Then there were half a dozen short wave ones also 20Kw to various overseas countries. The aerials were spread over many acres of farm land around the buildings. So there was plenty of variety. I had no fixed duties but arranged to spend most of my days there with one night duty. All the short wave transmitters, except one new one of 40Kw, were the originals designed by Mr Franklyn for the empire service which opened in 1926/27. They were very bulky by today's standards. Each consisted of four sections about six feet cube. To change wavelengths which had to be done twice daily, the coils had to be changed by hand and then tuned by turning control knobs. They were plastered with indicating meters, one in almost every circuit. I was so intrigued with this that I counted them and found there were fifty. Each one was logged daily on a sheet but the readings did not vary much. You could certainly see if anything went wrong but this was rare. The modern 40Kw is about a quarter the size and had wave-changing operated by two hand wheels.

I soon learned what had to be done and assisted the watch technicians. There were three on duty in the daytime and two at night. There was a deputy to Mr Hill and power house and aerial maintenance men.

Sylvia meanwhile occupied her time exploring the neighbourhood, especially Epping Forest. At weekends we visited Epping and Chipping

Ongar, going by bus. At the *Cock* public house at Epping we were much amused by the landlord's very small Yorkshire terrier who assisted local charities by unerringly finding pennies hidden anywhere in the lounge bar.

When the time came to move to the receiving station at Brentwood, Sylvia went there but was unable to find suitable digs. So we remained at Mrs Gow's and I went to Brentwood, about 10 miles, daily by bus. Mr Keen was the manager, evidently a very able man.

We then returned to Mrs Batt's in Hamptead. We found Mr and Mrs Fernie and their daughter Mrs Hadwen were living in a house in Haverstock Hill and went to see them several times.

Head office informed me I was appointed to Gibraltar as from the 1st January.

At Christmas we went by night train from King's Cross to Newcastle and on to Warkworth and spent a week with my parents, returning in time to go to an old year's night party at the Fernies in Hampstead. Remembering our first Russian style party at their house in Athens in 1923 we did not have anything to eat before going there at 9 p.m.

It was arranged with Spratts to send Paddy to our ship, and on 4th January 1935 we sailed from Tilbury in the P & O *Chitral* for Gibraltar.

CHAPTER ELEVEN

Gibraltar Again

The voyage to Gibraltar was uneventful. Paddy was kept on the stern in his kennel and we could visit him and give him exercise on the raised poop deck. For some reason, perhaps connected with feeding, it was the custom on passenger liners for dogs to be looked after by the ship's butcher.

On arrival we learned that we were to go straight into one of the company's furnished flats, the previous occupant having already left.

Like Malta, the introduction of automation had completely altered the station. The old mess building and quarters in South Barrack Road where I had lived as a bachelor during World War I had been turned into flats, five in the former and six in the latter. These were rented out, mainly to officers in the services. The old manager's house next to the mess was now a boarding house run by one of our senior men who had been made redundant. The foreign service staff now consisted of the manager, engineer, the latter's assistant, a mechanic in charge of the workshop, and five watchkeeping supervisor/engineers. The station itself had been demoted; the manager was now in the second grade and was officially designated manager/engineer and under him a third grade deputy engineer. In practice the latter was in charge of the engineering side, the manager only concerning himself with administration.

Near the top of Scud Hill which ran up from the lower main road the company had acquired two houses, called Patio Momo nos. 1 and 2, for the manager and the engineer, and next to them had built a block of seven flats, called Electra Flats for the others. They had splendid views of the bay and main harbour. There were four flats on one side and three on the other, with a common stairway. Behind was an open space where it had been intended to build another block. It made a place to park cars as the Patio Momo and Electra Flats entrances opened on to it and there was a short drive to Scud Hill.

The original instrument room was still there, all the old tables being used for the automatic regenerator repeating apparatus. One corner accommodated the local circuits to Tangier, our branch office in the town, and landlines to Madrid and Cadiz, operated by the local staff.

The flat allotted to us was one of the best, being on the first floor, seaward side. It had a lounge with outside verandah, dining room, three bedrooms, kitchen, and the usual offices. As already mentioned, Gibraltar's only piped water supply was what was called sanitary water slightly salty especially in the summer. Electra flats had two large underground water tanks filled by rainwater from the flat roof. There was a service tank on the roof, and fresh water was pumped to it two or three times a week. So we all had large earthenware jars (of Ali Baba size) in the kitchen and kept them full of fresh water from the only tap there. Towards the end of the summer the underground tanks used to get nearly empty and we had to ration ourselves.

For the bath we could soak in sanitary water and rub down with a small tin bath of fresh on a board across it. We called this a "P & O bath" after shipboard practice in those days.

We unpacked all our gear and soon got the flat habitable. We had bought a crate full of glassware and other things from Woolworths in

Spanish Revolution, July 1936, Frontier Gates.

London, where, if you bought enough, they packed and sent it to the docks free of charge. Very convenient and economical. Sylvia engaged a maid, a Spanish girl from La Linea, the border town, called Bella and she stayed with us the three years we were in Gib and proved a good servant.

Gibraltar cable station, while not as large as Malta, was still an important one as most of the main line cable circuits, i.e., London to Singapore, Bombay, Alexandria, etc., ran through it, while there were also circuits to Carcavellos near Lisbon, which connected with South America. The foreign service staff was fairly senior, only two being junior to me, so I now found myself back on watch-keeping.

El Cobre, the house in Spain previously rented by the company, had been given up but the mess library had been retained and the bathing place with hut next to the cable tanks at Camp Bay was still in use. As the weather grew warmer we went there regularly. We had the usual Rock passes issued by the garrison adjutant allowing us access to Camp Bay, the Dockyard and the upper Rock, except for the areas where the guns were mounted.

We often went for long walks on the upper Rock and introduced ourselves to the famous apes who lived there. There are magnificent views from One Gun Battery at the north end and from a signal station, not then in use, on Signal Hill in the centre. Sylvia christened this her country cottage and often walked up with Paddy when I was on duty. The highest point is at the south end but our passes did not allow us to go there, as its gun batteries were operational.

Quite a few of our axed men had joined Italcable. They were eventually all dismissed when the Italian-Abbysinian war broke out which was condemned by Britain and sanctions imposed on Italy by the League of Nations.

This happened not long after we got to Gib and led to the sudden arrival of HMS *Renown* and a flotilla of destroyers from the home fleet. The names of the latter all began with the letter F, e.g. *Fearless, Foresight,* etc. These were later replaced with eight more destroyers with names beginning with G, and after that H.

There was much coming and going of naval vessels which we could observe from our balcony. This interested us so we borrowed a copy of *Jane's Fighting Ships* from the staff library to identify them, and later got a more up to date illustrated book of the British navy.

The Italians had built two fine Atlantic liners called the *Rex* and the

Conti de Savoia, each 35,000 tons and they ran from Genoa to New York calling at Gibraltar. Their upper works, funnels, etc. were floodlit when they came in at night. *Rex* held the Blue Riband of the Atlantic for some time until the British *Queens* were built by Cunard White Star.

The Gordon Highlanders were at Gibraltar and we watched them beating the retreat one day on their parade ground. They were suddenly ordered to Malta and left on a transport. Nearly a year later they returned to Gib in a battleship, and it was extraordinary to see the hundreds of soldiers clustered all over her upper decks, on turrets, and wherever there was space, as she steamed into the bay and docked in the harbour.

There was a scare that Mussolini might lose his head and attack Gibraltar by air. There were no anti-aircraft guns, so a number of mobile AA guns were hastily shipped out and positioned at strategic spots. Later on fixed AA guns were put on the moles surrounding the harbour. Anti-submarine nets and booms were fixed across the two entrances to prevent torpedoes being fired through them.

During 1935 Mary Cooper, our friend from Malta, came out from England and stayed with us for a couple of months. N. J. L. Jefferies, his wife Helen and small daughter arrived and took over the flat below us.

On going to bathe at Camp Bay early one afternoon we found the pebbly beach near the cable tanks full of soldiers from the regiment at South Barracks sitting there in bathing costumes. After putting on my costume in our hut, I dived off the pier and swam about. An army sergeant came on to the pier and told me to get out of the water as bathing only started at 2 p.m. I pointed out that I was not in the army, had bathed there for years, and he was on our company's private pier. However, in the interests of army discipline we decided when bathing in the afternoon to wait until 2 p.m. before going into the water, as probably the soldiers would not understand why we could and they could not. Why this rule was made was a mystery.

The ceremony of locking up the fortress and carrying the keys with a military escort and band through the town to the governor's house was regularly carried out. They are carried on a cushion from the north gates and placed next to the governor as he has dinner.

There was a notice in Spanish outside a toilet near the north gates which read: "Retreté por los soldados". When a new regiment (the Cheshires) arrived someone thought this should be translated, so the words "Other ranks" were chalked up on the wall—the briefest translation I have seen.

The old battleship *Centurion* came to Gibraltar with her attendant destroyer *Shikari*. The former was a fleet target ship and could be controlled by wireless signals from the destroyer. The latter had had her forward gun removed and replaced by a small raised platform. This had a pedestal on which was mounted a telephone dial, similar to the ones on automatic telephones. By dialling various numbers, *Centurion* could be steered, her speed controlled and even made to emit a heavy smokescreen. She had a small crew who normally lived on board but were taken off by *Shikari* prior to firing at her.

Once she went out of control and had to be chased and boarded at speed. She was covered in patches where she had been hit and repaired. After a shoot she was put in the dry dock below our flats and the shot-holes plated over by welding and riveting.

We invited my mother to stay with us for a month and she came out in the P & O liner *Strathmore* in May.

We showed mother all the sights of Gibraltar. She tried painting in water colours but said the colours and light were very different from England and she would need a little time to get used to them. She did a picture of Europa point lighthouse at the south end of the Rock with the straits and a mountain known as Ape's Hill on the African coast behind.

I took a few days off and we went for a long week-end to Ronda in the hills which I had visited with Drucquer in World War I. We travelled by car to Los Barios station just north of Algeciras and caught the train there.

Mother was a bit startled in the train when she saw some blood oozing from under the seat opposite where a man was sitting. It was a recently killed goat which he was taking home. We had a pleasant stay in the Reina Victoria Hotel. Sylvia and I went for long walks and mother pottered about the garden and town, and talked to the English manageress.

While in Ronda we noticed many groups of men standing at street corners talking, and learned that there was a possibility of political trouble in Spain. The socialists had seized power the previous year, throwing out the king and his prime minister, and since then law and order had steadily deteriorated.

When we returned the cableship *Mirror* came in and I took mother to see over it .

A law had been introduced soon after our arrival requiring all dogs to have muzzles on public roads, and Paddy soon got used to wearing one. It was kept in the bottom of the hatstand and sometimes when we had visitors and he thought it was time for a walk, he would fetch the muzzle and plonk it down in front of us in the sitting room—a plain hint to our guests.

Owing to the continued slump in world trade the company had to call for further economies and we had another cut in our pay by everyone's seniority in their grade being put back one year.

On Sunday, 19th July 1936 Sylvia, Paddy and I walked up the Rock to her country cottage and sat there looking at the view, as it was a bright cloudless day. We noticed a small gunboat steaming across the bay from Algeciras. It came close to the shore at La Linea and suddenly started firing its guns at the barracks on the outskirts of the town. It was the outbreak of the Spanish civil war.

It was learned that the officers at the barracks, after trying unsuccessfully to get their men to mutiny, had come into Gibraltar and then gone to Algeciras which had joined the troops in Cadiz who had started the revolt under General Franco. In the next few weeks Franco ferried a large number of Moroccan soldiers from North Africa to Algeciras. Some came in flying boats lent to him by Mussolini; while others were shipped over in small steamers which had to run the gauntlet across the Straits. The Spanish navy sent several destroyers to try and stop them, and once or twice we saw the troopships being chased and fired on, but none was sunk. From our balcony we had a grandstand view of what went on.

The civil war interrupted our landline to Madrid, but the line to Cadiz through country in Franco's hands was still working. One of our cables to England landed at Vigo in north Spain where we had a relay station. As Vigo was also in the rebel's hands but had no landline communication with Cadiz, the Franco-ites started sending messages between these places through us. The Madrid Government must have found this out for it informed the International Telegraph Bureau at Berne that all telegraphic communication with Spain was suspended except through places controlled by it, so we shut down the Cadiz circuit. Next day the Portuguese Government which was sympathetic to Franco told the Berne Bureau that the Spanish government's message was incorrect as they were in communication with Spain. The Cadiz circuit was then re-opened.

Gradually Franco's men overran all the countryside around Gibraltar. This led to an influx of refugees from Spain but only those who could claim British nationality were allowed into Gibraltar. Many others, however, camped on the so-called neutral ground, a strip about half a mile square between the British and Spanish wire fences. We were thus cut off from Spain except by sea, and it was more than six months before we could go there.

The government troops made a big raid down the Mediterranean coast from Malaga and reached the hill-top town of San Roche in sight of Gibraltar, but were soon driven back. There was much brutality on both sides as they were all trigger-happy. Spanish sailors had murdered their officers and thrown them overboard, and declared for the Madrid government. They continued patrolling the Straits to stop Franco from bringing more troops from Africa, but without much success as many came by air. We saw one of their ships fire at a Dutch liner one morning. So the British navy brought a battlecruiser and some light cruisers to Gib to reinforce our destroyer flotilla.

The Bland Line ran a steamship service to Tangier. One afternoon when we were bathing at Camp Bay we heard HMS *Hood*, the battlecruiser, sounding her siren to recall men on shore. About half an hour later she came steaming past at full speed for the Straits followed by a cruiser. We heard afterwards that a Spanish cruiser had tried to arrest the Bland Tangier ship which had radioed for help. On arrival of HMS *Hood,* the Spanish warship made off.

We were told that a destroyer, HMS *Griffin* was coming to Gib for refit and her engineer officer, Lt Weston Smith, was looking for accommodation. We had one flat in our block vacant at the time, so when Weston Smith came, I took him to see the manager. The former said that Lt Williamson, their 1st Lieutenant, also had his wife coming and wanted to share the flat. The manager seemed a bit doubtful about this, but Weston Smith said it was only for a couple of months, so it was agreed that they could rent it.

The German pocket battleship *Deutschland* arrived at Gib and stayed for two or three days. Later she went up the east coast of Spain and was bombed by the Spanish government air force as they suspected her of supporting General Franco which she probably was. The bombs went through her forecastle into the mess decks below, causing many casualties. She returned to Gib and landed her wounded who were taken

Gibraltar dockyard from our balcony.

to the Military Hospital, the naval one having been closed some years before. The dead were buried in the north front cemetary. The hospital being shorthanded, a number of nurses came out from England in a large flying boat. About a month later *Deutschland* returned, re-embarked any men who had been wounded, exhumed the dead and took them away. It was noticeable that when the German ship was at Gib and their officers and men came ashore there was much photographing of the Rock. But there were no real secrets they could have seen. To avoid being accidentally bombed, all the British warships had wide red white and blue stripes painted across the tops of their gun shields or turrets.

I was now the next senior to the engineer and became his assistant, the same job as I had had in Malta.

As I had never been on board an aircraft carrier, Williamson said a friend of his in HMS *Hermes* which was expected after *Griffin* left, would show me over her. When she arrived Fl Lt A. J. D. Harding invited me to come and see him. In those days the RAF provided most of the pilots and service crews on aircraft carriers and it was rather odd to see them in their light blue uniforms mixed up with the naval officers on board. Harding and one or two of his friends came to dinner.

One week the civil war in Spain erupted all around Gibraltar. A squadron of Spanish government warships arrived in the bay and anchored off the Rock. They comprised a battleship, the *Jaime Primero* and several destroyers. We learned that they tried to buy stores in Gibraltar but could only do so for cash, of which they were short. They then went across the bay and anchored in the north west corner near the mouth of two small rivers and sent foraging parties ashore. While there a squadron of Franco's aircraft appeared and started to drop bombs on the ships who replied with anti-aircraft fire. Neither side hit the other but one of the planes flew over the north end of the Rock to escape. The ships continued firing at it and some pieces of shell fell on the upper Rock.

The governor sent his military secretary in a launch to the *Jaime Primero* and told the captain, reported to be a jumped up petty officer, that if this happened again the Rock guns would fire at him. Next day they were gone but a few days later they returned and engaged with gunfire some batteries of field artillery brought up by the Franco troops to Carneiro Point at the south west end of the bay. While watching this through field glasses, I suddenly saw the Martello tower on the promontory disappear. It had been hit by a twelve inch shell and disintegrated completely. Drucquer and I had visited this tower in 1918 on one of our walks in Spain.

They then went on to shell Algeciras town at point blank range. After doing this for about an hour, they steamed out of the bay and we did not see them again. One of the twelve inch shells from the *Jaime Primero* went through the roof of Vice Consul Beckinsale's house in Algeciras, across their bedroom and sitting room and out again the other side without exploding. Mrs Beckinsale was slightly hurt. There was considerable damage and he put in a claim to the Foreign Office; but it was disallowed on the grounds that he was not a career vice consul! He had been most vigilant about British subjects who occasionally got arrested and thrown into jail there. The Falangista young men, supporters of Franco, had developed the habit of going to the jail in the evening and shooting a few prisoners, so it was an unhealthy place to be in overnight. Beckinsale went there daily and bailed out any Britishers, usually Gibraltarians, who might have been arrested by mistake, or for misdemeanours.

As one could not go into Spain we decided to visit Tangier. With a few days station leave and a weekend we went by Bland Line steamer and stayed at a pleasant hotel. We bathed on the beach, visited the

Moorish castle, and the famous market and saw all the usual sights. While we were there Paddy was looked after by Jefferies. Mrs J. remarked how intelligent he was. When taken for a walk if he heard a car or other vehicle, he would immediately go close to the side of the road. She pointed this out to her small daughter, Jinker, as a good example of what to do as most roads were narrow and had no footpaths.

But he was also a bit artful. To get to Camp Bay one had to pass Rosia Bay, then climb up through the naval victualling yard and go down a double ladder with handrail. One day some boys were larking on the ladder and Paddy got a fright and fell about twelve feet or so. We took him to the vet who said one leg was badly sprained. For about a week Sylvia used to carry him up the stairs to our flat. But one day she heard the telephone ring as she was at the bottom so hurried up to answer it. Soon after she looked out of the window and saw Paddy chasing a cat *with all four legs in perfect order!* When she went down, up went the supposedly hurt leg but she told him he was a fraud and could get up the stairs himself.

The Italian cableship *Citta Di Milano* also called and two of their engineers came to our office to check cable charts. This was to verify that they had our cables plotted correctly so they would not damage them while working on their own. I enquired after Signor Del Grande who came with us in *Levant II* in 1919 and they told me he had retired and was living in Milan. I asked them to give him my regards if they should see him. Some months later they came again and told me they had seen Del Grande who remembered his trip in *Levant II* very well, and sent his regards to me.

During 1937 the sun had its eleven-yearly "spots" maximum, and this gave us much trouble in the office. On cables running east and west the magnetic storms generated by the spots caused strong and variable earth currents. On one occasion it was estimated that the electrical pressure difference between Malta and Gibraltar changed by about 50 volts in about a minute. As this was the voltage of our batteries, it disrupted the signals temporarily.

The next civil war incident was when one of our destroyers, HMS *Hunter* struck a mine while patrolling off the Spanish east coast. One side under the bridge was blown in killing a couple of men in the forward boiler room and flooding the lower deck forward. She was towed stern first to Gibraltar, looking a sorry sight with her foremast damaged and oil fuel all over her fore funnel, and put in the dry dock. This was a tricky operation as she was heavily down by the bows. We learned it was a marvel she had not been cut in two, her stout construction saving her. The ship's company was accommodated on shore, and, soon after, HMS *Active* arrived to replace her and they went to take her over. After temporary repairs *Hunter* left for Malta where permanent ones were to be carried out.

We went to visit the fresh water reservoirs inside the Rock. Not far above the Moorish Castle at the north end, there is a narrow tunnel right through to the other side. Here there are large concreted slopes for catching fresh water, the lower edges having a small canal for carrying it to the tunnel, where it was distributed to chambers cut in the solid rock, each holding a million gallons. A new one was being made and we looked down into it from the tunnel and saw the workmen excavating it. The previous year it had been discovered that fresh water could be had by sinking relatively shallow wells just inside the British wire fence on the north front. Several had been dug and the water pumped up to the Rock reservoirs. This water came underground from Spain, perhaps the run off from the low hill to the north. The city engineer said he thought it likely that these wells would eventually turn brackish owing to sea water seeping in, but in the meantime they provided a welcome addition to his supplies. The brackish sanitary water, was drawn from other wells on the north front.

Williamson came back in another destroyer for a short visit. At the time we had a freight ship berthed at our cable tanks on the north mole in the Admiralty harbour and I had been down there superintending the discharge of some cable. I invited the chief officer Mr White, to dinner and Williamson also came that evening. Sylvia was not feeling well and went to bed early, and we three men were yarning in the sitting room, when Williamson rather startled us by saying he thought his expectation of life would only be five years. He explained he was sure there was going to be a war with Germany and as he was a fleet air-arm pilot, he was likely to be one of the first casualties. He was nearly right—but not quite. He was in the carrier *Illustrious* when her aircraft attacked the Italian fleet at Taranto and he led the first squadron over the harbour mole. He was shot down and listed as missing, believed killed. But he wasn't killed and became a prisoner-of-war. Later he served at the Admiralty after the war. I wonder if Mr White was as lucky.

The aircraft carrier *Courageous;* flagship of Vice-Admiral Royle, came in and Fl Lt Harding whom we had known in *Hermes* was in her with another friend, Charleton-Jones and they both came to dinner. They said their ship had a guest room in which ladies could be entertained and would we come to lunch on Saturday as they were sailing soon after?

They both wanted to buy presents to take home, so Sylvia took them shopping on the Saturday morning. They returned with several parcels done up in newspaper, and she said we would bring them to the ship when we came to lunch. Young Borg, the taxi driver, had recently bought a new car, an imposing black Packard saloon and we engaged him to take us to *Courageous* which was moored alongside the south mole. When we arrived at the after gangway there was a petty officer standing there, who opened our car door. When he saw our parcels, he said: "Let me carry them, sir," so Sylvia and I went up the gangway with the PO behind. She suddenly noticed a knot of brass-hats at the opening under the flight deck and imagining they might be waiting to come down, hurried forward. As we stepped on deck the pipes sounded and we realised we were being piped over the side.

What had happened was that Admiral Royle was expecting the Admiral Superintendent of the Dockyard to lunch. The petty officer was the admiral's servant who had been posted to open the Admiral Superintendent's car door. So when the bosun's mate saw him escorting

Sylvia, Paddy and the author on the company's pier at Camp Bay.

us up the gangway, he thought the admiral's guest had arrived and sounded the pipes. We found our hosts and went down to their guest room where we all had a good laugh over the incident. They said we had to admit they had welcomed us handsomely. Then we remembered the parcels and it was found they had gone to the admiral's cabin.

In 1937 Franco's men having driven the government forces a long way away from Algeciras and Linea, it became possible to visit Spain. The Spanish consul in Gibraltar represented the Madrid government, so an unofficial office which could issue visas from the Franco faction was allowed in Gibraltar.

The entrance to Electra Flats being rather bleak, consisting of a muddy car park and then a concreted forecourt on to which the kitchens looked, I suggested to the inmates we start a small garden. We bought half a dozen sherry casks from Baglietto's, cut them in half and distributed them around the forecourt. Mrs Jefferies planted geraniums in them, and also dug up a bank at the outer edge and put in nasturtiums. The inner end of the car park was turned into a flower bed.

G. N. Perkins, the senior instructor at the Hampstead Training School, visited us in 1938, head office having decided that instructors should go to large cable stations for a month or so to see how things went in practice. The company had published a technical work in three volumes on their engineering practice and he had written a lot of it. He was paid for it, but told me that it worked out at about fivepence an hour for the work he put into it. We were all glad to see him again, and he was entertained by everyone.

C. S. Norseman paid us a visit and Captain Oliver and his officers were also entertained. He was a most witty and amusing man. The ship arrived a few days before Christmas 1937 for fuel and provisions before going on a repair. Captain Oliver informed head office that he would be ready to sail on 24th December. The managing director replied that they could remain in port over Christmas—a thoughtful action.

The battleships *Nelson* and *Rodney* came to Gibraltar. They were familiarly known in the Navy as *Flatiron No 1* and *No 2* because of their odd appearance, having enormously long fore decks with nine 16-inch guns in three triple turrets and very short quarter decks. Their design was due to treaty restrictions after the first war, the guns having been made for much larger battlecruisers which were never built. We knew a Lt Cmdr Holmes in *Rodney* and both of us went on board to see him one afternoon. They had some small, very fast motorboats and Sylvia and I were brought ashore in one, much to her delight, as she had seen them shooting about the harbour.

Hopcraft asked me to make up a tennis four with two naval officers one afternoon. They were Captain MacKeag-Jones and Commander Storey of *Nelson*. Talking to the latter afterwards, I mentioned a book called *The Fighting at Jutland* which was in our library. This was a collection of eyewitness accounts of the battle with many photographs. Storey remarked that the survivor account of the sinking of the battlecruiser *Queen Mary* was not very accurate. I said, "How do you know? There were only five survivors." He said, "I was one of them." He was a midshipman and the only officer saved.

We were due to leave in January 1938 after the usual three year spell in places with not too bad a climate; but Hopcraft asked me if we would like to stay on another three months as he was reluctant to change both the engineer and his assistant together. It was a complex station and these two jobs needed experience. This suited us very well as it was much better to go on leave in the spring.

The British government seemed to be starting precautionary measures for the next war as arrangements were being made for anti-aircraft batteries on the Rock, including one at Sylvia's country cottage. We got orders to prepare an emergency office in a deep dug-out. This had been made during the first war under about fifty feet of rock, and a concrete building erected inside, and apparatus installed together with underground landlines to our cable houses. It was never used and had been derelict between the wars. It was now to be put in order and wired up to take the new equipment we used. An emergency power plant was installed in an extension of the dug-out.

In the spring of 1938 together with one of our local mechanics I spent many days there doing the wiring and general installation work. We took sandwiches for lunch, and sometimes Sylvia with Paddy joined us there. Just before going on leave we had a demonstration for all the foreign service staff of the dug-out office and its arrangements. This emergency office was used for a long time during the subsequent war and a powerful wireless transmitter was added to the cable circuits, as all the Malta cables were cut by the Italians when they joined Germany against us.

About this time there appeared in the *Illustrated London News* a very good photograph of the Rock with heavy cloud, called the Levanter, hanging over the top. This cloud causes severe humidity with consequent discomfort to the inhabitants in the hot weather, and is therefore much hated by them. Appropriately the picture was titled; *The Dreaded Cloud*. But what it really referred to was the political cloud hanging over Europe owing to Hitler's activities against Austria and other countries.

In April 1938 R. R. Bryant, a bachelor, arrived to relieve me. After a couple of weeks overlap, we packed up all our belongings, left the flat and spent one night at the Bristol Hotel before sailing on a Bibby Line ship. We had arranged as before for Paddy to go to Spratts kennels on arrival in England.

The voyage was uneventful. We met Dent on board who had been in the Egyptian Ports and Lights ship *Aida* in Suez but who was now a Suez Canal pilot. We landed at Tilbury and went to stay at the Exiles Club, Meadowbank, at Twickenham.

CHAPTER TWELVE

Penang

When reporting to head office I saw the new staff manager, Mr Edmonds, whom we had met in Malta when he was inspecting branches. On enquiring where I was to be sent after my leave, he said to Penang in Malaya.

I returned to Meadowbank to find Sylvia talking to Insall and his wife on leave from Bermuda. When I said we were to go to Penang, Sylvia said, "Where is that, in China?" The Insalls said it was a very pleasant place to live; they had spent their honeymoon there. They suggested we write to Conrad Docker who was there then.

We did and it caused alarm and consternation in Penang as no one was due for leave and head office had not told them we were coming, and who was to be moved. Later we heard we were relieving an Australian Eastern Extension Company's man called Hyde who was to be transferred to Labuan, an island station off Borneo.

We had decided to invest in our first car, and Jefferies in Gibraltar had given us the name of a friend who was manager of a motor agent. He said he would be able to fix us up with a cheap one which was all we could afford.

So we went to see Mr Charles Fairhead of the Brooklands Motor Co in Bond Street. In the forecourt was a Rolls Royce and other expensive cars and we thought we must have come to the wrong place! But no, Mr Fairhead was most charming and said he had just what we wanted, an old six cylinder Chrysler, going for £17. It needed only a new tyre and 3rd party insurance, and the total cost came to £24. It was what was known as a "tourer" with a hood which could be folded down. I got a driving licence by quoting the previous one I had in 1929, so we returned the next day and drove it to Meadowbank.

We went to the Straits Settlements offices in Cockspur Street and got numerous pamphlets about Penang. We then drove up to Warkworth to see my parents, making a one night stop en route. The car did about twenty-five miles to the gallon which only cost one shilling and one penny then.

We had arranged to rent a furnished cottage with meals provided from a man called Jarvis at Hope Cove about six miles from Kingsbridge in Devon. We drove there down the Great West Road. It was called Spray Cottage, and the little bay known as Inner Hope was just across the road from it. Jarvis lived in the adjoining cottage with his wife and daughter. It had two rooms upstairs and a sitting room and bathroom down below. The Jarvis family brought our food over from next door. Jarvis had been a fisherman but now ran a hire car service.

We stayed there a month and explored all the countryside around including a visit to Plymouth about twenty miles to the west, and to Torquay the other way. Our favourite picnic spot was on Bolberry Down, just to the east of Inner Hope, where one had splendid views of the coastline from the high cliffs. In a cove there was the wreck of the famous sailing ship *Herzogin Cecelie* which had run ashore a year previously. Jarvis said the captain, mate and helmsman had all been drunk. Her masts and rigging were still standing.

In the first week in July we returned to London. I had been told the staff houses in Penang were what was known as "fully furnished", that is complete with linen, crockery, etc., so we went to head office stores department and had a look at the inventory. We decided to leave about eight packing cases with various household gear at the Exiles Club. This could be done free of charge except for 10/6d. a year for insurance. In the event they stayed there for eight years.

While visiting head office to see the doctor for the usual check-up before sailing, I went to London Station and saw Bruford, whom I had known in Gib and Malta, and who was now deputy engineer. He had invented an ingenious method of using the regenerator system on wireless circuits which the company worked after the merger in 1930. This proved extremely useful because it enabled a wireless link to replace temporarily a broken cable and led to the integration of the working of cable and wireless circuits. In general the cables would carry the baseload of traffic because they had to remain open 365 days in the year at most branches, while the wireless links, working at a higher speed, could be opened up during peak traffic periods and closed when not needed.

In July 1938, having sent off our heavy baggage to the ship, we loaded our cabin cases into the car, drove to Liverpool Street station and put them into the left luggage office. We then went to Bond Street and handed over the car to Mr. Fairhead who said he would sell it for us. It fetched £6.9.0d and our total motoring expenses including petrol over three months leave came to £40—pretty reasonable. We returned to Liverpool Street by tube, and caught the boat train and embarked on the P & O *Chitral* for Penang. We had arranged with Spratts to send Paddy to the ship, and he was accommodated as before at the stern.

We arrived at Penang at the end of August and the ship went alongside the main jetty. We were met by Conrad Docker and his wife, Molly, and told that we were to stay at the Runnymede Hotel as Hyde's children had only just recovered from measles and the family would not be leaving for three weeks.

The manager, Mr Trudgian, and his wife now arrived in their car, a new Armstrong-Siddely with automatic gears—very smart—and they drove us to the hotel. From the smart new cars and general appearance of the Europeans, it was obvious that we had entered a new world which was much more plutocratic than that in Malta and Gibraltar.

The island of Penang, about fifteen miles long and nine broad, is off the west coast of Malaya in about five degrees north latitude. The strait between it and the mainland narrows to about two miles and the capital, Georgetown, is situated here. The island has a backbone of low hills

Cable Office, Penang.

covered in trees and tropical vegetation. It is about 360 miles north of Singapore which, together with Penang, Malacca and the islands of Labuan, Christmas and Cocos-Keeling, constituted what was then known as the Straits Settlements, with a governor at Singapore.

The climate is tropical, the temperature usually being in the eighties Fahrenheit day and night, and it is rather humid. But apart from this it was a delightful place in which to live, having handsome roomy houses with large gardens, and many flowering trees and plants. excellent servants, and many amenities. In fact, probably the best place we were ever stationed at.

The cable station was in the northern outskirts of Georgetown, about a mile from the quays and business centre where we had a branch office. It consisted of a large area stretching from the main road to the beach. Near the sea was the manager's house and next to it a building which had originally been the office and mess, but was now three flats with administrative offices underneath. The new office had been built just on the landward side of this, and behind two houses facing the road. There were gardens and trees and tall bamboos all around, and next door was the Penang Club with a large lawn between it and the road; altogether very pleasant surroundings.

Except for Trudgian and myself, all the European staff had belonged to the old Eastern Extension, Australasia and China Telegraph company. There were seven of us. Of the Extension men, Lawrie, the engineer, and Moss were Australians who had joined in Adelaide where the company had a training school some years before. Docker, Maunder and Gardiner (the mechanic in charge of the workshop) were from the UK. They were all senior to me except Maunder and Gardiner.

Moss and Gardiner lived in the flats at the ends of the old office building. Lawrie and ourselves had the two houses facing the road, and Docker and Maunder (the only bachelor) lived in two of three bungalows in Vermont Road, about a mile inland from the office. The third bungalow there was occupied by M. P. Rule who was in charge of our office in the town.

The local staff consisted of a mixture of Chinese, Malays and Eurasians, the latter being descended from Portuguese ancestors who had settled in Malaya and inter-married with the local inhabitants. They were all good workers, competent at their jobs. There were also gardeners paid by the company and these were Tamils from India. They had been originally recruited for work on the rubber estates.

The office had been designed by someone who had never seen the site or had no imagination. It was a handsome single storied building with a wide arcaded verandah all round. As it was placed within twenty feet of the two-storied building on the seaward side and had tall, heavily foliaged trees on the other, the verandah kept out most of the daylight and artificial light had to be used for a good deal of the time. It would have been very suitable for the middle of the Sahara desert but was gloomy inside where it was.

Penang was mainly a relay station although there was a good deal of local traffic from the business community. There were two cables each to Colombo and Madras which were relay circuits into four cables to Singapore. They were part of the through circuits to Singapore from London, Alexandria, Bombay and Madras. There was also a cable to Medan in Sumatra about 165 miles away across the Malacca Straits where we had a small branch. Our local traffic was all sent to and received from Singapore. To do this advantage was taken of one of the useful by-products of the regenerator system. As already mentioned, the speed of a submarine cable varies inversely as the square of its length, i.e., halve the length and it works four times as fast. It had been found that it was quite easy to work two entirely separate circuits in one cable using the regenerator system to combine and split the channels. As our Singapore cables were much shorter than the ones to the west, we easily worked two channels on one cable, the extra channel being for our local circuit to Singapore.

We four watchkeepers each did a six hour daily duty, 1-7 and 7-1 a.m. and p.m. We changed duties daily (instead of weekly), doing morning, night, evening and afternoon watches in that order. On Sundays two men were off duty, and, of the other two, one did night duty and the other eighteen hours, 7 a.m. to 1 a.m. but did not have to be in the office the whole time, paying it about three or four visits and being on stand-by at home for the rest of the watch.

Malaya then kept time that was seven hours and twenty minutes ahead of Greenwich Mean Time. As this was confusing to work out quickly, the clocks in the office had a small inset face (like the seconds hand on some watches) which was set to GMT and which could be read at a glance. After World War II, it was changed to seven and a half hours, probably to help the BBC overseas service fit in their programme.

It was essential to have a car, so Docker took us to see Mr Harry

Oke, the jovial manager of Wearne's Motors who showed us two new Morris Ten cars he had in stock. We had spent all our meagre savings on leave, but Oke said that was no problem, we could have a car at once on the never never and to my surprise, told us that as we were not trading in an old car, we would get a discount on the price which made it about £190 plus interest. We chose a two-tone grey colour Morris and I had to take a driving test the next day at the police station. The European inspector told me to drive through the town and then turn round in a rather narrow street with large open six foot storm drains on either side. I told him I would not turn in such a street but drive round the block, but he insisted on my doing it, and I gingerly avoided getting our new car in the drain.

We learnt that in addition to a fully furnished house, everyone got a servant allowance of 75 Straits dollars a month, so we really thought that this was a good place to live! As Sylvia did not drive we engaged a Malay driver—known locally as a syce the Indian term for a groom.

Docker was secretary of the Penang Swimming Club which had a sea water swimming pool about 150ft long, and a pleasant club house. It faced the sea about four miles north of the town near a place called Tanjong Bungah (which means Cape of Flowers). There were sandy beaches on either side of the pool and it was a delightful place with shady trees, a surrounding garden, and a terrace overlooking the pool and the sea. Beyond the sea was the mainland with a steep mountain, Kedah Peak, clearly visible. Practically all the Europeans in Penang were members and many rubber planters, etc., on the mainland were country members, making a total of about 500. So we joined the club, and having a car driver Sylvia was able to go there when I was on duty.

We stayed in the Runnymede Hotel for about three weeks until Hyde and family left for Labuan. Paddy had not quite completed the six months quarantine from the time he left Gibraltar so had to go to the quarantine kennels for two months.

Our house was a large roomy place with a covered porch big enough to take a car, a wide entrance hall and two large rooms about forty feet long on each side, i.e. dining and sitting rooms. There was a small kitchen behind the hall. Upstairs was a verandah room over the hall, and two bedrooms over the two rooms below, and a narrow verandah at the back. The rooms had large windows but without glass, the ground floor ones with iron bars. The interior doors were all of the kind we called pub doors, i.e., double half-height doors, the bottom edges being about a foot from the floor and spring closing. Thus there was the maximum circulation of air, and cooling was helped by large ceiling fans. Birds could and indeed did enter, and occasionally nest in upstairs rooms, and now and then a bat would hang from an electric lamp cord, but they made little mess. The beds all had mosquito netting over them on four metal posts and each three quarter size bed had a small bolster known as a "Dutch wife"! by propping your leg over it, you got more cool air.

Behind about fifty feet away were the servants quarters, a kitchen and a garage, with a covered way from the house. Our house together with the other one facing the road where the engineer lived, had a large garden in front and a small one behind. The two houses had originally belonged to the Penang Club to accommodate resident bachelors. It was a men's club to which most of the managers of businesses belonged.

We engaged two Chinese servants as head boy/cook and his assistant and a Chinese armah (woman servant) three days a week to wash and iron our clothes. We had our domestic linen washed by a dhobi from outside.

In the office I had to learn the local ropes, though the working arrangements were very similar to those at Gib and Malta. There was less to do than in those places, especially on night duty as the Chinese operators were expert at attending to calls for attention on the through circuits and only told you if local action was needed. So to while away the time I set to work on an idea which had been sparked off by my talk with Bruford on his system for wireless circuits. This was to utilise as far as possible our existing cable apparatus to obviate the expense of special equipment. I worked out a scheme for this and spent my spare time in the office making drawings and typing descriptions. It was sent to head office as a proposal to their suggestions committee. It was marked commended but did not win a prize as it was never used.

The army was building a new cantonment at a place called Glugor about six miles south of Georgetown, occupied by a contingent of the Royal Artillery and Royal Engineers. The former had places where guns were mounted to protect the north and south channel sea approaches to the island. Lt Col Gage of the RE was in command and Major Joy was in charge of the gunners. They lived with their wives and families at Glugor. Mrs Joy had her sister staying with her and she was engaged to a young gunner officer called Lt Prest, and we soon met them and other army people. At a dinner party we also met

Commander Alexander RN and his wife. He was seconded to the Malayan RNVR detachment which was being raised at Penang.

There was a battalion of Territorial volunteers and a regular army officer, Major Fielding, was seconded to it as full time adjutant and instructor. It was divided into four companies each from a different ethnological group, i.e., Europeans, Chinese, Malays and Indians. Harry Oke was major of the European company.

Our house at Penang.

Swimming Club, Snake Temple, pool and terrace at Penang.

On the voyage out in the *Chitral* I had become friendly with the two senior wireless officers and when the ship came out again we invited them to our house for lunch. Molly Docker (who was of Russian extraction) went for a trip to visit friends in Hong Kong and on her return showed us a set of five carved camphor wood chests, the largest being three feet long and eighteen inches square. The other four fitted inside making a nest of chests, the smallest being sixteen inches long.

In 1939 N. J. L. Jefferies and his wife passed through en route to Hong Kong. Later we asked them to buy us a similar set of chests and our friends, the wireless officers of the *Chitral,* brought them to Penang for us on their next voyage and the total cost was £5. We also bought locally two plain camphor wood chests for £1 each, and we still have all of them in our house.

Later in 1939 Docker became due for leave and asked me whether I would take over the secretaryship of the Swimming Club. I pointed out that I was new to Malaya, did not speak the language, and knew relatively few members. He said he had already mentioned this to the committee but they would still like me to take the job on. The fact was that it was very convenient for the secretary to have a shift job like ours.

So, after attending a club committee meeting with Docker, I accepted the job. A firm of accountants called Evatt & Co were treasurers and did all the accounts, bills, etc. including supervising the catering, so my job was really a sort of general manager. We had a handyman, gardeners and pool attendants as well as the head boy and his assistants. The head boy was Chinese, spoke English and was very capable, so my instructions to the club staff were channelled through him and everything went quite smoothly. Club correspondence was mainly done on night duty in the office, where there was not much work as already mentioned. I received a small petrol allowance for my regular visits to the club.

Sylvia was also keen on the swimming club and helped me by keeping an eye on the ladies' dressing rooms and reporting anything amiss. She went there with Paddy when I was on morning duty. The club had a Malay rowing boat (called a koli) and she used to row out from the beach with Paddy to a small island called Pulo Tikus (Malay for Rat Island) half a mile out in the straits between Penang and the mainland.

The clubhouse at the north end of the pool had men's dressing rooms on the ground floor; and the main club room with bar above had an open balustrade on the seaward side and both ends. At the other end of the pool on the land side was a building containing the ladies' dressing rooms, and on the seaward side was a roofed pavilion jutting out over the beach. This was known as the Snake Temple.

The head of the government in Penang was the resident councillor, who was a deputy of the governor at Singapore. He had two district commissioners under him, one as president of the town council of Georgetown and another who was rural commissioner for the rest of the island. The police had British senior officers and one or two British inspectors, the rank and file being Chinese and Malays. Their point duty traffic control amused us. The constable had what looked like a pair of flat black and white wings strapped to his shoulders which extended on either side. He stood in the centre of a crossroads and controlled the traffic by facing first one way and then another at right angles. He raised his arms above his head when about to change over. The Malay for policeman is Mata-Mata (mata means eye, so mata-mata is two eyes). There was another odd police post called the protector of chinese. This was to counter intimidation of individuals by the often powerful tongs or Chinese secret societies. A Chinese could get help from the protector against blackmail or extortion.

The Chinese are undoubtedly the most industrious and business-minded of the inhabitants of Malaya. The Malays are of a more happy go lucky type and like to sit about in the sun, though they can make good soldiers as the Malay Regiment shows and many are hardworking fishermen. The Indians, mostly Tamils from South India, but some Sikhs (who specialise as janitors and night watchmen) are also hard-working.

Sir Edward Wilshaw who had become managing director of our company, decided to equip a number of cable stations with a small wireless transmitter and receiver for emergency use, and J. A. C. Robins was sent to Penang to install them. The engineer-in-chief's department had the fond idea that interference to wireless reception from cable office apparatus could be suppressed by fitting certain components to it; this did not work. Later it was realised that the only remedy was to site the aerial away from the office and screen both the lead-in cable and the receiver completely. Even an inch of un-screened wire from the aerial could lead to interference.

Saturday evening dances were held regularly at the Runnymede Hotel which had an excellent orchestra conducted by a Hungarian, and we used to go frequently, often making up a party with friends. Dancing took place in the large oblong dining room. At the far end was a wall with mirrors, and in front were arranged banks of flowers producing a marvellously decorative effect.

In March 1939 Hitler occupied Czechoslovakia and war finally broke out in September when he attacked Poland. The immediate effect on Penang was slight, but gradually various restrictions had to be imposed. Petrol rationing was introduced but did not much affect us as we did not do any great mileage. We had bought a short wave radio receiver and could listen to broadcasts from the BBC and local stations. The Dutch had a very good short wave station called Nirom at Batavia (now Djakarta) which in addition to news in English gave continuous broadcasts of light classical music.

The army cantonment at Glugor was reinforced by the arrival of the 5th Battalion of the 14th Punjab Regiment. This was another batalion of my brother's regiment, and several of the 5th Bn officers knew him, and we met most of them.

Lt Col Stokes was in command. This battalion had originally been called the 40th Pathans and was still very fond of its old name. Col Stokes had it displayed on his house name-plate. They were known in the Indian Army as the "Forty Thieves", Pathans being noted for such proclivities.

We got a few days station leave and went to stay at a little hotel along the north east coast beyond the swimming club. It was called Mount Pleasant and was built on the lower end of a hilly spur which ran out onto a promontory. It consisted of a dining room, lounge and verandah facing the sea, and in front was a swimming pool with palm trees and sun shelters around it. There were fine views of the sea on three sides, the hill being about 200 feet up. On a ledge below were a number of small chalets as sleeping accommodation for the guests, and a road ran down the hill to the main coast road.

A British light cruiser, HMS *Dauntless,* paid us a visit and the committee of the Swimming Club decided that visiting RN officers should be invited to become honourary members. I went to call on the ship and met Captain D. G. Moore and his officers, and told them they could use the club's facilities. The captain was a Royal Australian naval officer serving with the British navy and the ship subsequently paid us many visits.

It was arranged we should have some lectures from a local police officer who had been to England for a course in civil defence and was teaching its rudiments in Penang. A blood transfusion service was also organised at the hospital and Sylvia went frequently with other women to help with this work. Later there were practice black-outs lasting several hours when lights were switched off to accustom people to air raid precautions.

Penang was the main port for shipping rubber and tin which were the principal exports from this part of the mainland. There were numerous rubber estates and tin mines further south. In the early and middle 1930s there had been a slump in rubber and tin prices which had led to the sacking of many rubber planters, and economies under which one planter would manage two estates. But prices had gradually improved before the war started and now they picked up rapidly. The government, on instruction from home, discouraged Europeans from leaving their jobs to join the armed services in the UK. Our staff was not allowed to leave their posts. Gradually the number of passenger ships dropped, until with the entry of Italy into the war, there were only occasional ones coming via Cape Town, as the Mediterranean route was blocked.

There were two other light cruisers on the Singapore station, the *Durban* and the *Danae* and when they visited us I went on board to invite them to use the Swimming Club. They were commanded respectively by Captain J. A. S. Eccles and Captain A. C. Collinson. The former became an Admiral and C-in-C of the Home Fleet after the war, and the latter was sent to Hong Kong in 1941 and became a prisoner of war of the Japs. It was also decided to organise some entertainments for the lower deck and both the Swimming and Sports Clubs participated. Lawes, the assistant chief of police, lent police buses to take sixty sailors out to the Swimming Club in the afternoon. They could bathe and were given a high tea followed by dancing on the club verandah with ladies whom Sylvia had recruited to entertain them.

Penang had two or three good cinemas and we used to go there, often seeing films which had recently been released, as some came to the Far East direct from America. We used to take the naval officers there after dinner or to the Runnymede for dances.

While staying at Mount Pleasure we met an Australian couple, Lou and Bob McMillan and invited them to our house. He worked on a tin mine at Taiping about fifty miles south of Butterworth, the mainland town opposite Penang. They asked us to come and spend the week-end with them. So we crossed over on the car ferry and drove down the main road to Taiping. The country was very green and pleasant with numerous paddy (rice) fields surrounding Malay villages with palm thatched wooden houses raised on stilts; and there were small boys driving water buffalos. Here and there were rubber estates with the trees all planted in exact rows whichever way you looked at them. One stretch of the road was dead straight for eight miles.

The McMillan's bungalow was one of a group of ten a short distance beyond Taiping, itself a pleasant place with the usual rows of Chinese shops, trees and pandang (village green). The Kamunting tin mine where he worked used a number of large dredges and he was a dredgemaster in charge of one. They are very similar to those used to deepen harbours, having an endless chain of buckets on a framework which can be lowered or raised as required. The dredge floats in a shallow lake and digs into the bank thus extending the lake area while the waste material is expelled from a long boom carrying a conveyor belt which protruded from the stern. It thus moves forward taking its lake with it. The buckets discharge into a big rotating round screen (sieve) which breaks up the soil and removes the larger stones. The earth then passes across a number of vibrating tables submerged in water and the heavy tin-bearing ore sinks to the bottom, is removed and packed in small canvas bags to go to the refinery; it is cast into ingots about the size of a brick and very heavy, and loaded onto ships in Penang. The dredges are driven by electric motors from a power overhead line. They work twenty-four hours a day and can be heard at night in the distance. This is the recovery method used by the large European tin mines, and needs considerable capital but can be very profitable.

We were taken to the Taiping Swimming Club. While smaller than the one in Penang it was delightfully situated in a valley down which there was a picturesque waterfall. Alongside it the club had built a watershute which ended in a small swimming pool, and the water flowed through it into another pool with diving boards and concrete surround. The clubhouse with palm leaf thatch, adjoined both pools and the whole was surrounded with palms, flowers and tropical vegetation.

On one occasion we went for a walk just before dark and returned to their bungalow as a heavy thunder and rain storm broke. There was suddenly a tremendous flash of lightning and all the lights went out. Bob McMillan who was tuning the radio for the six o'clock news, got an electric shock which knocked him over, and Lou, who was in her bath,

Lou McMillan and Sylvia at the Taiping Swimming Club, Penang.

thought the end of the world had come. We switched on our car headlights and got some fusewire to replace all the fuses which had blown but, strangely, not one lamp was burnt out, though one fusebox had its porcelain cover shattered. The lightning must have struck the overhead electric power lines.

The McMillans took us for some pleasant picnics and we drove to Kuala Kangsa, the capital of the state of Perak (pronounced *Peera*,) which has a handsome mosque with a white dome. We also went to Ipoh about thirty miles south of Taiping and visited the swimming club there.

There were two hill stations in Malaya where Europeans went for holidays and to get a little cooler. One, twenty miles from Ipoh, was called Cameron Highlands and the other, Frasers Hill, was nearer Kuala Lumpur further south. We were not able to get away long enough to make it worth while going to them.

We did spend a few days at Penang Hill in the centre of the island where there was a small hotel and a number of bungalows. It was reached by a funicular rack railway in two sections with a change-over station half way up. The hill has some pleasant walks along wooded paths at the top, the height being about 1,200 feet. Near the lower station of the railway were the Waterfall Gardens where there was a display of bougainvillea in four or five different colours. Not far away are a number of Chinese and Indian temples. The Indians hold a big annual festival called Taipusan in which there is a long procession of images on elaborately decorated palanquins. Dozens of penitents with barbs and pins stuck into their flesh march from the town to the temples where their torments are removed.

A man called Newington who had originally been with our company, but who was now the manager of an insurance company, offered to devote his spare time to improving the Swimming Club garden. The committee gave him an allowance for labour, plants, etc. It was a great success. He made a pergola down the steps to the club with various coloured bougainvillea and erected a three-tier stand for flower pots behind the terrace where he kept a continuous display of various blooms which was very impressive.

Tin dredge at Kamunting Mines.

Another warship which paid Penang a visit was HMS *Terror,* a monitor with two enormous fifteen inch guns and large blisters along each side to protect it from torpedo attack. I went on board to visit the captain, Commander Haynes, RN, and he later came ashore to see us. Surgeon Commander Mansel-Reese of HMS *Dauntless* often visited us. A rather short man, he was a most cheerful extrovert and good company. After the war he became a Surgeon Rear Admiral.

Captain Catt and his wife went to live in a house they had rented from a rich Chinese. It was near the entrance to a valley and had an open swimming pool in the centre with the rooms of the house built round it. Sylvia often went to see Mrs Catt and probably caught dengue fever there as she had one or two attacks of this. It produces bad pains in the joints and general debility and is believed to be carried by mosquitoes of which there were a good many in that neighbourhood. In the town and immediate suburbs it was an offence to leave stagnant water about for mosquitoes to breed in, and Inspectors came round every now and then. They took samples of any water found, especially in flower vases, to check for mosquito larvae.

Northam Road, where our house was, was lined with what are known as Angsana trees. They are as large as big oaks, heavily leafed and produce small bright yellow flowers all over. There were also flame of the forest trees, and when the blossoms from both dropped onto the road they made a carpet of red and gold which was very beautiful. Those who had been to Hawaii said that Penang was not unlike it with its gardens, trees and flowers. It was certainly the prettiest overseas place we ever stayed in. The drawback was the damp heat and I got prickly heat which took some time to get rid of with ointment the doctor prescribed.

Trudgian, our manager, went on leave and was relieved by F. J. R. Glass. In 1941 Glass was transferred to Hong Kong and replaced by R. F. L. La Nauze, an Australian. Glass was afterwards a prisoner when Hong Kong was captured by the Japs but survived. La Nauze unfortunately died in a prisoners' camp in Singapore.

A Major Vetch and his wife invited us to have supper with them at the Flying Club, south of the town. He was the secretary and flying instructor. Early in the evening a Mr Nixon, the Manager of a firm called Guthrie & Co appeared and said he was going up in one of their Tiger Moth light aircraft and enquired if anyone wanted to come with him. Vetch asked me and, after consulting Sylvia, I went up with Nixon on my first flight. We flew over the narrows to Butterworth and then back and over the town and returned to the club. It was just dusk and very clear, and we could see the whole of Georgetown and the mainland with lights just beginning to come on.

The strange question of "When is a carpet not a carpet?" Answer: "When it is a rug," cropped up. We were allowed to requisition items for our furnished houses annually, so we put in for three carpets to cover our tiled ground floors. The divisional manager in Singapore exploded and said he had no carpets at all, only rugs, which, of course, we should have asked for and which we eventually got. The carpet designation had fitted our previous houses—much smaller than those in Malaya.

Tommy Marsden and "Baron" Westworth were transferred to Cocos Island and relieved by W. H. Lampen-Smith and Bassett, both of whose wives came with them. Several of our men who had been axed in the early 1930s passed through Penang on their way to Singapore to take up jobs as cable censors. When the war broke out the company, at the instigation of the government, circularised these axed men, asking them to volunteer for such jobs, and about a dozen or so went to Singapore.

We met Rex and Madge Phillips. He was a civil engineer working for a firm of contractors who were building airfields in Malaya. They came to see us and invited us to spend weekends with them in a rubber planter's bungalow which they had rented at Sungei Patani about fifteen miles north of Butterworth on the mainland. Rex took me to see his airfield and for the first time I saw the large mechanised earth-moving equipment used, enormous twenty-ton scrapers and other gear. A number of these airfields were being built all down the peninsular in preparation for the arrival of Spitfire fighters which were expected to be available soon. In the event, Prime Minister Churchill had to send these aircraft to assist Russia when it was attacked by the Germans. So they never arrived in Malaya and the airfields were seized and used by the Japs in the invasion at the end of 1941.

The government introduced an income tax but to placate public opinion called it a war tax and said it would be dropped when the war was over; which it was not. Our company had always paid local income tax for their staff abroad but as it was called a war tax said we would have to pay it ourselves. Later they reversed this decision and paid it for us. Compulsory war insurance premiums were also introduced for stocks of business firms. The local newspaper, *The Pinang Gazette* (probably the old spelling of Penang) contested assessment on stocks of paper alleging they sold news and not newsprint, but lost when it came to court. When the Japs arrived they were probably glad.

We met a young rubber planter called Abbot who was manager of an estate in Kedah and he stayed with us once or twice at weekends. We paid him a visit on his estate and saw how the rubber trees were tapped by making incisions into the bark and letting the white liquid, known as latex, run down into small cups. The Tamil labourers collect the latex into large containers and take it to the sheds where it is mixed in a long shallow tank with formic acid which coagulates it. It is then rolled into flat strips and finally baled and shipped to the rubber factories in Europe and elsewhere.

We were told that E. E. Story, an Australian then at Cocos Island, was to relieve us for furlough. His wife and family would come from Australia as no wives were allowed at Cocos Island cable station. Head office had recently sent out a circular saying that staff could apply to spend their leave in countries other than the UK provided the climate was reasonably cool. Leave in the UK started on arrival there, but if one went elsewhere now, it would start when one left one's station and the time normally taken to get to the UK would be added to it. The amount of leave depended on the climate, amenities, etc., of the station one had served at, and varied from three months for three years service in the Mediterranean to five months for the same period in the tropics. As Sylvia had not seen her family for thirteen years we applied to spend our leave in South Africa.

Conrad Docker had returned to Penang so it was arranged he should take over the secretaryship of the Swimming Club. The committee gave us a farewell supper party and presented me with a silver cigarette box suitably inscribed in appreciation of my work for the club. Sylvia was given a small sapphire and pearl broach. The job, entailing contacts with contractors, government officials and meeting a large number of people, was very useful training in management which served me in good stead later.

Story arrived in the middle of September 1941 and took over our house at the end of the month when we went to stay at Mount Pleasure to wait for a ship. There was a service of large Dutch cargo liners which ran from Japan via Malaya to South Africa and South America. It was the custom then for staff to leave their household goods at the cable depot in Singapore if they were returning to the Far East. Head office declined to say where we were to go next, so we decided to pack up everything and take it with us. We sold our car for the amount we had paid for it as owing to the war there was a great demand for good second-hand cars.

We had a month at Mount Pleasure before we were told to go by train to Singapore to catch a ship there. One evening some friends were dining there and had as a guest a staff officer from GHQ Singapore. He said that the Japs, having invaded French Indo-China in September were expected to move against Malaya in about three months time. I said, "Good heavens, we had better get away as soon as possible," and he agreed.

On 28th October we left Penang by ferry to Butterworth where we caught the night express for Kuala Lumpur. We had decided that as it was quite impossible to take Paddy with us and he was now old and nearly blind, the kindest thing to do was to put him to sleep and I took him to the vet and saw it done on the day we left. It was very sad, but he had had a good and happy life with us for fifteen years.

The island of Singapore is about the same size as the Isle of Wight but flatter, with the town at the south end. The channels separating it from the mainland are narrow and there is a causeway with road and railway joining it to the Malay state of Johore to the north. The naval base was east of the causeway. The town with a mixed population, mainly Chinese, then about 800,000, is a busy trading and shipping centre. In the roadstead and at Keppel Harbour on the south west side, dozens of ships anchor and discharge or load cargoes from all over the east. It was founded on a drained swamp by Sir Stamford Raffles whose statue near a tree where he is supposed to have landed, stands near the Padang (grassy park). There are fine shops, offices and banks centred around Raffles Place, and pleasant houses in suburbs very similar to Penang.

I went to see our divisional manager, Mr Rickwood, and pointed out that it seemed that we would be spending nearly two months of our leave in Malaya.

In North Bridge Road near our hotel we saw dozens of shops displaying gold teeth in the windows. The Chinese are fond of them and you can have solid gold teeth to replace ones you have lost or dentures. If you are not so well off, thin gold covers for teeth or dentures are available—a wonderful sight.

The making of large Chinese lanterns, usually round with enormous ideographs in red, intrigued us. You could watch workmen painting them in open shops. Many streets with tenement blocks where Chinese lived had hundreds of wooden poles protruding from windows and verandahs overhead and festooned with washing hung out to dry. They are undoubtedly a very industrious race.

We dined at Raffles Hotel one evening and met some of the officers from HMS *Dauntless* who took us to a dance at the Tanglin Club, the European club in Singapore. HMS *Danae* was in drydock at the naval base and Captain Frank Butler invited us to a cocktail party at the naval barracks. We were introduced by him to Admiral Sir Geoffrey and Lady Layton and he told them we had done more than anyone to entertain the navy in Penang. The commander-in-chief was a very impressive character, rather short but with very sharp eyes which looked right through you. Lady Layton was charming. In 1942 he was placed in charge in Colombo after the loss of Singapore, and by his forceful leadership saved many lives and ships when the Japs bombed the harbour and town.

We had a small dinner party at our hotel with a nurse, Miss Butcher whom we had known in Gib and Engineer Commander Ham of HMS *Danae*. The latter arrived in a uniform mess jacket and I told him we thought of going to *The Happy World* and *The New World* later, and offered to lend him a civilian mess jacket as officers in uniform were not supposed to visit these allegedly low haunts. But he beckoned me into the cloakroom and produced a civilian one from a small valise. The navy was always prepared for anything! These places were large permanent fairs run by the Chinese and had booths and buildings with every kind of entertainment. There were two or three Chinese theatres with continuous performances, shooting galleries, hoop-la, the dodge-ems and all the shows one expects in such a place. They were crowded with all races.

On the 24th November, we left Singapore from Clifford Pier to join a Dutch passenger ship for Batavia where we would catch our ship to Cape Town. Mrs Joy came to see us off. At the last minute she had forgotten to give us the address of her husband's sister in South Africa but said she would send it. Owing to the Jap invasion she never did, but we met the sister and her family by chance.

CHAPTER THIRTEEN

South Africa

Our ship, the *Bysskus* of 3,000 tons left Singapore on Monday, 24th November 1941 with a dozen passengers.

We arrived at Tanjong Priok the port of Batavia (now Djakarta) about three miles from the town.

We stayed at the famous *Hotel Des Indes,* a large building facing one of the main streets. A covered way at the side led to a quadrangle at the back enclosing a garden containing some deer. Around it was a two-storeyed row of bedrooms, each with a separate entrance, verandah sitting-room and bathroom. There were several of these quadrangles with similar rooms for guests. This is a very good idea for a large hotel in the tropics before the days of air-conditioning as bedroom windows can be kept open at night without fear of being disturbed by noise from the public rooms; but it needs plenty of space. Everything was well appointed and the food, of which the Dutch are very fond, was superb. When serving one of their famous dishes, such as *Reisstaffel* or *Nasir Goreng,* there would be a dozen Javanese waiters each carrying a separate item to go on your plate.

The next day we went to the shipping offices at Tanjong Priok about our passages and to our cable office where we found that Bryant had arrived from Australia.

In the foyer of the hotel were glass showcases and in one Sylvia had spotted a crocodile-skin dressing case with tortoise shell fittings. She said: "I would like that". It was about £20 in Dutch guilders but we had only a limited amount in that currency to pay our hotel bill and not enough to buy it. So next day we went to the cable office and Bryant let us have enough to buy it in exchange for a cheque on London.

We walked round the town the next day. The main streets all have canals running down the centre with much washing of clothes by the Javanese women. In the evening Bryant came to dinner with us. He had earlier shown us his nice bungalow, one of several rented by our company.

Next day, Sunday, we went in a hired car with a friend we had met on the ship and had lunch at a very good Dutch chalet type restaurant in the hills about 3,000 feet up, and then on to Buitenzorg where there are well known botanical gardens. It was a pleasant outing and we saw numerous Dutch houses, painted in bright colours—very picturesque. The country was hilly with terraced rice fields.

The following day, Monday 1st December, we embarked on the KPM liner *Tegelburg,* 14,000 tons, which sailed for Mauritius about 5 p.m. She carried up to 600 passengers, including 100 first class. She passed through the Sunda Straits between Java and Sumatra during the night so we did not see the famous island of Krakatoa whose volcano erupted in 1883. The ship had comfortable first-class cabins and spacious public rooms and decks. There was a swimming pool at the after end of the promenade deck and on the boat deck, a small tennis court with net surround. Being smaller than usual, one played with special rackets which had plywood instead of strings. This, strangely, made the game very similar but—as it were--smaller than usual. One could hit with about the same strength as on an ordinary court.

Also on the boat deck was a gymnasium in which Sylvia spent much time riding bicycles and rowing a boat on special machines. The food, as is usual in Dutch ships, was excellent. The dinner menu had eighteen items to choose from and there was a note at the bottom inviting you to contact the chief steward if you fancied something special.

The voyage was uneventful until we suddenly learned on the radio of the attack by the Japanese on the United States' naval base at Pearl Harbour, and later of their assault on north Malaya, Hong Kong and the Philippines. This was a shock as we thought of all the friends we had left behind.

We arrived at Port Louis, Mauritius, on 9th December. Just before we got there a male passenger jumped overboard and started swimming towards the shore. The ship was stopped, a boat lowered and he was picked up. He was handed over to the police at Port Louis as the captain refused to take him further.

We went ashore by launch as the ship was anchored some way from the town, and visited the cable office where we met H. Biron, the brother of Basil Biron who had been in Suez with me. We hired a car and drove to Curepipe, about sixteen miles from Port Louis, at an altitude of 1,800 feet which is the chief European residential centre. It is supposed to be a fine town with good houses and gardens, but I am afraid we were not very favourably impressed and the tea we had at the hotel was badly served. There were also hundreds of flies.

The ship sailed the next day and arrived at Durban four days later. We went ashore and had a look round at our old station.

We reached Cape Town on 17th December and put up at the Grand Hotel in Strand Street, just off Adderley Street. Netlam Miller, the husband of Sylvia's eldest sister Mercy, had retired from the bank at Robertson and they had gone to live at Pinelands, a suburb on the east side of Table Mountain. When they heard we were coming to South Africa it was arranged that they, and her other sister, Gertrude and husband Arthur Steer from Graaff Reinet, should all spend Christmas at a seaside resort called Hermanus about eighty miles from the Cape on the south east coast.

We telephoned them on arrival and they said the hotel could take us on 20th December. We bought an old green Ford V8 tourer for £91, but it was not a good buy as it gave a lot of trouble at first, though I got rid of its defects eventually. Large American cars are common in South Africa as they are more suitable for a big country where the climate is

1941 Christmas party at Marine Hotel, Hermanus, Arthur, Gertrude, daughter Ann, Mrs. and Mr. Sproat (Mrs. Joy's in-laws), Mercy, Netlam, Sylvia.

warm, as one keeps much cooler in a roomy car.

On 20th December we left Cape Town and drove to the Marine Hotel, Hermanus. It was a pleasant journey over the Hottentot's Holland mountains by the Sir Lowry Pass on the other side of False Bay to the east of the Cape Peninsular. Near the pass is the large Steenbras reservoir, three and a half miles long, used to supply most of the water for Cape Town and its suburbs.

We were greeted by the Millers and Steers whom Sylvia had not seen for close on fourteen years. They announced it would be no use our romancing about Malaya as someone staying at the hotel had been there. When we met her, who should it turn out to be but Major Joy's sister, her husband and their daughter, Anne—the Sproat family whose address we never received from Mrs Joy! Their home was in Johannesburg and they had only met Sylvia's relations by pure chance as they had originally intended spending their holiday at another hotel.

We all spent Christmas together at Hermanus returning to Cape Town on 29th December. Mercy and Netlam Miller gave us a party on New Year's eve at a restaurant in the town. The next day Netlam had a heart attack and was in bed for over three weeks. Gertrude and Arthur Steer returned to Graaff Reinet.

A week later we moved to the Outspan Hotel at Fishoek, a seaside resort on False Bay eighteen miles from Cape Town on the east side of the peninsula. We met a Dr Mackenzie and his wife who were on holiday from Salisbury, Rhodesia. He invited me to go up Table Mountain with the Curator of the Kirstenbosch botanical gardens. With a party of students, we went up Skeleton Gorge above the gardens and then along the back of the mountain. We finally reached the flat top and walked to the upper station of the aerial cableway where we met Sylvia and Mrs MacKenzie and their small daughter. They had come round to Cape Town in their car and up the cableway. We all had tea in the restaurant, and went down the cableway to Kirstenbosch to pick up our car.

We later moved to the Hotel Lanark, at Fishoek, which was run by a Miss Knowles, an Englishwoman from Broadstairs with whom we became friendly. Kate Gain, the wife of Sylvia's cousin in Shanghai, and her three children were living at Fishoek and I joined them for tennis at the club several times.

Wallace Donaldson and his wife who had been relieved by us in Lourenço Marques in 1930, was also on leave in Cape Town. He was to go to St Helena and we exchanged visits with them.

Our bank in Cape Town telephoned us one morning and said a naval officer, Commander Goodfellow, wanted our address. It was the ship's doctor from HMS *Durban,* and he came out to Fishoek and told us he was on board the troopship *Empress of Britain* which was full of women and children who had escaped from the Japs in Malaya and were on their way home. He had been ordered home and was helping the ship's doctor—very suitable as he was a gynaecologist in civilian life. Malaya was gradually being over-run by the Japs and Singapore surrendered on 14th February. Most of the European women and children were evacuated either to England or Australia but hardly any of the men. We heard later that our Penang staff, after destroying all the cable apparatus, went down to Singapore. A number of them and some of the Singapore men, among them the divisional manager were ordered to embark on a small ship but she was bombed and nineteen of them, including the DM were killed. Bertie Banks and Conrad Docker who were on board this vessel became prisoners with all the staff left behind and others in Borneo and Hong Kong. Strangely enough, the only one to escape was Eric Story who had relieved me in Penang. His wife and children arrived from Australia just in time to be evacuated back there. Head office ordered him to go to Karachi and he left Singapore by air before the surrender.

Ebenezer Farm, South Africa, old homestead on right.

In Adderley Street one morning we suddenly saw the English magistrate from Penang and his wife. Over morning tea they told us she had escaped with other women and children on a ship to Colombo. He was in the Volunteers and they were holding a rear line of defence in Singapore when the surrender took place. He and another man escaped in a Chinese boat to Sumatra where they found a British warship which took them to Colombo.

We stayed at Fishoek for two and a half months. It was the summer time and we bathed and enjoyed our holiday with visits to Pinelands to see Sylvia's sister and her husband who gradually recovered from his heart attack.

On 24th March we left Cape Town by train for Graaff Reinet to visit Sylvia's other sister and husband Arthur. On booking two first class train fares, one could rail a car for four guineas; so we delivered the car to the railway before leaving. We arrived at Graaff Reinet two days later, and put up at the Drosdty Hotel. I had previously obtained a visitor's driving licence, valid for three months, but I now got a permanent one. This has a photo on it and is valid for life, one has to take driving tests but they were not very severe.

In April, the cable office wired us that I was appointed to Accra in the Gold Coast. I wrote at once to the manager sending two copies, one by air and one by sea mail which was just as well as one never arrived. He was J. B. McRury and he replied there would be a flat for us over the office but it was not fully furnished, so needed linen, crockery, etc. As we had left ours behind in England we had to buy another lot in Cape Town, when we got back there. Fortunately it was easily obtainable.

In the meantime we enjoyed our stay in Graaff Reinet, going for drives and picnics round about. We drove up a road to what is known as the Valley of Desolation on top of the mountains overlooking the town. The Van Ryneveld Pass Dam which had been under construction across the Sundays River when we were on our honeymoon, was now finished but owing to recent drought, the dam was only half full. South Africans use the word dam in two senses, one for a wall across a river as we do, and another for a water reservoir either behind a dam or just any large artificial pool or lake.

Sylvia met Vera Hobson and her husband Barry. She had been at school with Vera and had also known Barry years before. They had a sheep farm called Ebenezer about forty miles south east of Graaff

Reinet in the middle of an area known as the Platteland, i.e., the flat lands. They invited us to come and stay with them for a few days. Barry Hobson's farm was about 40,000 acres. There were two houses in one of which his mother lived, a small detached building for guest bedrooms and a farm shop. He had electric light from his own engine and battery, windmill for pumping water and a telephone, most of the usual amenities even though miles from town and other farms. He was descended from one of the 1820 settlers, about 4,000 of whom had come out from England in that year. They landed at Port Elizabeth and settled in the area to the north and west known as the Great Karroo, a vast plateau about 350 miles long and 3,000 feet high.

The sheep, mostly merinos, feed on what is known as Karroo bush, an unpromising looking dark green bush which nevertheless affords nourishment to them even in the dryest season. There is practically no grass. It is a rather barren looking landscape with about eighteen inches of rain annually and sometimes less, with low kopjes. But with large farms running about one sheep to from two to four acres, farmers can make a fair living. Barry told me that during the slump years in the early thirties they were very hard up and could rarely afford even to go to town. He had three sons, Sandford aged seventeen (Vera's maiden name), and twins aged about fourteen. The price of wool was now good but he wanted to save money to buy additional farms for the twins if they wished to be farmers. One of the difficulties in South Africa had been that many of the early Boer (Dutch) farmers had large families and when they died their farms were split up until they got too small to support a family. So some sold out and went to the towns, producing a class known as poor whites who worked as labourers.

Barry had a number of black farm hands whom he employed. Most of them came from families who had worked on the farm for generations and seemed a happy lot. He was, in fact, a good employer and he and Vera took great trouble to look after his men and their families.

We stayed four days and had a pleasant time. Barry took me on a springbok shoot on his cousin Robert Hobson's farm. All the farms were divided by wire fences into what were known as camps, each of several thousand acres. Every now and then the springbok would become too numerous, eating up all the karroo bush, and the farmer would have a shoot to thin them down and invite his neighbours to come and participate. Owing to the war there was a shortage of rifle ammunition so the farmers were using shotguns to kill game. To kill a springbok with a shotgun one must only fire when it is close.

There were about a dozen or more farmers at Robert Hobson's shoot. We lined up as directed by him and his African boys drove the springbok towards us. They can travel at quite a pace with their extraordinary hopping gait and one has to be quick and accurate to shoot them.

We returned to Graaff Reinet and a week later left by train for Cape Town, our car going as before on the train.

We set to work sorting out our household effects which had been stored by a firm of shipping agents, and buying crockery, linen, etc. Fortunately we had taken our canteen of cutlery to Penang. We decided to leave our camphor wood chests with some fancy table linen and various other things we had collected in the Far East, in store in Cape Town. Our leave was now up.

We sold our car for £50—not too bad as we had had good use of it. We met C. V. Williams and his wife who were on leave in Cape Town. He was an "Extension" man but had been in Accra just before the war when there was a bad earthquake, and he told me all about it. We continued to stay at the Lanark Hotel at Fishoek. It is a pleasant seaside resort with magnificent views of the Hottentot Hollands mountains on the other side of False Bay.

On 16th June we embarked on a ship called the *Pierre Loti* of 5,000 tons. There were about eighty passengers including a few children, nearly all British bound for Nigeria or the Gold Coast but one or two Frenchmen returning to their colonies south of the equator which had been taken over by General de Gaulle's Free French.

The ship was an odd one. She had been built by John Brown's of Clydebank for the Tsar of Russia, so we were told, then sold to the French Messagerie Line in the Mediterranean, finally being employed in the Pacific between the French islands there. She had escaped the Japs and fetched up in Australia where she was taken over by the British Ministry of War Transport. They arranged with the Blue Funnel Line to provide British officers and engineers to man her. The crew was Chinese, mainly from Malaya, but British loss of face due to the fall of Singapore made them mutinous and difficult to handle. One of them tried to knife the chief steward and had to be put in confinement. However, they had to work as they had nowhere else to go.

As we were now where German submarines were operating, there was a blackout at night, and we had to carry our lifebelts with us wherever we were and also had blitz-bags. These were haversacks containing toilet and other necessities, passports, money, etc., in case we had to leave the ship in a hurry. There was regular lifeboat drill and at one port en route we even practised abandoning ship. The lifeboats were put into the water and we all got into them and rowed about.

Three days later we arrived at Walvis Bay and moored alongside the jetty. This was about the most God-forsaken spot we had ever seen. Apart from the port and railway buildings there was nothing but a short row of houses with a couple of shops and one pub. Everything was flat and arid with not a tree or blade of grass to be seen, and it was very hot. Its only asset is its good harbour. We went ashore for a walk that evening and again the next morning and the ship sailed at noon.

Four days later we arrived at Pointe Noire in French Equatorial Africa. We stayed there alongside a jetty for ten days, discharging and loading cargo.

We got to Port Gentil about 24 hours after leaving Pointe Noire. This was much more picturesque with lots of trees and gardens. We stayed

Table Mountain and the Cableway, Lion's Head on the right.

there for three days and had some pleasant walks ashore.

The next place was Libreville in a wide estuary, where we arrived the following day. I had been here before in the cableship *Transmitter* in 1922. This time we saw the signs of war. Lying on a sandbank on her side was a 5,000 ton French cruiser. She had been damaged and beached in a sinking condition in a short battle when the Free French came to Libreville supported by the British Navy, and siezed the place from the Vichy French.

Four days later we sailed for Duala in the Cameroons where we arrived the next day, but anchored at the entrance to the estuary, a long way from the town. Cargo and passengers were discharged into lighters and tender respectively.

There was a couple who sat at our table in the saloon called Carman. He was an accountant with the United Africa Co (Unilever) in Nigeria. I mentioned to him one day about reading Major Tilman's book describing his exploit in riding a bicycle across central Africa from Uganda to the mouth of the Congo. "Impossible," said Carman, and though I told him that Tilman was a famous Everest climber, he refused to believe the story was true.

There were three other married couples who, like us, had come from Malaya. They were rubber planters and had been on leave in Australia when the Japs arrived. They were going to the British Cameroons to take over rubber plantations there to help make up for the loss of rubber from Malaya.

We left early the next day and arrived off the mouth of the Bonny River in the evening. On our way from Duala we had passed the island of Fernando Poo on our left, with its magnificent mountain peak which rises to 9,350 feet.

The next morning we entered the river and passing the small town of Bonny where I had had my first palm oil chop while in *Transmitter*, proceeded up the winding channel which had many branching ones, and arrived at Port Harcourt where we went alongside the quay to coal. We remained there for four days and went for walks into the town and visited the native market, very picturesque with the Nigerian mammies in gay colours selling local produce.

We went to the post office and sent cables to Sylvia's sister Mercy in Cape Town, and to my parents in England. We had been so long on the voyage that I realised that McRury, in Accra, would be wondering what had become of us and when we would arrive, so I let him know without giving away shipping information. A man called Crouch who had been one of the supervisors in Suez and with whom I had played much cricket, was manager of our station in Lagos, not far from Port Harcourt. So I sent an inland telegram telling him to tell McRury that we would be with him in about five or six days. I knew Crouch would send this on to Accra by coded service message and no one else would know.

The day before we left Port Harcourt there was nearly a riot amongst the African labourers who were putting the coal on board from railway wagons. Some idiots amongst the passengers started throwing small coins on to the quay causing the Africans to scramble for them, and stopping all the work until the captain appeared and told them off. He was a rather peculiar character who usually walked about the ship in khaki shorts and a none too clean singlet, and seemed eccentric. We heard later that the eccentric captain ran the ship ashore at Duala and she became a wreck. So we were lucky to complete our voyage safely.

We left Port Harcourt on the morning of 21st August and arrived at Takoradi in the Gold Coast three days later. This was the new harbour the building of which had been contemplated when I was in *Transmitter* in 1922. It is about three miles west of the old town of Sekondi where earlier we had a cable station, now closed.

Takoradi harbour was proving too small and a large anti-torpedo net had been installed outside to make a bigger safe anchorage in war time.

CHAPTER FOURTEEN

Accra

Although we arrived at Takoradi about 3 o'clock, it was 9 p.m. before we got through the customs and immigration control; too late to get to Accra about 130 miles away. Mr Robinson of Elder Dempsters, the shipping line, kindly drove us to a small Greek Hotel called *The Acropolis* in Sekondi where we put up for the night.

I telephoned McRury who said we should hire a mammy car for ourselves and luggage, and the company would pay for it. This is a light lorry chassis on to which has been built a wooden body with three or four rows of seats behind the driver and a space for goods at the back. It is a sort of glorified station wagon with a roof but no sides where the seats are. We hired the whole vehicle and our packing cases, trunks, etc. were put in the back and on the rear seats and we travelled in the front row behind the driver. We took some sandwiches and the journey lasted seven hours, with a couple of short stops. The road runs parallel with the coast and passes through flat country with heavy jungle and trees. There are a number of small towns; Cape Coast Castle where there is a medieval fortress built by the Danes; Saltpond and Swedru, the latter a fair sized town.

Sylvia bought a wooden stool and some baskets from children at a Catholic mission station. These stools are made of wood carved in many shapes. We later bought a large mahogany one in the shape of an elephant and still have it. African chiefs sit on carved stools when they appear before their tribesmen to dispense justice or receive petitions, and in West Africa the word stool has become a synonym for the seat of government, much as we refer to Whitehall.

We got to Accra about 4 p.m. and passed through the town to our office on the east side and into the entrance drive. Sylvia said: "What's this, the post office?" "This," I said, "Is the cable office and where you are going to live". "Good heavens," she said, "I've never seen a cable office like this. I thought it must be the GPO at least." It was Broderick House, a handsome building which had been completed in 1922 and was named after Lord Middleton's family, directors of the old African Direct Telegraph Co, a subsidiary of the Eastern Telegraph Co.

We were taken by McRury to the manager's flat at one end and had tea. Mac said that on getting news of us from Port Harcourt, he had sent Stevenson on leave as he was ill. At that time there were only four foreign service staff at Accra; Mac, Barnes (assistant manager), and two assistant engineers, Stevenson and Balls. I was appointed to relieve Barnes but he had volunteered to stay on until Stevenson's relief arrived.

While we had been on our way from Cape Town, head office had decided to start a direct wireless service to London, and an engineer was being sent out to install it. Two senior operators to supervise, and an operating instructor were also being sent to run the wireless circuit and train the local staff. So Mac decided to get a house for himself outside the office and we were to move into his flat, the assistant manager's flat at the other end of the building being used to enlarge the bachelors' mess in the middle.

Accra had only two cables, to Freetown (Sierra Leone) and Lagos (Nigeria), and was what was known as a third class station, i.e., the manager was a third grade officer. His assistant, a fourth grade man, in addition to attending to the engineering side, arranged duty lists and generally supervised the staff, both European and African. The manager dealt with administration and did the cash accounts. In all stations the traffic accounts (and traffic statistics called for by head office) were done by one or more local clerks and their department was known as the Abstracts. These men were on a special salary scale slightly lower than that for the operators. There were about twenty of the latter, two supervisors (all Africans) and a number of delivery messengers. There were also a workshop assistant who looked after the batteries, and two gardeners. In war time cable censors, appointed by the government, were mostly European ladies, wives of government officials. They worked during counter hours at a desk behind a large screen at the back of the counter room. The chief censor was a post office man called Carriline whose office was in the GPO. He was a jolly, fat man with a Rabelaisian sense of humour and we got on well with him.

We unpacked and settled into Barnes' flat at the east end of the building, he having moved to the mess in the middle, and it was arranged we should have meals in Mac's flat until we moved in there the following Sunday. I proposed to Barnes that he should continue as assistant manager for two weeks and I would do office supervision to learn all the ropes. It was a very strenuous fortnight as, owing to traffic congestion we were doing schedules (called "skeds") of wireless reception from Ascension Island station. Our apparatus was very primitive consisting of an old Hallicrafter wireless receiver and an amplifier to record the signals on tape. This needed some skill and experience to operate which the Africans did not have, and had to be done for a couple of hours morning and afternoon by the assistant engineers in addition to their six hour duties in the main office. After the fortnight I took over my proper job as assistant manager and engineer.

Our flat had a sitting room dining room, two bedrooms and another one used as a store room, kitchen and the usual offices. We had a verandah at the side, and another one in front overlooking the double entrance drive and garden, with a flagpole wearing the company's house flag. We got a bit short of these during the war and Sylvia spent much time mending them—one of many unofficial chores. She engaged three Africans as house boy, his assistant and a cook to run our establishment. The cable shore ends which I had helped to land in 1922 came into the office underground from the beach. So we could walk down in our bathing costumes for a dip. There was always a heavy surf running as we faced an enormous expanse of ocean, and we had good surfing.

Across the road from the office was the British Bank of West Africa, a large handsome building, and Barclays Bank was a short distance up the road. Then there was a small square with the General Post Office facing it, and another street called Horse Road with Indian and Syrian shops in it. There were a good many Syrians in Accra, mostly shopkeepers, and the usual Indians selling silks, cottons, watches, trinkets, etc.

About half a mile out to sea there was a cargo ship of 7,000 tons which had been torpedoed, brought in and beached. She was sitting on the bottom quite upright and only up to her usual marks in the water. Later an enterprising Britisher salvaged her, and she was towed away to Lagos for repairs. Owing to the danger of being torpedoed in the open roadstead hardly any ships came to Accra during the war.

Next to our building on the town side was the Anglican church and the bishop's bungalow in a large compound. On our other side was an African girls' school, known as the Bishop's School run by the church. There were two cricket grounds and the polo ground and, in the far distance, Christianborg Castle. This, like the one at Cape Coast, had been built by the Danes on the sea front and was an imposing castle with a large walled garden on the landward side. It was the official residence of the Governor of the Gold Coast.

We were told it was not a very pleasant place to live in, being damp and salty with the surf reaching to its seaward walls. In fact, with the hot damp climate and sea spray, everything made of iron or other metal rusted or corroded at an alarming rate. The beach had thousands of small crabs, many of them white and almost transparent which appeared just before sunset. The Africans used to bury four gallon kerosene tins with open tops in the sand and then collect the crabs that fell in.

Johnny Balls had a small Morris car which he had taken over from the previous manager and he and Barnes took Sylvia for a drive to Aburi about twenty miles inland on a small range of hills where there was a Scottish Mission and girls' school for Africans. Sylvia instituted a regular practice of being at home for morning tea, and Mac and I nearly always came upstairs from the office.

The West African Army Command had taken over part of Achimota College about eight miles inland, and in Accra there was a Brigade HQ. They were training a division of African troops which later went to Burma to fight the Japs. Shortly before they left a Major Foote, second in command of GHQ Signals, asked me if a telegraphic address could be registered for them in Bombay and I got Mac to arrange it by coded message sent only via cable. Two days later an officer appeared who identified himself as a security officer at GHQ. He wanted to know about Foote's request and appeared extremely relieved when he saw me extract the papers from the safe in my office. I told him we always exercised careful security and he went away apparently satisfied.

Lord Swinton who was Resident Cabinet Minister in West Africa was also at Achimota. He had a staff of half a dozen or so Europeans with some local English ladies who did cipher work. All their overseas telegrams were sent through our office and they were our largest customer with a despatch rider service from Achimota. We referred to them as "Resmin", their telegraphic address, and we soon met most of the men on their staff. We also had a teleprinter line to GHQ Signals.

In addition to morning teas, we frequently invited members of our mess, Resmin staff, army officers and others to small dinner parties in our flat, and had card games after dinner, or just talked.

The Accra airport had been greatly extended during the war and, as part of Lend Lease a large number of Americans employed by Pan American Airways had been sent there to carry out the work and run it. When America entered the war it was arranged that the American army air force should operate it. The Pan-Am Americans were all drafted into their army and their camp was enlarged to take many more. Their chief signal officer, Colonel Brooke-Sawyer and the chief postal officer, Harold Young, came to see Mac on business so we invited them to dinner. They were both soon to become close friends. Brooke-Sawyer brought his deputy, Captain Dessallett to see us and he also joined our regular circle. Brooke-Sawyer was a tall genial man, much liked by everybody. He was a Californian and in civil life worked in insurance, but had served briefly in Europe in World War I. Dessallett was a telephone engineer from New Jersey and was rather shy. It was noticeable that the two were inseparable and our mess christened them "Tom Sawyer and Huckleberry Finn". Harold Young was a postal official from Montana and Sylvia said he had very intelligent feet, i.e., was a good dancer, when we took him to Saturday night dances at the Accra Club.

Dawson, a Colonial Office man, was Lord Swinton's cipher officer and he and a man called Kesby frequently came to see us. Kesby was at the time a temporary civil servant and had been in the cabinet secretariat before coming to West Africa. He later relieved Dawson as cipher officer.

Mac was in hospital with malaria for about three weeks in December and I also went down with it for about a week, but did not go to hospital. The company's medical officer was Dr Gillespie, the senior specialist at the European hospital. He was a charming Scotsman, much liked, but he had a peculiarity. He never sent in his bills until he was going on leave, i.e. about once every fifteen months. Mac forgot to press him for bills for a year, and had to explain to a suspicious head office why a large medical bill suddenly became due for payment.

A. R. Harrison, the wireless installation engineer, J. B. Hewett, assistant engineer, and Rooks, operating instructor, all arrived in December and Barnes left for England. A fortnight later W. W. C. Harrisson and Lardeaux, the two wireless supervisors, arrived. Soon after they both went down with jaundice and had to go to hospital. This was due to a faulty yellow fever inoculation, and we heard of several other cases. We all had to have these inoculations, be regularly vaccinated, against typhoid and sometimes others. They seemed to be effective as no one ever contracted these diseases. Malaria was hard to avoid, but I only got it twice in many years in Africa, and Sylvia only once.

Our Ascension station advised us that their matron would be passing through so Mac arranged for her to be put up for the night with the hospital matron. Sylvia and I went to meet her at the airport and A. R. Harrison who knew her came with us. I had an airport pass and got one for Sylvia and when we went in Harrison got in too—more of a mix up of the various passes including the taxi driver's. When we came out an African guard spotted there were more persons than passes and began to get difficult. However, an American sergeant came over and said: "Wal, you let them all in so you had better let them all out".

The cable to Sierre Leone was a long one. It had originally called in at Sekondi but had later been put through at sea, and our office there closed. To work a cable in both directions simultaneously one had to maintain a balance with various electrical adjustments. During the night I often got pulled out of bed by the African supervisors to adjust the balance so something had to be done about it. This was to rearrange the apparatus to enclose it to prevent dampness, such enclosures being kept dry with electric lamps continuously on. Johnny Balls, Hewett and I planned the alterations for a Sunday so that each of us was allotted a part of the work to complete it in one day. We got it done in about fourteen hours and the result was successful.

Meanwhile most of the wireless apparatus had arrived, together with parts to erect two 100ft towers in opposite corners of the office compound and four 70ft ones for a large rhombic (diamond shaped) aerial on the nearby old cricket ground. The government had given permission to put it there as a temporary war measure. A. R. Harrison was fully occupied in getting everything installed. Mac had a small building erected at the back as a store for the gear, thoughtfully with double doors so it could be used as a garage later, and we were a hive of activity. A ground floor room at the east end of the building was made into a transmitting room for the five kilowatt main transmitter, and the receiver and amplifier installed in the cable instrument room. With a completely screened receiver and lead in cables from the receiving aerials, no interference from the cable apparatus was experienced.

Mr and Mrs Howard who lived nearby were friends of the mess and we soon met them. He worked in the British Bank of West Africa and they had a small ancient German Opel car. Mrs Howard was rather deaf and Johnny Balls spent a lot of time mending her electric hearing aid.

One day I was called to our public counter and who should be there but Mr and Mrs Brady who had seen my signature on a notice. They were Australians and he had been in the Public Works Dept in Kedah in North Malaya building a bridge over the Muda river before we left Penang. We had met them at the planters bungalow occupied by our friends the Phillips. They told us they had escaped the Japs, she going early on to Australia while he had been ordered to blow up the bridge he had just finished, and escape to Singapore from which he had got away to Australia. He was now seconded to the PWD in Accra. A number of other men from Malaya came to the Gold Coast, one being appointed as engineer to the post office telegraphs.

In April Charles Rodbourne arrived and Johnny Balls went on leave. He had done nearly two years in Accra and worked hard, with hardly a day's sickness. As mentioned earlier, Ascension station used to send traffic to us by radio. Being received on morse tape, it had to be typed on to forms by our local operators. As we had not enough of them, messages were often delayed. We had a cable code printer but it could not be operated by morse signals. We asked Ascension if they could send the type of cable code signals that Bruford had invented for use on wireless circuits and they agreed. So Johnny Balls got an old blue spot loudspeaker and turned it into a sensitive relay and I devised an electrical circuit to de-code the Bruford type signals. The result was excellent, and we could print all the telegrams sent from Ascension by radio automatically.

Harold Young departed and was relieved by Captain Lyon from Baltimore, a charming man who came to dinner with us several times. Dining with the Howards of the bank we experienced our first earthquake tremor, not a severe one but it set the hanging electric lamps swinging.

An ENSA concert party which included some very pretty girls came to entertain the troops and they were entertained by the young officers. Two of the girls were from near my parents' home at Warkworth in Northumberland, and came to one of Sylvia's morning teas, and later to dinner much to the satisfaction of our men in the mess, pretty young girls being unknown in Accra.

Captain Dessallett was one of the most modest Americans we ever met. Colonel Sawyer having gone away temporarily, I phoned Dessallett and asked him to dinner. He said, "You know the colonel is away?" I said, "It is you we are inviting, not the colonel". He said he would be delighted to come.

Colonel Sawyer was remarkably able at pouring oil on troubled waters. At a local communications conference attended by representatives of the three British services, the post office telegraphs, the Americans and ourselves, the Royal Corp of Signals man got into a heated argument with the PO man. Sawyer stepped in and deftly suggested a compromise which was at once agreed. He was helpful in other ways. One afternoon Harrison asked me if I thought the Americans would lend him an oscilloscope as he had a problem. I telephoned Sawyer and he said: "Yes, when do you want it?" I told him when convenient. At 4.30 p.m. that same afternoon he suddenly appeared in my office with oscilloscope and he and Harrison departed to use it.

In the middle of July head office told Mac that a Western Telegraph man called Hunter would relieve him. Hunter had been on his way by sea to another station but his ship had been torpedoed in the South Atlantic and the survivors landed at Lagos in Nigeria. The following Sunday morning about 8 a.m. the phone rang, and it was Hunter at Accra Airport. I got a taxi and collected him and took him to Mac's house on the Ridge and later they both came down to the office. Hunter said he had lost all his kit—even his false teeth—when the ship was sunk, and he had had to fit himself out at Lagos. That same day we got a letter from head office saying that I had been promoted to the third grade and Harrison to the fourth grade, so we had a party that evening to celebrate.

Mac left for England on 15th August. Before his departure we all went to a dance at the Army School of Artillery mess. We did our best after he left to keep everyone happy and I think Sylvia helped a lot. She was a sympathetic listener to the odd troubles of life which the men brought to her, and our parties for them and others helped to make things cheerful.

In October Captain Elwood, RN, the naval liaison officer at Resmin and his deputy Lt Bowman, gave a dinner party at Achimota on the occasion of a visit by Admiral Rawlings, commander-in-chief West

Africa, and his staff who came from Sierra Leone for a conference with GHQ, and Resmin. It was held out of doors and we sat at small tables in his garden. Owing to lack of crockery, the menu was avocado pear with sardines inside; steak and kidney stew served in a large coconut with the top as a lid and eaten with a spoon; sweets served on plantain leaves. It was rather fun as everyone entered into the spirit of it, and afterwards our host amused everyone by dancing a hornpipe to his own whistled accompaniment.

He came to dinner with us and we played a round of poker at which he professed to be a novice, but was much better than we were.

Just before Christmas Lt Butters, RNVR, Lord Swinton's Secretary, who had come to dinner with us several times, invited us to dine with him at the Accra Club. On our arrival we were introduced to his chief and an American, Colonel Logie. On hearing that Sylvia's mother's maiden name was Logie, he at once claimed cousinship. Lord Swinton was a tall thin man, very active and an interesting talker, and the colonel was witty, so we had an entertaining evening. I asked Butters if he thought that Lord Swinton would care to come to our flat for a nightcap, and he said he was sure he would. So we asked him and we all got into his Rolls Royce. On arrival Lord Swinton pointed to the lighted instrument room windows on the ground floor and enquired if that was where all the work went on. I said, "Yes, you have not seen it?" and he said, "I haven't been invited." I told him we should be delighted to show him round. After a drink and some conversation, he and Butters left for Achimota.

We heard a rather amusing anecdote about Lord Swinton which the latter used to tell against himself as showing what not to do. A certain district in Nigeria was growing groundnuts and it was desired to increase production. Two shillings and sixpence per load was being paid to the African farmers. So it was decided to increase the price to five shillings. The next crop turned out to be only a little over half the previous one. This elementary lesson in economics might have application in this country, even though we are more sophisticated than West Africa.

On Christmas day we had a cocktail party before lunch in our flat. Our guests included Colonel Jones the chief signal officer from GHQ and Major Foote and Dawson from Resmin, together with Hunter and all our men from the mess. In the evening we had a dinner party with two American officers and a sister and doctor from the British Military Hospital.

Christmas card 1943 from Chief Signal Officer GHQ Accra.

Harrison had got the wireless apparatus installed and aerials erected and we had commenced working a high speed morse circuit to London daily from 8 a.m. to about 9 p.m. We asked Resmin whether their cipher messages could go by radio and they agreed unless otherwise marked.

As readers of the American writer, Mr Kahn, in his book *The Codebreakers*, shown recently on television, will know, the "one time pad" method of encoding, which is impossible to crack, was used. In those days this was done manually. Nowadays it can be done electrically using special one time tapes.

I suggested to Hunter that as the Government had given us special permission to put the large rhombic aerial on the old cricket ground, we ought to invite the governor to come and see the new London circuit working. We found that he was away on a visit but the Colonial Secretary, Sir George London, who was acting governor would come. We showed him all the works and he seemed to be impressed. He and his ADC, Hunter and Harrison came upstairs to our flat afterwards.

Two days later we went to a wedding at the artillery mess. One of their officers was being married to a sister at the hospital. At the party afterwards, the colonel told me they were grateful to us for sorting out a problem between them and Brigade HQ Signals. A few weeks earlier two gunner officers came to see us and asked whether our wireless man could help them. They had recently received from the UK a caravan housed radar set for training with AA guns and it had been sited on the sea front about a mile east of us. Not long afterwards Brigade HQ Signals had complained of radio interference and suggested it was from the gunners' radar. I sent for Harrison and we went to inspect the radar van. He thought it unlikely the interference was due to it after making one or two tests, and went off to Brigade HQ Signals. Later he told me he found the trouble, a sparking generator in Brigade HQ's own office! Harrison was undoubtedly the most competent wireless engineer in Accra and later helped diagnose a fault for GHQ Signals at Achimota. One of the young gunner officers, Lt Hawkey, was the son of a man who used to keep a hardware store in Bushey, Herts when I was a boy and from where I bought wire for my ham wireless aerials.

One Saturday evening some of the men in the mess went to the dance at the Accra Club. When they returned they found an American soldier in Harrison's bed. He was apparently dead drunk so they moved him to their sitting room and made him comfortable in two large chairs. Next morning as he was still asleep they got some large crayfish (lobsters) which Lardeaux had bought for the mess cuisine and arranged them tastefully around him. Later they gave him breakfast and put him in a taxi for his camp. He did not remember and they never found out who had put him there but it was probably some British officer who had visited them. The following Saturday Sylvia sketched the features of a young lady on cardboard and we arranged "her" in a night gown and boudoir cap in Harrison's bed while he was at the Club.

In January 1944 he was transferred to Lagos to install wireless sets there. We were sorry to lose him as he was always bright, cheerful and full of fun.

One of our American friends was Captain Pritschke who came from California and he often visited us. He was good company having an apparently endless stock of stories. One I remember was really a parable. It was about a man who had moved to the west during the period in American history when thousands of settlers were trekking westwards looking for new places to settle. He set up a small hotel and restaurant on one of the main routes. Families would stop over and asked him what the folks were like thereabouts and he would always say, "What were they like where you came from?" Whatever the answer, good or bad, he would then say, "They are much the same hereabouts."

We went to dinner with the Bradys our PWD friends from Malaya and met a Scotsman called Robertson who was in the railways department. The Bradys were occupying a railway bungalow near the station. Robertson was bewailing the happy go lucky attitude of his African staff who were always having accidents when we heard an almighty crash nearby. Robertson philosophically said: "That's number thirty this month".

Almost opposite the cable office was *the* posh African club, known as the Rodger Club, and we were often spectators of the arrival and departure of members when they gave a dance. The men usually wore dinner jackets and some of the women's creations were marvellous. Their dance bands were very good, as Africans have an excellent ear for rhythm. We went to the races and observed some African ladies dressed up to the nines, but carrying their handbags (or their shoes even) on their heads.

Mr S. E. Brown, recently arrived as American Consul was an amusing man with a fund of stories. He had been in Saigon in French Indo-China when the Japs arrived and had taken refuge in the British Consul-General's house. When the time came for them to embark on the ship taking diplomats to be exchanged, they wondered what they should do with their national flags. They had one bottle of gin left, and Brown said they solemnly burnt their flags and then consumed the gin.

The hundred foot towers put up in our compound were to keep receiving aerials away from interference. For the office, they did this but we suffered trouble from motor cars entering our drive in front. Harrison had acquired from the army a couple of 30ft portable masts which he had erected at the rear of the office and tried an aerial on them. After he had gone we moved them right to the top of the low cliff overlooking the beach. I asked Colonel Jones at GHQ if he could lend us about 300 yards of feeder cable and he agreed. We trenched it into the office from the top of the cliff, connected it to our small aerial there, and found it provided us with interference free signals from London. So the two 100ft towers were a waste of time and money.

Early in March we got tickets and went to the opening session of the

Gold Coast "Mammy".

Legislative Council presided over by the Governor, Sir Alan Burns. There was an imposing array of African Chiefs all elaborately dressed in native costume, and a tremendous flood of long speeches from them. Particularly remembered was an interminable one by a chief about another who had recently died; we got his whole life story. Throughout all this the Governor sat impassively, and we began to realize that he earned his salary.

On 3rd April we heard that our relief, A. T. Wood, was on his way to Accra from the UK. We had again applied to spend our leave in South Africa, and were told there was a ship leaving in about a week.

We telephoned friends to tell them, one being Butters, Lord Swinton's secretary. Soon after Butters phoned and said Lord Swinton would like to see over our office as promised, so after consulting Hunter, it was arranged for the next day. Butters must have told his boss that we were leaving.

So Hunter and I showed Lord Swinton and Butters all round the office. Our guest had a phenomenal memory for people. When we got to the counter where Mrs Surridge was the censor on duty, Lord Swinton said at once: "Wasn't your husband in Cyprus when I was

Colonial Secretary some years ago?'' He could not have known he was going to meet her. While looking at the direct London wireless circuit, as London was not transmitting, I said to W. C. Harrisson, ''Ask him to send some specimen signals'', which he did, using the hand key. When they had seen everything we went upstairs to our flat where Sylvia was waiting, and had drinks. Before leaving Lord Swinton thanked Sylvia for all she had done to entertain his staff in the nineteen months we had been there.

I had a pass to go to the airport to collect tapes of messages sent by air from Ascension. Hunter said it had better be transferred to him. We went to see the Assistant Superintendent of Police who issued them but he was reluctant to give Hunter a permanent pass, but said we could always get one on application. We pointed out that sometimes we had to go there in the middle of the night, but to no avail. Finally I said that in that case we would refer the matter to Lord Swinton's office. This did the trick and he gave Hunter a pass. Lardeaux who was due for leave wanted to spend it in Bermuda where his wife was living, and had been canvassing American friends with a view to thumbing a lift on one of their aircraft. He told me they could not promise anything so I suggested he telephone Resmin and ask if they could help. He did so and they telephoned back and asked him when he wanted to leave. This cheered him up no end, a useful by-product of our friendly relations with them.

So Sylvia and I finally packed all our gear, mostly done by her, hired a mammy car and on 11th April left for Sekondi arriving by tea time at the Greek Acropolis Hotel where we spent the night. Next day we went to Takoradi docks after lunch, where we had a long hot wait before all the formalities were gone through. We had provided ourselves with two thermos flasks of tea which we shared with as many others as possible. Finally at 4 p.m. we went on board our ship SS *Marudu*, of 4,000 tons. She belonged to the Straits Steamship Co and normally ran between Penang, Singapore and Borneo, and who should be in command but Captain Caithness whom we had known in Penang.

The *Marudu* did not sail until the following morning so we had a quiet evening in the harbour. The ship was very full. In adjacent cabins there were three men in one and their wives in the other.

The ship arrived at Lagos the following afternoon but we were not allowed to go ashore. On the far side at Apapa where the new quays had been built since I was last there in 1922, we saw the Dutch liner

Tegelberg in which we had travelled from Batavia to Cape Town two and half years before. She was now a troopship. The *Marudu* left Lagos just before dark the next day. The captain addressed all the passengers and asked the men to volunteer to assist with submarine look-out duties, two at a time on the bridge as the ship was travelling unescorted. Everyone agreed and duties were arranged. We were also reminded to carry with us always our lifebelts and blitz bags. A strict blackout at night with no smoking on deck was enforced.

We had excellent weather and the voyage was uneventful. When on watch on the bridge one morning I spotted what might have been a submarine but turned out to be a whale spouting water at intervals.

Sylvia and I compared notes after the voyage and agreed that, had we been torpedoed, we both hoped we would not land back in West Africa. We had had enough of that country for the time being. Sylvia went through her diary and found we had entertained an average of at least 100 people a month.

We arrived at Cape Town on 26th April. Before leaving the Gold Coast I had asked the Mount Nelson Hotel to reserve a room for us but could not tell them the time of arrival. The agent asked me where we were staying and said he thought the hotel was full. So I telephoned; they had a room for us, and we drove there at once. This is probably the best hotel in Cape Town and was owned by the Union Castle Mail Steamship Company. It stands in extensive grounds in the residential area above the town and has been famous ever since the South African war in 1899. Louis, the head porter, who had been there for years showed us some uniform trunks in the basement store which he said belonged to long dead officers and had never been claimed.

CHAPTER FIFTEEN

South Africa Again and Portsudan

After settling in to the hotel we went next day to see Mercy Miller, Sylvia's eldest sister at her house in Pinelands in the northern suburbs. The following day Sylvia's brother Douglas—with whom I used to go up Table Mountain years before— and his wife, Edna, arrived from Pretoria to stay with Mercy.

Westcott was still running his branch staff department in the offices of the South African Cable Co. He told me that Lightning Smith, ironically so-called because he was slow moving, was branch engineer there. I had known him in Suez. He had transferred from Cable & Wireless Ltd to the South African Co. When they took over from C & W in Cape Town and Durban, it was announced that they would like a few C & W men to join them, preference being given to those with South African wives of whom there were quite a few as our men sent there had got married to some of the attractive girls. I considered joining the South African Co but decided against it as the prospects of promotion appeared limited.

Smith took me to see their chief engineer, Mr S. Turner, a large jovial man who invited me to come and see their wireless stations at Klipheuval and Milnerton. So Smith and I went with the chief by car to Milnerton, seven miles away, where we had lunch, and then on to Klipheuvel about twenty-five miles north east of Cape Town. This was the overseas transmitting station for telegraph and telephone working, mainly to England. It was very similar to the Marconi built station at Ongar in Essex where I had been in 1934, and Ongar's Manager, Mr Hill, had actually chosen the site as already mentioned. We then returned to Milnerton where we saw the receiving station. Next door to it was the South African Broadcasting Company's medium wave transmitting station and I asked about interference from it. The engineer-in-charge said that as long as all their aerials, masts, stays, etc., were properly bonded together, there was no trouble. In fact, he said it kept them up to scratch in this respect. A bond failure caused a spark from the induced currents from the broadcasting station and immediate interference on their receivers. This was similar to conditions in Accra where we had what is known as commonsite working, i.e. transmitting and receiving aerials rather close but working on different wavelengths.

We had a pleasant month in Cape Town, visiting various local beauty spots, etc. It was arranged that Mercy, Sylvia and I should all go to Graaff Reinet to see her other sister Gertrude and husband Arthur. Douglas and Edna returned to Pretoria after their holiday in Cape Town and we set off for Graaff Reinet on 1st June by train. We went by the usual Garden route, Mossel Bay, George, Oudtshoorn and arrived about 7 a.m. on 3rd June, i.e., one day and two nights travel.

We stayed as before at the Drosdty Hotel and were welcomed by Gertrude and Arthur who took us to visit all their friends. Three days later the news broke of the D-Day landings in Normandy, and the Mayor of Graaff Reinet immediately called together the English, Dutch and Wesleyan Church Ministers and arranged a joint service in the Town Hall which was packed with people from the country all around and was very moving.

We had a pleasant stay in Graaff Reinet and on 2nd July Sylvia and I were invited by our former hosts, Vera and Barry Hobson, to stay on their farm, Ebenezer, forty miles away, and he fetched us in his car.

A day or two later, Barry, Sandford, their uncle, William Hobson, and I went to Belmont Farm about thirty miles away, owned by Archie MacNaughton who had invited his friends to an all day shoot of rooi (red) buck which were plentiful on the top of a large kojpe, in fact, a small plateau. We left Ebenezer Farm about 6 a.m. and were given breakfast at the MacNaughton's farmhouse. We then drove to the foot of the plateau and had a long hot walk up paths to the top. Our host allotted us positions in line for a drive of the red springbok. On my left I had a Dutch farmer and Barry warned me he had a habit of firing sideways so I esconced myself with a large boulder between him and me. We were now using the .303 Lee Enfield service rifles as the shortage of ammunition previously mentioned had been overcome and plenty was available. After the drive during which I managed to shoot one red buck, we all came together for a picnic lunch and in the afternoon there was another drive in a different place. When all was over we gathered below the plateau and MacNaughton distributed some of the game to his guests.

The next day there was bad news. On our earlier visit to Barry about two years before, we had visited the large farm, Wheatlands, owned by Tom Parkes. Well, he telephoned Barry that his only son had been killed in action in Italy. We all went over to see them at once. They had two sailors from the Royal Navy staying with them, and after talking to Parkes and his wife, we brought the sailors back with us to stay at Ebenezer. At that time most of the farmers put up sailors from naval ships at Port Elizabeth so as to give them a complete change and a holiday, and we met a number on farms round about. It was very sad about young Parkes as they had no other son to carry on their farm.

The following day we got a telegram from Westcott in Cape Town telling me I was appointed to Port Sudan cable station and was to go to Durban unaccompanied to arrive there by 22nd July. I replied asking him why without my wife, but he said those were head office's instructions and it was no use asking them.

Barry Hobson had a shoot on his farm and the two sailors came along and had a bang at the springbok, much to their satisfaction. They were nice young lads and gave us an impromptu sing-song one evening in the farm sitting room. Barry told me that when he was very young, about three years old, during the Boer War in 1901, Commandant Jan Smuts (General Smuts) came to Ebenezer farm with a commando of mounted Boers and demanded food and forage for their horses at rifle point.

We returned to Graff Reinet on 10th July. Except for asking Barry and Vera for lunch at our hotel when they came to town, we could not do much to return their hospitality. Owing to our nomadic way of life in the cable service this happened more than once, where we met people that we liked but did not see again. Farm life in the Karroo is lonely and it is no doubt pleasant to have friends to stay. Some farmers liked solitude and it used to be said of the old Dutch Boer farmer that he thought the country was much too crowded if he could see in the far distance the smoke from his neighbour's fire!

Barry and Vera later had to face the same tragedy as Tom Parkes and his wife. Their eldest son, Sandford, joined the South African army towards the end of the war. While serving in Italy he got appendicitis and died of peritonitis. Keith, his younger brother now runs Ebenezer farm as Barry died in 1960.

It was decided that Sylvia and her sister Mercy would stay on in Graaff Reinet after I left. The booking clerk at the railway station said when I went to get my ticket, "Oh, I thought you were a soldier returning to the Middle East and have booked you on a train carrying troops." I said, "That's all right, I *am* going to the Middle East and it's the same as war service."

So on the 20th I said goodbye to Sylvia and her sisters and Arthur, and left Graaff Reinet. In my carriage was a handsome young officer of the South African army, Captain Ritchie Moffet, a pleasant companion until we changed trains that evening for another going to Durban. In a four-berth compartment I was with a SA naval lieutenant and an LAC of the RAF. The former told me he was a chemist in Durban in civil life. We arrived at Harrismith the next morning. Our naval companion knew all the ropes, telling us to nip out of the train on the wrong side, cross the line and get to the restaurant the other side so as to have breakfast before the train went on half an hour later.

The next sixty miles is downhill for the first thirty as the railway traverses a mountain pass and then zig-zags down from 5,500 ft to 3,300 ft until it reaches Ladysmith. We got to Ladysmith for lunch and then had to wait until about 6 p.m. when the train from Johannesburg via the northern line was due. I had read a lot about the seige of Ladysmith in the SA war, so went to explore the town in the afternoon. It is not a very large one and except for a low ridge of hills on one side, looked a hard place to defend.

Half of our train was attached to half the incoming Johannesburg train and we left Ladysmith about 8 p.m. and arrived at Durban the following morning early, so I was not able to see anything of this part of Natal. The line drops from 3,000 ft to the coast.

I went to the cable office and saw Theobald, a South African, who was acting manager, F. R. Spray, being on leave. Spray had been manager at Lourenço Marques when we had been there and was another Eastern man who had joined the South African Cable Company. Theobald said he had booked me in at the Mayfair Hotel in Smith Street, and I had better go and see Mr Duncan of the Ministry of War Transport. At the Mayfair I found Eric Bailey and his wife waiting for a ship to Malta. Mr Duncan said he expected me to go on a ship leaving in about a week but it was not calling at Port Sudan. It would call at other ports before reaching Aden so he was seeing if he could arrange for me to transfer to another ship; otherwise I would have to go on to Suez and come back.

Cameras had to be given up to the ship's purser. I nearly lost mine as

I forgot it when I changed ships, but Bailey rescued it and sent it back to me later in the voyage. The ship was an Anchor liner of about 10,000 tons and quite comfortable.

We sailed in a convoy of a dozen ships with two or three small escort warships. This was the only time I sailed in a ship in convoy. Being the largest vessel our ship was the commodore's ship and in command. The voyage to Beira was uneventful except that one morning there was a submarine scare and two of our escorts dropped depth charges which exploded with the usual fountains of water thrown up.

We got to Beira in three days, and before breakfast, Mr Fraser, the Union Castle Line agent, came down to my cabin and said he represented the Ministry of War Transport and had got a cable from Durban about me. There was a Dutch cargo ship at Beira loading coal for Port Sudan and he would ask the captain if he would take me. Next day I packed my bags and went over to the SS *Vermeer*. She was a British built cargo ship of 7,000 tons, being one of a war-time class known as Commonwealth ships, as all the ones wearing the British flag had this word in their names. I was allotted a cabin in the bridge superstructure close to the dining saloon. She was covered in coal dust as they were loading 10,000 tons for the Sudan Railways. The Anchor liner departed but we did not finish the coal for another two or three days, then the whole ship was thoroughly washed down and cleaned up.

The captain invited me to his cabin for a whisky and soda after dinner. He spoke excellent English as did most of the ship's officers. The other officers were a pleasant crowd and made me welcome to their dining saloon.

I noticed that before retiring for the night most of the officers jammed a doormat in their cabin door to keep them ajar, and was told there had been cases where, after being torpedoed, men found their cabin doors stuck and could not get out. When a ship is in drydock, as I had noticed in cableships, there is a tendency for cabin doors to jam due to slight distortion of the ship's hull or framing, as it is not uniformly supported by water. Several of the *Vermeer's* officers had survived torpedoings so I heard a lot about them.

About this time (August 1944) General Montgomery's army had broken out of the Normandy bridgehead in France and was advancing into Belgium and Holland. I had bought a school atlas in Durban and after a tussle with an officious Customs officer ("no maps allowed") had brought it on board. No one had a map of Belgium and Holland so

I left my atlas on the saloon table so that everyone could follow the progress of Monty's troops. Many of them had homes thereabouts.

We got to Zanzibar and I went ashore with the captain and visited the cable station. The manager was Mr Tresidder, an Australian man of whom I had heard when in Penang, but had not met before. We left at lunchtime and reached Mombasa the next day, and anchored in Kilindini harbour. At Kilindini was a Royal Navy escort aircraft carrier, a cruiser and some destroyers. Next morning we tied up near the oil tanks and I went ashore and took a taxi to the town. At the cable office I met the manager, L. C. Robinson. He was a UK extension man who had been manager at Penang before we went there in 1938.

The next day we left for Aden. As we passed Cape Gardafui Captain Brouwer drew my attention to the ocean currents which met at this most easterly point of Africa. It was a calm evening with the sun just about to set over the shore line and, as we altered course slightly, to round the Cape, a definite line of large ripples extended from it to far out of sight to the east. It was very striking.

Three days later we arrived at Port Sudan and I was met and taken to our office. H. B. ("(Wimpole") Martin whom I had known in Suez was manager and he invited me to live in his house instead of in the mess, as his wife was in England. Port Sudan was a second class station, Martin being in the second grade, and I, as his assistant manager and engineer, in the third grade. I relieved A. Crump, a "Western" man who was overdue for leave, and head office had told Martin I was only to be there for about six months and was then to go to Mauritius. This explained why Sylvia was not allowed to accompany me. There was only one company's houser for the manager.

The office was at the front of a large rectangular garden compound with the bachelor's mess and manager's house all in one building along the rear of it. There were five cables each way to Suez and Aden, all worked automatically as part of through chain circuits, and a cable to Jeddah in Saudi Arabia where it was operated by their government.

There were five other foreign service men, A. G. Hill, Graydon, Hooper, B. P. Hampton and A. Boa, about ten local operators and ten men for the workshop, traffic accounts, etc. Hampton, his wife and small son lived in a rented furnished flat about three quarters of a mile from the office, and the other men were in the mess.

Port Sudan harbour consists of a lagoon formed by a sand and coral spit of land about a quarter of a mile from the shore. The quays where ships go alongside have been built on the inner side of this spit and are connected to the shore near the north end by a steel drawbridge carrying road and railway. The land stretches inland flat for several miles when it reaches a low range of hills which lead to the higher plateau beyond. The town, about a mile long, and half a mile wide, is flat and consisted of three or four long streets with cross roads at intervals. It has only been in existence from the early 1920's. Previous to that the main port on this coast was at Suakin about thirty-seven miles south which had a natural harbour. This became silted up and the government decided to build a new harbour and town to replace it. So Suakin was abandoned and all its inhabitants left it and came to Port Sudan.

The climate is very hot in the summer when the shade temperature goes up to 114 degrees Fahrenheit or more, but is dryer than West Africa though more humid than inland towns like Khartoum. There is a small public garden in the centre, but little grass or other greenery. Most of the buildings are of coral rock which is plentiful but tends to soak up the heat in the day and give it out at night. As there was no air-conditioning in those days, many houses had a small roofed area on their flat tops, open on all sides, which was used for sleeping.

I settled into Martin's house at the south end of the quarters building. To return Captain Brouwer's hospitality, I asked him, the chief officer and chief engineer round for drinks the next evening and we sat out in the garden as it was very hot. Martin kindly lent me some whisky as it was rationed and one could not draw one's allowance, one bottle a week, until after seven days residence. He also introduced me to the Red Sea Club, the senior one there and put my name down for membership.

B. P. Hampton had been ill and was to go on leave shortly, so I asked him whether his landlord would rent the flat to me.

I asked Martin to wire head office and say I had found a house and could my wife come up from Cape Town with the cancellation of my later transfer to Mauritius. This was approved so we wired to Cape Town to get Sylvia a passage. She and her sister Mercy had left Graaff Reinet and gone to stay at the Lanark Hotel at Fishoek near Cape Town where we had stayed in 1942 and which was still run by our friend Miss Knowles. As soon as Sylvia was told she could come to Port Sudan, she set to work re-packing our effects.

She left Cape Town by train on 10th October for Durban where she had to wait a month in the Balmoral Hotel before sailing for Port Sudan on 10th November via Beira and Aden, also on a Dutch ship, and arrived on 9th December.

Meanwhile I settled down to my new job and began to meet members of the local community. The weather was still pretty hot in September, and the regulation evening attire for men was white shirt, white duck trousers without turn-ups, black socks, shoes, and bow tie and a cummerbund, black for ordinary civilians, but green for government officials. This was known as Red Sea kit, a very sensible form of evening dress. Our Aden mess wore the same with red cummerbunds. When it got very hot at a party, the host would say, "Off ties"; our black bows would be removed and top shirt buttons undone. It was often supplemented by a small sweat towel to mop up perspiration. In the winter white or black dinner jackets were worn in addition.

Four of the men in the mess did six hour shift duties round the clock, the fifth, A. G. Hill was my assistant and did office reliefs if anyone was sick or for local leave in the summer when we all got fourteen days at a hill station. I did 8.00 a.m. to 1.30 p.m. in the office and then went there for about half an hour after tea to see that all was well; but I was on call at any time if something went wrong or a cable was interrupted.

In November B. P. Hampton and his family departed. He was relieved by two young assistant engineers, Ellum and Gritten. Looking back it is clear that we had a remarkable number of able men in Port Sudan at that time. Hill, Hooper and Ellum became managers later and Graydon and Boa went to head office and rose to be heads of departments—Graydon as staff manager and Boa as head of organisation and methods.

Martin had a bridge party one evening soon after my arrival. His guests were McDowell, the deputy commissioner, and Gwen and Ian Anderson, manager of Barclays Bank. Gwen was expecting a baby and told us that she had been in the WRNS, had got permission to marry Ian, and was now pregnant in order to be sacked from the WRNS! They were a jolly couple and we kept in touch with them long after we left Port Sudan.

Just before I was taking over the flat, head office wired Martin that his wife in England would be leaving for Port Sudan in about a week. She arrived and I left Martin's house and went into our flat, so was able to get everything in order before Sylvia arrived. It was not possible to get a refrigerator but I managed to buy what looked like one but, was in fact an ice chest, half a block of ice being put into it to keep food cool. Ice was delivered twice a day so it served us quite well.

One could not get a motor car unless it was essential to one's job and tyres were also controlled, so I decided to get a bicycle and one for Sylvia. Our chief mechanic, a Greek called Sultanian, was transferred to Athens so I bought a bike from him. The only one obtainable for Sylvia was a rather old ladies' bike, which Sultanian took into the workshop and overhauled, and it served her quite well. It was a good place for bikes being all on the level. I used mine to go to the office and we both regularly had rides after tea. We had to leave them under cover in the day time or they got too hot to touch.

The Sudan was different to other places ruled by the British as it was run by the Foreign Office, not by the Colonial Office. From our rather limited experience, they seemed to do it rather well. How this came about is a long story, but it was mainly due to Lord Cromer who, in effect, governed Egypt from 1882 to 1912 and is described in his book *Modern Egypt*.

It started in Turkey where the Western Powers had forced the Sultan to allow their consuls to have legal jurisdiction over their own nationals, the local courts being inefficient and corrupt. Egypt, being nominally a dependency of Turkey, it applied there. After the British occupation of Egypt in 1882 the courts, police, etc., were reformed and the legal jurisdiction of foreign consuls was unnecessary and greatly hampered the police, especially in putting down drug smuggling. So when the Sudan, originally an Egyptian colony, was reconquered by Lord Kitchener in 1897, the country was re-constituted as a condominium between Britain and Egypt and no foreign jurisdiction was admitted. The Foreign Office appointed the governor-general and virtually ruled the country. Ironically one could not get or renew a British passport in the Sudan. When mine ran out a new one had to be obtained from the British Embassy in Cairo and sent to Port Sudan by safe hand, i.e. some well-known person coming there.

Sylvia soon settled into running our flat. Our head boy was a tall Sudanese called Fadl Said and there were two others to help him. There was rationing of some items of food notably tea, coffee, sugar and whiskey, but we never really went short.

The Red Sea Club had a small swimming pool. This got rather warm in the summer but was very pleasant at other times. The club had originally been formed for senior British officials but had gradually admitted to membership managers and others from commercial firms.

The commissioner was a man called Thomas and soon after Sylvia's arrival his wife came out from England. Tommy Thomas was a very pleasant fair haired man, and his wife who was French, was charming. She had been caught by the war in France and had only recently got out after it was liberated by the British and American armies. A previous medical officer of health, Dr Cruickshank, had started a small dairy with a few cows to supply milk to the hospital. As there was soon a surplus, it was now being sold to Europeans. Dr Cruickshank had left and Thomas had taken over running the dairy.

Sylvia became friendly with Mrs Cummins, wife of the Railways and Port Manager, and Mrs Davies, whose husband was manager of the Shell Co. Christmas 1944 was celebrated by having lunch with the Martins and in the evening there was a dinner dance at the club.

January, February and March were relatively cool but we were much plagued by strong winds usually accompanied by tremendous sandstorms known locally as haboobs. The air is thick with sand and dust, and it gets quite dark.

On 12th January we were at an evening party when we got a telephone message from the docks that A. R. Harrison and his wife were on a ship just arriving and leaving at daylight, so we got a taxi and went on board to see them. It was the first time we had met her. They were on their way to Colombo. Another visitor in February was Mrs Kirby, wife of A. A. (Peter) Kirby who was en route to Seychelles to join her husband. Her ship stayed several days and she spent a good deal of time at our flat as it was hot on board.

We used to go for rides on our bikes after tea and visited a village nearby, the inhabitants of which were practically all West African negroes. We were told they were Mohammedans who had been on a pilgrimage to Mecca and had run out of money and settled there.

We often had men from our mess to dinner or cocktail parties as we had done in Accra, and also exchanged similar hospitality with other friends we made. The mess gave regular parties to which we and others were invited. So life was cheerful even though physical conditions were uncomfortable. The British community was one of the most friendly we ever came across. There were weekly dances at the Red Sea Club, topped off with ham and egg suppers which were quite fun.

We had one or two cable interruptions which kept me busy testing, attending to the cableship and subsequent re-balancing the cable when it was restored. Port Sudan had a low power radio transmitter and receiver, known in our jargon as a Col Set (i.e. colonial radio set) which had been supplied early on in the war for emergency use. It was used in case the Jeddah cable was interrupted to work either with their airport radio or Mecca, usually the latter. We had been informed by head office that Sir Edward Wilshaw had offered to give a similar set to the Saudi Arabian Government for use at Jeddah when the cable was broken. The offer had been made through British diplomatic channels and accepted. Martin was instructed to send someone over to Jeddah to find a site for it, meet the local telegraph superintendent, and make tentative arrangements for its installation later by one of our engineers. It was decided that I should go to Jeddah and Mr Warner, the manager of Gellatly Hankeys, kindly arranged with their manager in Jeddah to put me up in their mess as at that time there were no European hotels of any kind.

My birthday was celebrated with a heavy haboob and the next day I left Port Sudan for Jeddah by a BOAC aircraft, a twin engined Lockheed Lodestar and arrived in an hour, the distance being 150 miles. I was met by Sandy Cran, one of Gellatly's men and taken to their building. The town at that time was still surrounded by its wall about 30ft high on the three landward sides, except that two large holes had been knocked in it to the north and south. Practically all the buildings inside the walls were three or four storey old Turkish houses built of coral stone with numerous windows with wooden jalousies. The streets were sandy and mostly unpaved, and there was a large market roofed in with stalls along a central roadway.

Gellatlys had one of these large houses. On the ground floor was their garage for a Land Rover and the manager's car, together with water pumping equipment and an electric light plant as Jeddah had no public utilities. On the first floor was the business office and the second floor was the bachelors' mess. The top floor was a flat for the manager and his wife, Mr and Mrs Miles. I was made welcome and taken that evening to a large party at the house of the British Consul, Mr Ellison, where I met his two vice-consuls, the Dutch Consul, Mr Van der Meulen, and a number of the foreign residents, mostly British and American.

The next day I called on the British Minister to Saudi Arabia, Mr L. B. Grafftey-Smith. He told me the Saudi government had sent an official down from Mecca to meet me. He spoke English and the superintendent of the telegraph office would give me all the help he could.

I went to see the superintendent of telegraphs, Saleh Kial, and met the official from Mecca, El Sayed Juniad A. Bajuniad. The former, who spoke no English, was a tall dark man with a pleasant manner, and the latter was a rather short, lighter haired gentleman, also very courteous, who spoke good English. They were dressed in the long flowing robes of the Arabs with head-dress.

I stayed a week in Jeddah and it was decided the radio set should be in a small building a short distance from the telegraph office where there was room to erect masts for aerials. They tried to get me to say that we would put up the building, but I told them they must do that as we are only supplying the set and installing it. The superintendent was obviously very keen on having it as it made him independent of the airport, Mecca radio and other government departments.

I also met the postmaster, Abdul Kader Muhtasib, a most genial man who spoke English. He told me he had kind recollections of the visit to Jeddah of Mr J. Broadbent (then the manager at Port Sudan), whom he described as a most excellent gentleman. This was Joe Broadbent who had been engineer at Suez and Malta with me.

On the Friday, the Mohammedan Sunday, Cran and two others in their mess took me in their Land Rover for a picnic and bathe. He told me that it behoved one to drive carefully as the law was "an eye for an eye, etc." if you injured anyone. There was no shortage of alcohol in their mess as they had a system which I never came across anywhere else. All the expenses both food *and* drink were paid for by Gellatlys. No doubt this was a sort of fringe benefit for service in such a place. However, they did not drink to excess but in that hot climate consumed a good deal of light ale.

One evening a week the whole foreign community were invited to a party at the American embassy where they were entertained by the U.S. Minister, Mr Eddy, a tall cheerful man, and his staff. They had a new building outside the city walls, and the party ended with the showing of a film. One of our vice-consuls, Mr Ousman, told me all about the new oil wells which were being drilled at Dhairan near the Persian Gulf and said that the Arabian American Oil Co (known as Aramco) was providing fully air-conditioned quarters and other amenities for the American staff. The Saudi Arabian government were not at all rich at that time as the oil had not yet started to flow. The main source of revenue was from the pilgrims who came in their thousands by sea and land to visit the holy places, Mecca and Medina. A tarmac road from

Jeddah to Mecca had been built by Egyptian engineers and they took me to see the Jeddah end where there was a barrier and police post, beyond which non-Mohammedans were not allowed to go.

I went to see the suk (market) and bought a dozen teaspoons which were made of silver rials (Saudi Arabian coins) bent into shallow bowls and attached to silver handles with a camel emblem at the end. These were a present for Sylvia when I returned to Port Sudan.

I wrote a report which Martin forwarded to head office; they made no comment so presumably were satisfied with what I had arranged. Not long after there was an interruption to the Jeddah cable and we worked by radio to Mecca. The Saudi Arabian operators were very particular about whom they would work with and always asked who the Sudanese operators were. If they had heard by the grapevine that one of these was not a good Mohammedan, they would refuse to communicate with us while he was on the circuit.

I found that the Col Set radio had been installed in a room at the north end of the bachelors' mess with the aerial nearby to get away from interference by the office. This was inconvenient as it was a hundred yards away. Examination of the Col Set receiver showed that it had two fairly large screw terminals protruding from the back of the metal case to which the aerial and earth were connected. From my Accra experience I knew they could pick up interference so the workshop made a small metal box, screwed to the case, to cover them with a small hole at the back for the screened feeder cable to the aerial. This reduced electrical interference considerably.

We had a wedding in April when the assistant commissioner of police, D. G. Brown married Jean Yates, one of the sisters at the hospital, and we all went to the celebration. The weather was beginning to warm up. Sylvia joined one or two ladies who were sorting clothing and sewing for the Red Cross, and the swimming pool at the club was becoming very popular.

On the 8th May there was a dinner at the Red Sea Hotel, near the harbour front, to celebrate VE Day which was attended by the European community, followed by a dance at the Sports Club. In June a good many wives went away either to England, or the local hill station at a place called Erkowit, 3,500 ft up, about ninety miles away by rail and road.

Thomas and his wife invited us to go for a day's outing by car to Suakin, thirty-seven miles south of Port Sudan. He paid it visits now

*The Old Suakin
Residency, Sylvia, the
author and "Tommy"
Thomas.*

and then as it was in his jurisdiction. As already mentioned, it was once the main port but was abandoned when Port Sudan was built. The town is built on a small island in the middle of the large harbour and connected with the shore on the landward side by a causeway. It was built by the Turks as a slave exporting port and many of the houses are similar to those in Jeddah. When the Mahdi conquered the Sudan in the 1880's it was the only place which continued to be held by the British until the Sudan was re-conquered by Lord Kitchener in 1898.

We drove to the residency which is kept in order by the government as a rest house and police post. It is situated at the edge of the town on the seaward side and its verandah is built right over the water. Several famous people have lived in it, Gordon, Wingate, Kitchener, etc., and we were invited by Thomas to sign the visitors book. We walked through the town which was deserted though most of the old Turkish houses were still standing. Thomas said that many were still owned by residents of Port Sudan and elsewhere as they refused to sell them, not that there would be many buyers. On one of the seaward arms of the harbour was a quarantine station for pilgrims to Mecca, only used during the pilgrim season.

There was a large black plaque on the wall of the residency courtyard. It was a memorial to the men who fell in the battle of Tokar, about fifty miles south. This was against the so called "Fuzzy-Wuzzies", members of the Hadendoa tribe who, led by a chief called Osman Digna, supported the Mahdi and fiercely attacked the British troops landed at Suakin. Their nickname stems from their luxuriant hair. We saw some of them in the docks area of Port Sudan.

E. E. Story the Australian extension man who had relieved me in Penang in September 1941 and got away from Singapore, passed through Port Sudan en route for Massawa in Eritrea where the company had established a radio station working to Aden. Bishop Gwynne, bishop of Egypt and the Sudan, paid us a visit. I had met him in Suez in 1928. He was now over eighty but still active. After preaching in the church on Sunday, he attended a dinner given by our mess at which Mr and Mrs Martin, Sylvia and I were guests.

We had some trouble with the land cables to our cablehouse. They ran south from the office, crossed a creek and then reached the cablehouse south of the harbour entrance. It was very hot and working outdoors in the sun was trying, and one realised how easy it was in such a climate to collapse from heat stroke.

In July Martin and his wife went to Erkowit hill station for two weeks local leave, and I acted as manager, speaking to him on the phone once or twice to tell him how things were going. On their return, Sylvia and I took our leave. We were due to depart by train at 4 p.m. but on the previous two days there had been rain in the hills and when we got to the station we found that departure was postponed for some hours until the line had been inspected for washaways. The railway manager's house was nearby and Cummins and his wife rescued us and gave us tea and drinks until the train finally left at 8.30 p.m. It was very hot until about midnight by which time it had climbed up a bit. We arrived at Summit station at 4 a.m. and found a station wagon waiting to take us and others on to Erkowit which we reached an hour later. We passed a large prisoner-of-war camp where Italians from the Eritrean campaign were confined. We were at 3,500 ft and it was much cooler.

The hill station consisted of a central building with dining room, lounges, kitchens, etc., and a number of small stone bungalows dotted around, each with two or three bedrooms with bathrooms.

We had hardly got there when we heard on the wireless the news of the dropping of the atom bombs on Hiroshima and Nagasaki, and on VJ Day (14th August) there was a celebration dinner at which Tommy Thomas made an excellent speech. On 22nd August we left before dawn to catch the train at Summit and reached Port Sudan at 10.45 a.m. The day after we got back was about the worst for the year with a noon shade temperature of 119 degrees F. and high humidity and we all felt knocked out.

A week later we got a thunderbolt. Head office cabled Martin that Wallace Donaldson would be leaving the UK by air to relieve me, and that I was to proceed by air to Colombo for orders for the Far East, unaccompanied.

Sylvia decided she would return to South Africa and head office approved this, so she cabled her two sisters who were now living together in the elder one's house near Cape Town. Gellatly Hankey were deputed to find out if there were any ships going to Durban and a week later said that an Egyptian cargo boat called *The Star of Alex*, 5,000 tons, would be leaving in ballast for Durban in about five days and had accommodation for Sylvia. As there was little chance of another ship, she decided to go and started packing her things.

On 15th September she sailed at 2 p.m. and I went on board to see her off. The accommodation was primitive, but there was another English lady on board. She was the wife of the general manager of the Palestine railways, Mrs Norman, and she and Sylvia liked each other. They had a pretty rough passage as coal had been put on deck and the ship was filthy. The captain, although English, had lost his UK master's ticket for some offence. They struck a bad storm and the ballast shifted but she finally put into Lourenço Marques where Sylvia and Mrs Norman disembarked. They had trouble in getting money as their sterling travellers cheques could not be cashed. Fortunately Sylvia found the South African consul general was a man who had been in college with her in Cape Town and all was arranged. They went by train to Johannesburg where Sylvia had friends and then went on to Cape Town to stay with her two sisters at Pinelands in the suburbs.

Meanwhile Donaldson arrived to take over from me. I gave a farewell party in our flat, and Donaldson helped me pack up all our household effects. They were shipped to Durban where they remained in store for some time. I moved to the Red Sea Hotel for a few days and after saying goodbye to the Martins and all the staff, left Port Sudan on 1st October by BOAC service for Karachi. I could only take one suitcase so left all my luggage with Gellatlys to be sent on later to wherever I fetched up.

CHAPTER SIXTEEN

Cocos—Keeling Islands

BOAC used two-engined Lockheed Lodestar aircraft on their Cairo to Karachi service. They carried about twenty passengers and had four rows of seats at the back and two long seats on either side at the front. There was a crew of two, pilot and navigator/purser. We left Port Sudan about 4 p.m. and arrived at Asmara, 320 miles away, two hours later. The airport and town are on a high plateau, 8,000 feet up, so it was much cooler. We were driven to a hotel in the town and I got a good night's sleep.

We left the next morning and had a splendid view of the steep hill roads down the plateau to the sea coast near Massawa. We flew down the Red Sea to the Straits of Bab el Mandeb and arrived at Aden. After refuelling we went along the south coast of Arabia. The weather was fine and sunny and from 10,000 feet one could see for miles inland, a welter of barren hills, very forbidding. We stopped for lunch and refuelling at Mukalla, an RAF staging post, and then went on another 360 miles to Solala in Oman where we stayed the night at the RAF base; a total distance of 1,130 miles for the day.

The RAF were very hospitable and took us for a drive to the town where there were guards of the Omani army, picturesque Arabs with ancient rifles and long daggers ornamented with silver mounts.

Next morning we left at 8 a.m. and came down three hours later at Masira Island, south of the entrance to the Persian Gulf, where we had lunch. The next leg of 600 miles was all across the sea to Karachi which we reached about 5 p.m. There were two airports there, one run by the RAF and the other, Karachi airport, on the other side of the town by the United States Air Force. We landed at the former and I was immediately in trouble with my yellow fever certificate which they refused to accept as it was out of date and said I would have to go into quarantine. I rang our cable office and spoke to C. G. Gott, who said he did not think anything could be done about it. However, I was not alone as the pilot of our aircraft, Flt Lt Humphreys, was also told that his certificate was not properly authenticated.

So Humphreys and I were put in a rickety station wagon with mosquito netting over the windows and driven across the town to the other airport where the quarantine quarters were situated. This was a long single storey building with very wide verandahs on two sides, all mosquito-netted, and doors locked. A reply came from Cairo the next day and the pilot was released. An Indian doctor came in the morning and gave me a fresh yellow fever inoculation and said I would have to stay there for nine days. Actually it was not a bad thing. I had had a strenuous time in the last three weeks what with getting Sylvia away to South Africa, packing up, handing over and then travelling. The nine days I spent there was a complete rest and did me a lot of good. The food was good and we were dished out one evening whisky a day. The matron was competent and ran the place smoothly. But the inmates were an extraordinary menagerie.

There was a brigadier of the Gold Coast Regiment who seemed to spend most of the time on the phone and departed two days later. There was a chief officer of the WRNS called Miss Cheetham, a very Girton college type. There was an RAF Leading Aircraftsman called Jackson

Direction Island—viewed from the air with flying boats and Air Sea Rescue launches, cable station buildings in left centre.

and an Egyptian army doctor, Captain Mahagoob, who had been in charge of a Green Crescent hospital in the Abyssinian war and told us that the Italians bombed it more than once. He was an interesting man to talk to. Finally there were half a dozen Persians, two families of men, women and children from Jask in Iran.

My brother Miles had been captured in the Western desert in 1942 and sent to Italy. When the Italians capitulated he escaped but was recaptured and sent to a POW camp in Germany where he had a rough time before being released by the US Army. He was now back in India doing staff work at GHQ, New Delhi. So I sent him a telegram to ask if there was any chance of his being able to come to Karachi. He could not but told me our cousin, Derrick Foster, a group captain in the RAF was in Karachi in charge of the base at Clifton. I telephoned to Derrick whom I had not seen since we were children in 1913 and he invited me to have lunch with him as soon as I was let out. Finally on the ninth day the doctor gave me my certificate and I arranged to get a taxi after lunch to my hotel.

This had been taken over for service and civilian personnel arriving and leaving by air, and was crowded with men in various uniforms with a few civilians. In the main lounge was a board on the wall and on it was chalked daily the names of those due to leave the next day. I found myself in a bedroom with two other men, one Indian officer and one British. The latter was Major Mathews-Killam, RA, the son of Mr Justice Mathews who had been a judge in Penang when I was there.

Next day I went to our office and saw Gott who invited me to his house. Also there was D. T. Cox and Boultwood who had been in charge of the workshop in Gibraltar before the war. My cousin Derrick was very hospitable and gave me a lunch and also a dinner at the Sind Club, an imposing building with every amenity. On that occasion Gott said he was dining there with his wife and two guests and would my cousin and I join them after dinner. We did so and Gott told Derrick that his daughter was in the WRAF in England and was anxious to be posted to Clifton in Karachi. I heard later that Derrick helped to get her sent there and Gott was pleased.

After six days in the hotel, my name came up and I left Karachi in an RAF Dakota. We got to Santa Maria airport near Bombay about tea time and were accommodated in a RAF rest house nearby. After tea I went for a walk and came to a long sandy beach with bathing chalets. On my return the rest house manager said someone had been enquiring for me. On the verandah I found "Baron" Westworth who had been in Suez with me in the 1920's and in Penang. He was on his way to Colombo from London and told me what news he had gathered in head office a few days before. It was not much but I was supposed to go to Penang. He said they wanted him to go to Cocos Island as manager but he told them he was not keen, having done one spell there during the war.

We were called at 4 a.m. and, after breakfast, taken in a mini-bus to our plane. But it had a fault and we all returned to the rest house. The next morning we were again up at 4 a.m. and took off in our DC3. After flying for about twenty minutes we returned to Santa Maria. The aircrew in the cockpit said they had a leak in the heating system and were being par-boiled. Next day it was mended and we were away early. We flew right across India from Bombay to Bangalore at about 10,000 feet. It was fine and clear and all the country-side was visible.

At Bangalore the RAF gave us some brunch about 10.30 a.m. and we took off again, crossed the rest of India and saw the narrow strait between it and Ceylon where the railway crosses Adams Bridge then landed at Ratmalana airport on the outskirts of Colombo.

I took a taxi to our office and went in to see the manager, A. J. Whiteside. He had just got a letter from head office about various appointments and I was to go to Cocos Island to relieve Harry Moss as Manager.

He sent me to the Galle Face Hotel with one of the staff, as the head receptionist had one of his family in our office, and there were several of our men staying there. At the hotel we found they had not a room to spare but just then Alan (Hampstead) Heath appeared and said if they would put in another bed, I could stay in his room and this was arranged. Heath whom I had last seen at Gib en route to Alexandria in 1935, was waiting for a visa from General MacArthur's HQ in the Philippines to go to Manila to re-open our office there.

Our Colombo office was a hive of activity. H. G. (Tufty) Baker was assistant manager and had two other men crowded into his room doing accounts and clerical work.

At the hotel there were half a dozen of our men waiting to be sent on to Far Eastern branches. The company had assembled at Colombo a great deal of new cable apparatus which had to go on to branches captured during the war, as most of the old equipment had been destroyed to prevent the Japanese using it.

A. R. Harrison was in charge of the wireless station at Negombo about ten miles outside Colombo. He came in to see Whiteside and invited me to spend the weekend with him and his wife at their bungalow. I went by train and had a very pleasant time as they were close to the beach and there was good bathing.

On 30th October Whiteside told me I was to leave by air the next day and that the RAF said flights by civilians now had to be paid for in cash and had refused a cheque. He gave me five hundred rupees and I went to their HQ and demanded a receipt.

Early next morning I went to Ratmalana airport, and at 8 a.m. we took off in a four engined Skymaster. There were about ten passengers plus a handful of RAF men and a lot of packing cases. The only seating was canvas covered metal frames along the sides. As we left Colombo there was a good view of the inland mountains all clothed in heavy vegetation with large patches of tea gardens here and there. We then left the land and started the 1,600 miles hop to Cocos. There was a lot of cloud but we could see the sea at intervals. We were flying at 10,000 feet at 220 miles per hour.

About 4 p.m. Cocos island came into view and we circled and landed on the 3,000 yard runway on West Island. I was met by two of our staff, Sims and Griffin, both Australians. The runway was four miles from the landing place, whence we had to cross the lagoon to Direction Island where the cable station was. At the landing was our staff sailing boat *Daphne* and we embarked in her and set sail across the lagoon. The wind fell light and it took us nearly three hours to reach our pier on Direction Island. Moss took me to the manager's bungalow known as *Top House.*

The Cocos Keeling islands are a coral atoll consisting of five principal and some smaller islands arranged in a rough circle with a central lagoon about six miles across. All of them are low, long and narrow and covered with trees, mostly coconut palms. There is a barrier reef a hundred yards or less from the outside edge of the land. Direction Island, the most north easterly of the circle, is in the form of a crescent moon three quarters of a mile long and 200 to 300 yards wide. There is a separate atoll called North Keeling Island about sixteen miles to the north. There is only one entrance to the lagoon, to the westward of Direction Island. Near the latter to the south is Home Island where the owners, the Clunies Ross family lived with a Malay village of 1,600 inhabitants. South Island is uninhabited and West Island which is the biggest, had the airstrip on it.

The islands were discovered by Captain Keeling, an East India Co
mariner in 1609. John Clunies Ross, the owner of a trading schooner,
settled there in 1827 with his family. He turned the islands into a
coconut plantation. Charles Darwin in the famous voyage of the *Beagle*
visited the islands in 1836 and, from soundings, propounded the theory
that these atolls were originally volcanic craters which sank in the sea.
George, the son of Ross I, succeeded him in 1854 and in 1857 was
recognised as governor when Captain Fremantle in HMS *Juno*
proclaimed the islands as part of the British Empire. George died in
1872 and his son succeeded as Ross III. In 1878 they came under the
control of the Ceylon Government but were transferred in 1886 to the
Straits Settlements government. In 1902 the cable station was opened to
connect South Africa with Australia by cables to Perth, Western
Australia, and Durban, Natal, via Rodriguez and Mauritius Islands. In
1908 a cable was laid to Batavia (now Djakarta) in Java giving a route to
Singapore and in 1926 a duplicate cable was laid to Perth. Ross III died

Malay House, Cocos Islands.

in 1910 when his son, Ross IV took over. He died in November 1944 of a heart attack after a Jap air raid. During the First World War the German cruiser *Emden* came in 1914, but owing to the prompt wireless alarm given by the cable station, and the proximity of an escorted troopship convoy, she was put out of action by HMS *Sydney* and ran ashore on North Keeling Island.

In March 1942 when the Japs invaded Malaya and the Dutch East Indies, they sent a ship and shelled the cable station, but only slight damage was caused. The company withdrew all the staff except four men but later sent others when the Japs failed to occupy the islands. To make them think the cable station was destroyed, no reference was made to them in messages or letters, and it was referred to by the code name of *Brown,* later changed to *James.* Thereafter there were several air raids on Direction and Home islands, and a few people were killed, but none of our staff. In March 1945 an expedition was mounted by South East Asia Command to occupy West Island and build the airstrip to bomb Japanese occupied Java. They were all ready to do this when the atom bombs were dropped and the war ended. So the Liberator bombers were used to drop supplies to prisoner of war camps in Java. It was then expected that the RAF Navy and anciliary services would soon be evacuated and this was the position at the time of my arrival.

Moss handed over to me and left by air for Australia ten days later. The staff at Cocos consisted of W. J. Stubbs (assistant manager and engineer), and Croger, Griffin, Jenkins and Moore as office watchkeepers. Of these all but Moore were ex-Pacific Cable Board men, Stubbs being a New Zealander and the others Australians. Sedman was in charge of the workshop, a London station man who had volunteered during the war to go abroad, and Sims, another Australian, who was known as the outside engineer. His job was to run the engine room and manage the gang of six Singapore Malays who did maintenance, painting bungalows, looking after water tanks, etc. He had four Malays from Home Island as engine room assistants. We also had a Malay clerk called Arshad for traffic accounts.

Besides ourselves on Direction Island there was an RAF airsea rescue service consisting of three officers and some two dozen men. They had three large high speed launches powered by Napier Lion engines for picking up anyone who fell in the sea. There was also a detachment under a naval officer with a staff of three or four officers who acted as pilots for ships entering the lagoon with the use of two motor launches and a direction finding station.

The managing director in London had laid it down some years before that managers should put their names on service telegrams to head office so that he could visualise who was sending them. When Moss handed over to me he sent the customary message as follows: "Moss/Cocos to MD.—Date/time Stray in charge." It happened that an hour later Dan Griffin who looked after our mess canteen stores came in and reported we needed more vitamin pills. These had been supplied to Cocos as it had been unable to keep its vegetable garden going during the war for lack of fertilisers. So I sent the following service telegram: "Stray/Cocos to MD—Date/time please send six dozen bottles of vitamin pills." The juxtaposition of the two messages struck me as amusing.

The cable station buildings were all of an early pre-fab type having been sent out in sections on the original cable-laying ship. They had galvanised iron walls and roofs, and were lined inside with teak match-boarding. The floors were raised three feet above the ground on steel posts and girders, and there were wide verandahs on three sides. There were no windows proper, but several teak double doors with glass in the upper parts. There were heavy wooden cyclone shutters, normally kept stacked under the buildings, which could be firmly clipped over the French doors, and each roof had four wire ropes attached to the peak which could be fastened to concrete anchor blocks and tightened with rigging screws to prevent the roof being blown off.

The main buildings were all in a line facing the lagoon about fifty yards from the sandy beach which lined the latter, and behind them were the servants quarters, workshops, stores, etc. There was a trolley railway at the rear which ran down to the jetty.

As well as a staff sailing boat, there was a library, billiard room, two tennis courts, electric light and small Electrolux refrigerators in each bungalow and the mess buildings. But owing to the war and lack of our normal quota of Singapore Chinese servants, all meals were served in the dining room at Top House, where Stubbs had his bedroom. I had two rooms, bedroom and sitting room and we all had Singapore jars and commodes in our bathrooms attached to each bedroom.

Fresh water was caught on our galvanised iron roofs which were painted with a non-lead paint and piped to large tanks around the buildings.

The cables from Australia and South Africa were worked as an automatic through circuit between Durban and Adelaide in South Australia. The Batavia (Djakarta) cable which had been cut during the war was still not restored owing to troubles between the Javanese and the Dutch, so our second cable to Australia was idle at that time.

Cocos station had a system by which the European staff carried out various community jobs. The holders of these were called jaggers, a Malay word meaning watchman or keeper. There was a boat jagger, a library jagger, billiard room jagger and so on. This was a good idea as it gave everyone something to do when off duty. The services had an open air cinema show once or twice a week to which our staff had been invited. Our lagoon beach was excellent for bathing but it was dangerous to go out of one's depth owing to sharks and barracuda. It was said that one man had a bite from a barracuda in his behind when only standing breast deep in the water.

Shortly after, two British destroyers arrived from Fremantle, the port for Perth. The Admiralty had a fleet oiler, the *Belgol,* anchored in the lagoon to re-fuel them. Our manager in Perth, Mr Smith, was very helpful in sending us stores by any ship which might be calling and these two, HM ships *Norman* and *Nizam* were bringing some for us. So I went with Sims to *Norman* and while he was collecting the stores, called on the captain, Commander Saumarez, who invited me to stay to dinner. Captain Stack also came to dinner and Saumarez made a signal to *Nizam* for her captain, Lt Cmdr Hopkins, to join us. So it was a pleasant evening. The ships were on their way home from the Pacific Fleet which had been operating with the US Navy against the Japs, and Saumarez told us stories about the fighting and especially the surprise of the Americans when our aircraft carriers survived kamikazi (suicide) attacks by Jap bombers. If hit directly, most American carriers caught fire and several were lost. The British carriers, however, had three inch armoured flight decks and always survived. I recollected reading in the annual *Jane's Fighting Ships* criticism before the war about these armoured decks, there described as a useless waste of weight. It was ironic they should prove invaluable against a form of attack never envisaged when built.

Commander Moore, RNR arrived as new naval officer in charge (NOIC). I called on him at once and established cordial relations. He had retired from the Royal Indian Navy but had rejoined in the RNR during the war.

Before Moss left he took me one night to the services open air

cinema. We carried light cane chairs and sat at the back. But after Cmdr
Moore and I became friends, he said to come on cinema nights to his
mess. Then he and I would walk over to where everyone was gathered
and sit in the middle of the centre row of front seats reserved for the
officers. The show only started when NOIC arrived, a very VIP way of
attending.

There was an Indian Dock Operating Co on West Island and they ran
a regular ferry service from there to our island using River Landing
Craft (RLC). These were a sort of lighter with a short deck at the stern
and fitted with two Ford V8 car engines underneath and a tiny
wheelhouse above. The forward end had a ramp which could be let
down so that a lorry could be driven straight onto them from the beach.

We were very friendly with Captain Perry, the master of the oiler
Belgol and his officers and they often came ashore to see us. The chief
engineer, Mr Fielder, presented us with a few new records for our old
wind-up gramophone.

Moss had been acting as mess president so we had a meeting to elect a
new one. Croger and I were both proposed and the voting was a tie so I
used my casting vote to elect him. It was much better for the manager
not to be mess president and Croger was a good one. At my suggestion
there was a good clear out at Top House by removing all the old blackout shades, cleaning up the mess silver, challenge cups, etc., having
curtains made for the French windows and generally sprucing the place
up. Jenkins was mess caterer and Dan Griffin ran our general store
where drinks, sweets, toothbrushes and all the sundries were obtainable.
We did not use money at all. Everything was signed for and put on our
mess bill, even our losings/gains at bridge, and minor debits and credits
between individuals as well as anything bought from Home Island.
Moss had been doing the mess accounts and Croger the company's
accounts and we continued this for a month and then swapped over.

We had a system by which the mess gave a lunch party every Sunday
morning. One week Croger would invite as mess guests a few officers
from units on West Island who had been helpful to us with our mail,
stores, etc. And the next week was for private guests when any member
could invite his particular friends by letting the mess president know so
as not to have more than we could seat. Wee Kee Lin, our cook, made
marvellous Malay curry and our parties were very popular.

In addition to getting our stores by naval vessels from Australia and
this included our drinks, mostly beer and gin, we could buy from the

Naafi on West Island and even from the Indian RASC unit but generally Australian stores were cheaper. Our whisky was a special brand Victoria Vat which had been supplied from the UK in bottles and we still got some. One consignment came soon after I got there. Most of our food came from tins but we kept some free range chickens and had a piggery with four or five pigs. These were fed partly on coconuts for which we paid a small monthly sum to the Ross estate as, by the terms of our lease, all the coconuts belonged to them. One of their Malays supplied us with fish, and now and then turtle from the lagoon.

As Christmas approached NOIC told me a light aircraft carrier, HMS *Queen,* was coming from Colombo bringing special food for the occasion. She was due at 6 a.m. but did not turn up until 2 p.m. He went off to her and next day told me that when their late arrival was mentioned, they became very uncommunicative and he thought they had missed the islands altogether and had had to turn back. This is not difficult to do if the navigation is a bit out. There was a homing radio beacon on West Island to prevent aircraft doing this in bad visibility, i.e. tropical rain. We had a big party in the mess for Christmas dinner with eight guests from the navy and RAF rescue service.

After the death of Ross IV in 1944 the Ceylon government had sent a Military Administrator to run the estate. After a couple of changes, he was now Lt Col E. Lloyd-Jones, a tall lanky man with a marvellous flow of expletives when riled. He had been a rubber planter in Malaya before the war. He was a cheerful soul and I liked him and we corresponded for some years after I left Cocos. He had one or two NCO clerks to assist him.

We usually dressed in shorts and open neck shirts or even singlets for tennis. Most of the RAF men went about in shorts only. While one could go bare-foot on the beach, light shoes were advisable otherwise one could get cuts from the coral pebbles and there seems to be some sort of infection in coral as one could get what was known as coral sores which, while not serious, were very troublesome to cure. I had told Gellatly Hankey in Port Sudan to send on my trunks via Colombo but they only arrived in April 1946, so my wardrobe was minimal. I bought a tennis racquet in Colombo and a few extra things but one did not need many clothes as things were washed as soon as taken off.

Lloyd-Jones invited me to lunch at his bungalow, one of two for European estate assistants. He showed me over the Ross house, a rather amorphous pile, with a lot of small rooms. The best was the large library panelled in mahogany. Many of the Malays on Home Island had been taught how to make curios to sell to the troops. There were model dukongs, the single sail type of boat they used for fishing on the lagoon; Malay parangs with vicious-looking steel blades, about 18 inches long, as sharp as a razor; model parangs in brass as paper knives, and pin jewellery made from tortoise shell in the shape of fish, etc., with safety-pin fasteners. The model boats were about eighteen inches long of a hardwood known locally as grongong, much like mahogany, and which took a high polish. They were fitted out with masts and sails complete with tiny blocks and ropes. I bought two and sent them to Sylvia and my parents, also some jewellery and two parang paper knives.

As there was a regular service of RAF aircraft between Colombo and Perth we got our letters by them. I put Colombo stamps on letters to Sylvia and others, and on the Australian mail their own, obtainable from the mail officer on West Island. The RAF would also bring small parcels from Australia for us.

Hatch and Da Silva, two Colombo operators, returned there and were replaced by two young Telcom operators, Faulkner and Barnett.

In peace time the company had a resident doctor who also looked after the Ross family and their Malays, but now there was an Indian Medical Service Hospital on West Island with medical orderlies on Direction and Home Islands to which one of the doctors made visits. As they were allowed to take private patients, the company paid them for any attendance required by us. Soon after my arrival, the IMS doctors and staff were sent back to India and replaced by RAF personnel. Squadron Leader Greene, the PMO, came to see me and said they were quite ready to look after us, but were not allowed to charge fees. I suggested asking the company who agreed to make a donation to the RAF Benevolent Fund at the rate we paid our doctor. They had a dentist, Flt Lt Corless, and when we had them all over to a Sunday lunch, he said to come over and see him if we had any teeth trouble. Not long after I had toothache and went to see him. His tent was pitched in a coconut grove and his assistant had put the chair under the trees, it reminded me of scenes out of *South Pacific*.

Group Capt Stone told me that the evacuation of the services had been postponed indefinitely on account of the fighting in Java which made them short of shipping. Owing to this fighting Quantas Airways transferred their civilian air service which had been operating through Batavia to Cocos and sent three or four of their staff to West Island.

Airstrip Control Tower, note height above sea level.

The RAF agreed to re-fuel and service the aircraft. They were converted Lancaster bombers and one of them fell into the sea about 500 miles north west of Cocos en route from Colombo. Two special rescue Liberators were sent to search for it and our own air-sea rescue launches went out, but no trace was ever found.

Stone asked me if we had any records of severe cyclones as he wanted to issue instructions as to what should be done. In our files was a letter from the superintendent to head office giving an account of the cyclone which struck on 29th November, 1909, the worst experienced for forty years, so a copy was made and sent to him. We had one or two bad "blows" during the year, and once rigged our cyclone shutters and roof stays, but nothing like the one in 1909 when the barometer dropped below 28 inches and the eye of the storm went right over the islands. Twenty-five thousand coconut trees were blown down and the damage cost Mr Ross a great deal of money.

A Major Montgomery was the Eurasian officer in command of the

Indian Dock Operating Co and had his office (a tent) at the landing place at the north end of West Island. Monty was a charming man and if you were waiting there for a ferry to cross the lagoon would invite you in for a chat and a cup of tea, which beverage he seemed to have on tap at all hours.

Lloyd-Jones went on leave and was relieved by D. A. Somerville of the Malayan Civil Service who was appointed District Commissioner.

Another visitor was Captain Stevens of the War Graves Commission who asked if there were any graves on Direction Island. I showed him where three RAF men had been buried, and an Indian soldier, all with improvised headstones. The former had died when a flying boat crashed in the lagoon when taking off in 1943, but I had no knowledge of the Indian and could not say what his religion was.

A party of magnetic survey men came to measure the magnetic variation and chose a site well away from all buildings near the West end of the island. We made an inscribed concrete block to mark the exact position for possible future surveyors.

We had six or eight visitors one day. A Quantas aircraft was delayed by engine trouble and one of the passengers was Group Captain Warren of the Royal Australian Air Force. He borrowed Stone's motor launch and came over from West Island with other passengers including a pretty Australian girl called Miss Phillips. We entertained them to drinks and Miss Phillips told me she had been in the WRNS at Sydney. I had heard that my friend in Penang, Captain D. G. Moore of HMS *Dauntless,* had been promoted Rear Admiral so I asked Miss Phillips if she had met him. She said; "Yes, he is now working at the Pacific Fleet HQ at Sydney." This information was to prove useful later. She asked if she could send a cable and I told her that was what we were here for, so she wrote it out, addressed to her parents, as follows: *On a coral island with a thousand men* stop *having a whale of a time.*

The Air Sea Rescue Service ran a picnic on a Sunday to North Keeling Island, sixteen miles away, and invited some of our men to go with them in a large launch. They reported there were bits of the German cruiser *Emden* still visible where she had been beached after being put out of action by HMS *Sydney* in 1914.

At this time there was a mutiny of the Royal Indian Navy at Bombay and other ports. It was put down without difficulty but while it was on, one of their ships, the *Llanstephan Castle,* arrived at Cocos and stayed for about a week. She was an old Union Castle liner fitted out as a troop landing ship with special landing boats, and I went with NOIC to call on her captain, Commander Fickney, RNR. I told him the last time I had been on board his ship was in Cape Town in 1921 when I went from the Cableship *Britannia* to visit the *Llanstephan's* chief wireless operator. Whilst she was there NOIC told me there had been a fear her Indian crew might mutiny in sympathy with their fellows in Bombay and he had arranged with the Fortress Commander to give us an armed guard.

Stone told me in early April they would probably all be leaving in early May and I reported to head office that we would be doing our best to stock up with supplies for about five or six months, but that we should need a doctor. I requested the divisional manager in Melbourne, Mr Holmes, to ask the navy whether any of their ships passing nearby could bring us about twenty tons of stores. The oiler *Belgol* had left and there had been no naval vessels calling from Australia for some time, though we knew some passed close to us by listening in on our radio.

Mr Holmes replied that the navy said they were unable to help, so remembering what Miss Phillips had told me, I suggested to the DM Melbourne that he telephone to Rear Admiral Moore at Sydney, mention my name, and ask him if he could assist. Next day Holmes replied that Admiral Moore had promised help and a few days later we got a cablegram, repeated to NOIC from Naval HQ at Sydney to HMS *Holmsound* ordering her to lift 20 tons of stores at Fremantle and deliver them to us at Cocos. I sent a telegram to thank Admiral Moore.

Holmsound arrived and NOIC and I called on the captain who said they were en route to Aden and he was only too pleased to break the voyage at Cocos. She was a special aircraft repair ship and had workshops to maintain electrical and mechanical equipment for carrier borne planes. In collaboration with NOIC we arranged entertainment for her ship's company and she left the next day.

We now had a good stock of stores of all kinds and arrangements were made with Captain Phillips, the OC of a petrol platoon on West Island, to supply us with several thousand gallons of petrol, diesel fuel and paraffin. We had three engines for our electric light plant, one very old paraffin one, a diesel and a recently acquired petrol engine.

As we had to be independent once the services had gone, our stores were divided between various buildings, and our fuel supplies in large drums separated into two or three dumps in case of fire. The same applied to our stationery stores which comprised a large amount of slip, the paper tapes used in the office.

The Fortress Commander on a visit to DI asked me whether we would like to have our photographs taken. He had a photo reconnaisance section which had not much to do, and lots of film to do it with. So two of them came over and took group photos of the foreign service staff and our Chinese and Malays and gave us all prints.

Before the Jap war there were six rifles belonging to the cable station but these were given to the army in 1941 to prevent accusations of our being armed civilians in case of capture. No receipt could be traced for them, so NOIC agreed to leave us six Short Lee-Enfield rifles and ammunition.

The evacuation of army vehicles on West Island started with the arrival of LST 3502 commanded by Lt Cmdr Vernon, RNR. I had not seen a tank landing ship before and he kindly showed me all over her. They filled her up with all sorts of jeeps and trucks. She did not put down her ramp on the beach but was anchored in the lagoon and vehicles were brought one or two at a time to her open bow doors by the RLC's already described, and driven straight into her lower hold, and then up a slope on to her upper deck. A small tanker also came and took away surplus aviation spirit from two large tanks which had been built amongst the palm trees on West Island.

Stone said that a disposals officer was coming from Singapore to decide what was to happen to various stores and equipment, and did we want to buy any? He said he would send him over to see me, and in due course Wing Commander Garwood arrived. I told him the company might be interested in two SWB8 wireless transmitters the RAF had on West Island. These were the same as the one A. R. Harrison had installed in Accra in 1943. He said they would be available but it would be handled through the Air Ministry in London, so I wired head office to contact them only to receive a reply that the Air Ministry said that the offer was unauthorised and they were not for sale.

NOIC and his mess threw a farewell party and a lot of officers from West Island came over for it. My trunks, etc., from Port Sudan had suddenly arrived from Colombo on a cargo ship and I was able to wear Red Sea kit for the occasion.

Stone sent an officer and a couple of NCO's from their meteorological section with the barometers, thermometers, rain gauges and other instruments for us to use as I had agreed to take over their duties, and they spent a week setting them up and teaching our watch keepers how to take readings and code them for cabling to Australia.

The barometer (a standard one) was put in my office and was stated to be six feet above sea level for correction purposes. The Australians offered our men a small remuneration to do wind balloons but it was less than our overtime rates and no one would take them on. Eventually when our doctor arrived he volunteered to do it. It was a twice daily messy job, making hydrogen from chemicals, filling a balloon and when released measuring its height and bearing every minute with a special theodolite mounted on the top of the long mess building. The results giving wind speed and direction at different heights, were coded and cabled. A month or so later when we asked Singapore to get us a further stock of balloons, the Met there and later in Colombo asked if they could have our reports, and the Australians agreed. So the resulting cablegrams, six a day, brought us in a revenue of about £3,500 annually.

NOIC asked us to look after the Direction finding hut and apparatus which was on the western tip of Direction Island, and some food stocks he left behind, as the Admiralty intended sending civilian operators later to work it. He also left us one of his motor launches, quite a large one, which was very useful as Sims was a very good engineer and could easily handle her.

Finally in early May the British India Line troopship *Aronda* arrived to take away all the remaining service personnel. She brought with her Dr C. A. Van Rooyen from Colombo. He was a medium height spare man, about forty-seven years old, and belonged to the Ceylon Burgher community , descendants of early Dutch marriages with the Singhalese.

Comdr Moore asked if he could be spared a bottle of whisky and I went on board after tea with it as a parting gift. I also gave him about 700 Ceylon rupees which he was to give to our manager in Colombo for my credit. The Army had had an account with us for odd cablegrams paid in Ceylon. But for the last payment they asked us to take cash so I debited my salary account with the bill and accepted the rupees myself which Moore was now to help me to get rid of. He duly handed the money over in Ceylon who credited it back to me in sterling.

I had dinner on board the troopship with Moore, Stone and the senior officers, and then said goodbye to them all and came ashore. She sailed early the next morning. Our Moore also left on the same ship.

Stone had asked me to go over to West Island to make sure no one had got left behind, so next day a large party of us went in the navy launch and Somerville from Home Island also came over. Near the landing we found a shed with a number of motor vehicles in it, so we appropriated a couple of jeeps and a light truck and drove the four miles to the airstrip. It was rather an eerie feeling, like seeing a deserted town.

I took the doctor to the hospital just beyond the airstrip and he collected the drugs left behind for him and we got several drums of DDT which had been used to spray around to kill mosquitoes. Cocos had quite a lot but fortunately they were not anopheles which carry malaria so though they occasionally bit us, we suffered no ill effects.

We were now back to pre-war conditions with only ourselves and the Home Islanders under Somerville and it certainly was very quiet after all the bustle of the services around us.

Before the war it had been the practice for the Orient liners on their way to Australia from Aden or Colombo to pass near to Cocos and drop a barrel containing letters, newspapers and some choice items of food. The passengers would then watch the bearded cable men in their sailing boat pick it up. The growing of beards was a sort of ritual. But now there were no liners to bring letters for us, and none of our men had beards.

We borrowed an RLC from Somerville and brought over some cement left behind by the Royal Engineers. There was a large amount of equipment left behind on West Island. Croger inspected an old Liberator aircraft without engines and inside found an Avometer (electrical test meter) in fair condition. There were some large diesel engines and dynamos but they were no use to us. Our two young operators, Faulkner and Barnett found a couple of motor bikes which they rode about on, and Sims got from somewhere a complete V8 Ford engine though I do not know what he did with it eventually. Our senior Australian staff all acquired electric household refrigerators, American ones. We had heard that the services were instructed to destroy all Lend-Lease equipment they could not take away, but no doubt our friends had forgotten to do this with refrigerators.

Sims told me my bungalow was next on the list for re-decorating—each building was done on a rota every two or three years, There were three or four large (and awful) pictures of lions and tigers in my sitting room. So I scrapped them. In the library I found a splendid book full of coloured engravings of famous French artists, Renoir and others, so I appropriated about six or eight, had narrow frames made for them, and put them up in my sitting room and bedroom.

In June we heard that Mrs Ross and her two elder children were coming from Singapore in the 10,000 ton cruiser *Swiftsure.*

Jenkins told me that for family reasons he would much like to go on leave for which he was due, so I wired the DM in Melbourne and he sent a bachelor, H. B. Sutherland, then at Perth, by air to Singapore to catch HMS *Swiftsure.* Sutherland had volunteered for Cocos having been there during the war.

Before her arrival, *Swiftsure* asked us by radio whether we had a large scale chart of Cocos and we replied, "Yes, and will bring it to you on your arrival outside the lagoon." We had a copy of the most recent Admiralty chart given to me by NOIC before he left and it had been put into a watertight metal can, an empty blue print paper container, so that it should not get wet. She got to Cocos at dawn and we went out in the navy launch and I went on board, clutching the chart can. I was met at the gangway top by Comdr Brown and handed the chart to a sailor who whisked off to the bridge with it. *Swiftsure* had what is known as a tower bridge and by the time I had climbed up the gangway from the launch, and then up numerous ladders, I had not much breath left. Captain McLaughlin met me on the bridge and she steamed towards the lagoon. Unfortunately the weather was not good as there was a strong wind from the south west, and the captain decided his ship was too big, 600 feet long, to enter so he anchored near the entrance.

We then went to the quarterdeck where Somerville had just arrived from Home Island and were introduced to Mrs Ross, John Ross aged nineteen, and his sister about seventeen. The captain said he had intended to stay for two or three days but the weather and anchorage being poor, he would leave that night. Somerville had brought off from Home Island model boats and other artefacts already described to sell and there was such a demand that lots had to be drawn for them. Comdr W. L. M. Brown and the gunnery officer, Lt J. G. Wells, failed to get model boats, so I told them that if they paid £2. 10s. each to our manager in Perth for my credit, I would order two and post them to England. The captain also failed in the draw, so Stubbs suggested that if I would give up the one I already had in my room, the mess would present it to Captain McLaughlin as a gift. I agreed at once and we gave it to him before they left. Wells told me that he knew Lt Cmdr Kenneth Williamson, who had bombed the Italians at Taranto, and that far from being killed, he was shot down and taken prisoner but was now home again. This was the first news that he was still alive and I was glad to hear it. I always remembered his prediction in Gibraltar in 1938 that his expectancy of life was about five years.

I had lunch in the wardroom with Wells, and Stubbs gave a lunch party in our mess to a number of the ship's officers, so we entertained them as best as we could though we were sorry their stay was so short. Sutherland came ashore and Jenkins left for Australia. His dog was to be looked after by his relief. Mrs Ross and her children settled into the bungalow next to Somerville's as she decided not to go into the big house for the present.

After all this excitement we went back to our quiet life. I had more time to myself so unpacked all my trunks, etc., and hung up my cold climate clothes to air in a small store room which opened off my sitting room. In Gibraltar I had bought some carpentry tools, and in Accra had had made a large tool box to my own design. It was about the size of a trunk in hardwood, and on opening the lid, the front folded down to disclose a nest of small drawers.

The food stores left behind by the navy were in a galvanised iron hut about 300 yards from the nearest of our occupied buildings, and we found it had been broken into and some stolen. I reported this to Somerville who tried to find out who had done it, without success. We nailed the hut up but it happened again, so I asked our two young operators if they would like to earn some overtime. When off duty they moved all the stores from this hut to the old hut which was surrounded by our buildings and we had no further thefts.

Our next incident was a message from Perth which said that Perth Radio coast station reported a cargo ship in our vicinity with a sick man on board and she wanted to know if we had a doctor. We got on the air with our radio at once and contacted the ship. Dr Van Rooyen was sent for and it was suspected the sick man had appendicitis so the doctor gave advice to the captain as to what to do and the latter said they would arrive off Cocos that afternoon.

The doctor and Dan Griffin made ready his surgery for an operation if necessary and I sent a message to Somerville that a ship was calling, in case he wished to despatch letters. About 4 p.m. we went out to the ship in the launch and the doctor went to examine the patient while we talked to the captain and his officers. Van Rooyen said the man had not got appendicitis but prescribed for him.

Mrs Ross gave a party and dance for the Malays. It was held in the big house and grounds, and there was dancing in the evening in the large library room. She, her family and guests from the cable station sat at one end of the room while an elderly violinist provided the music from the other end. On each side of the long room were the dancers, men on one side and girls on the other, and the dance consisted of each moving from the walls to the centre to meet their partners and then going backwards to the walls. After a time this stopped and the Malays made two lines down the room, men and girls, and danced the *Sir Roger de Coverley.*

Stubbs, as well as being a good cable engineer, was also skilled as a watch repairer. He told me that while on leaves during the war in Auckland he had assisted a watchmaker friend and he had certainly learned all the tricks of the trade.

One of our cables from Australia was interrupted near the other end but restored after about ten days. This was the one first laid in 1902. The other, laid in 1926, was a loaded cable, that is the conductor had some magnetic material incorporated in it which enabled the speed of working to be increased. Unfortunately this had the effect of preventing duplex working, i.e., sending and receiving simultaneously. This was not important here, as owing to the great difference in time between the UK, South Africa, and Australia, the peak periods of traffic in opposite directions, did not coincide. What was unique was an ingenious device whereby if something went wrong, one could operate an alarm bell at the other end to tell the man there to stop sending even though you could not send messages to him. It was known as a beam switch, perhaps because it had a lever like the old beam engines.

Cocos had a water distilling plant but it was only used about once a year to provide water for our batteries, and was heated by coal of which we had a small stock.

The doctor was a good tennis player and I had many enjoyable games against him, in which he nearly always beat me. We gave a return party to the Ross family but could not compete with their dance. Mrs Ross told me her husband had spent about £10,000 out of his own pocket to keep the Malay islanders in food, during the slump in the 1930s when the price of copra was very low. She said that as the population had now grown to about 1,600 it would be difficult to support them if copra prices were poor, and she thought some of them would have to be sent to Malaya or Java. Up till then the rule had been that any islander who left Cocos was never allowed to return. In this way old man Ross had hoped to keep them free from the contamination of civilisation, and he seemed to have succeeded up to 1945 as they were a happy crowd and perfectly satisfied with their lot. Contact with the troops, however, had not done them any good, but now they had gone things should settle down again, as in fact they did. She told me the government had paid the Ross estate £1 for each coconut tree cut down to make the runway airstrip and buildings on West Island.

Group Captain Stone had made himself unpopular in their last couple of months stay by insisting that the airstrip, roads, etc., should be properly maintained to the end. He told me he was sure that within ten years the island would again be an air staging post. And he was right as in 1951 the Australians came, re-built the runway in concrete (it had been pressed steel plate) and used it for their air service by Quantas to South Africa via Mauritius with a spur to Singapore.

We found two small cold chambers on West Island, each about fifteen feet square with refrigerator plant powered by a petrol engine. They were dismantled, brought over to Direction Island and re-erected on the foundations of an old store. We also brought over about 2,000 gallons of petrol left behind by the services. It was intended to use the cold chambers later to keep fresh food brought by the relief ship.

We organised a practice rifle shoot with our service rifles, firing at targets so that the bullets went right out to sea. So with these and other activities such as bathing, fishing and sailing in the lagoon we managed to pass our off-duty hours. We also played a good deal of auction bridge in the evening. Lack of letters and newspapers was the main drawback to life there, though we had some short wave radio receivers and could listen to the news, etc.

There were occasional hazards. Croger had a dukong which he hired from Home Island. It was blowing hard one afternoon and after tea Stubbs reported to me that Croger had gone over to West Island and had not returned. There was a considerable sea running even in the lagoon, so Stubbs, Sims and another man set out in the admiralty launch to look for him. He was not found as he had very sensibly decided to stay over night on West Island till the wind went down.

When not playing tennis I used to take our two dogs for a walk round the island after tea. They loved it and sometimes found an odd rat to hunt in dumps of coconuts and got very excited.

In October the divisional manager, Singapore, advised us the old relief ship, *The Islander* belonging to the Christmas Island Phosphate Co would be resuming visits and would arrive about the end of the

Cocos Cable Station staff 1946, front row, Griffin, Stubbs, Stray, Croger,
Jenkins, back row, Moore, Sedman, Barnett, Faulkner, Sims, Arshad.

month with reliefs for Croger, Sedman, Arshad and me; the two young
operators were to go without reliefs as they were no longer needed. It
would also bring three civilian operators for the admiralty direction
finding station. So we ordered reliefs for all our Chinese and Malays
and made lists of stores needed.

As the old Chinese quarters had been burned in March 1942 when the
Japs bombarded Direction Island, it was decided to use the old Lower
Quarters, now empty, for the additional Chinese expected and that the
staff should use the long mess for meals.

We also renovated NOIC's old officers' quarters for the admiralty
men. Singapore advised that they had booked me on the Dutch liner
Oranji leaving there in the middle of November for the UK. So I cabled
Sylvia that I expected to get to England early in December. She had left
Cape Town for a trip to Bloemfontein to visit friends and then gone on
to Durban. There was difficulty in getting passages from South Africa

to England but with the help of a friend in the Union Castle Steamship Coy's office, she got one leaving Cape Town on 17th October in the *Caernarvon Castle*, 20,000 tons. Arrangements were made for Singapore to send us some Straits currency so that we had some money in our pockets on arrival.

Our Chinese servants and Malays were now to return to Singapore; a completely new lot had been engaged to arrive in *The Islander*. Somerville was also to be relieved, so I consulted Mrs Ross and she said the pre-war rules should be introduced. So a leaflet in Chinese was prepared, written by our cook, a copy of which would be given to the new ones so they knew what the rules were.

Head Office told us to pay Wee Kee Lin and the other four Chinese who had been there since 1942 a special bonus and there was one for our Malays.

There was plenty to do in preparation for the ship's visit; as she only stayed about a day or so, the manager had to write a handing over report for his relief. I suggested to the mess that when I got to London I should get a modern radiogram and some new records to replace our old wind-up one, and try and get the company to pay for at least part of it. Before the Jap war the mess had been financed by every newcomer paying in £20 which formed a floating fund to buy stores. Four months' supply was necessary as there were only three ships a year. The company paid for an extra emergency stock covering another couple of months. On a man's departure his money was refunded.

The Islander went to Christmas Island, then came on to us and arrived at dawn on 30th October. We went out in the launch and gave them the chart and she came into the lagoon to anchor. We took all our reliefs ashore at once, as there was a lot to do. My relief was Hyde, an Australian whom I had relieved in Penang in 1938. There were two large mailbags from Singapore post office with letters and parcels to be checked and signed for. These included two or three letters addressed to "The Postmaster, Cocos", and asking for Cocos Island stamps. I answered that there were no such things. Hyde had served at Cocos before—but a lot had happened since then so it was a busy day and I only got finished about 8 p.m. when I felt quite exhausted. As Sylvia was due at Southampton the following morning, I sent a cable to her and went to bed.

Next morning I formally handed over and then finished my packing. *The Islander* sailed at 4 p.m.; most of the staff came out in the launch to say goodbye, and the Australians sang the Hawaiian farewell song as we steamed off.

We arrived at Christmas Island, a distance of 350 miles north east of Cocos, two days later and tied up at the Phosphate company's jetty. This island had been occupied by the Japs who tried to utilise the phosphate but they pointed out the remains of a sunken Jap cargo ship near the jetty which had been torpedoed by a British submarine while loading. The island is quite different to Cocos being roughly circular but no lagoon, and the interior gradually rising to a low hill. Near the jetty was a factory where the phosphate rock is crushed and bungalows for the staff. Most of the island is a mass of this useful fertiliser discovered by Captain Murray, who was a contemporary of the earlier Clunies-Rosses and Murray had given them a share in the business which was very profitable. I heard later that young John Clunies Ross had sold his share for about three quarters of a million pounds when the company was bought out by the Australian Phosphate Commission.

After a week there I began to think I should miss my ship to England and tackled Captain Stanton, but he said he would get me to Singapore in time. The island had thousands of land crabs, many red in colour and some over a foot long. They lived in holes in the hillsides and amongst the undergrowth, and as you walked by, retreated into their holes and then came out behind you, a rather horrid sight. Once a year the crabs became possessed of an urge to rush down to the sea, coming across roads and the company's railway lines regardless of how many get crushed and killed, like lemmings.

We stayed eight days and then left for Singapore. We passed through the Sunda Straits between Sumatra and Java in the morning and had a good view of Krakatoa, the island volcano which erupted violently in 1883 causing a tidal wave which drowned about 30,000 Javanese. One could see no sign of it being a volcano as it was clothed from head to foot in tropical vegetation.

We reached Singapore on 14th November and were met by several of our men including Harry Moss. At the office I met the new divisional manager, G. T. Edwards, and was told that a Commander Hudson, RN wanted me to call at his office. They had booked me in at the Seaview Hotel, near the Swimming Club, about four miles from the town as all the other hotels were full. Commander Hudson wanted some information about Cocos for naval intelligence records, and a visit had to be paid to the Netherlands Line office for my ticket.

Our assistant manager, E. Coates, kindly gave me lunch at the Adelphi Hotel where Sylvia and I had stayed for nearly a month in 1941. I heard she had arrived in England on 2nd November and gone to stay with my parents in Northumberland. I went to Thomas Cook's office in Raffles Hotel and asked them to book me a room in an hotel in London on my arrival. The Sea View Hotel was reached about 5 p.m. and there was Croger who was sharing a room with me.

Next day I went to the embarkation point near Clifford Pier and found a wartime infantry landing craft in which the passengers were to go out to the liner *Oranji* anchored in the harbour. The landing craft gradually filled up with a hundred or more passengers, men, women and children.

On board *Oranji* I was met by G. F. (Bacchus) Hollands whom I had known in Gib years before. He said, "I have arranged for you to be in my cabin with Leach. The ship is very full and we three have to share a two-berth cabin but it is air conditioned." W. J. Leach, a London station man had passed through Accra when we were there in 1943. There were two bunks and a settee and though it was a bit crowded we got on well together, as both Bacchus and Leach were cheerful souls. The former had come in the ship from Batavia (Djakarta). There were about 2,000 passengers in *Oranji*. She was a fine motor ship of 20,000 tons, 25 knots, completed in 1938 and used as a hospital ship throughout the war. These large Dutch liners built for the Far East service normally carried about 800 passengers, only a quarter of which were first class as many of the Dutch travelled second class. They had two sittings for lunch and dinner in the first class and one changed daily from the early to the late sitting. They did not serve early morning tea but one could put on a dressing gown at 7 a.m. and go up to the lounge and get a cup of coffee. The first class lounge was a large handsome room with a central circular floor for dancing, and tables and a varandah on both sides. It was marvellously lit at night by coloured fluorescent lamps concealed in the ceiling, which shed a soft but good light for reading.

As well as Hollands and Leach there was Tresidder, who was retiring as manager of Singapore and two young operators. The ship called at Colombo and I went ashore and telephoned Whiteside, our manager, and invited him and his wife for dinner on board as guest of the six of us. They came and we had a jolly evening as we had all been at Colombo at one time or another.

Before leaving Singapore I had laid in a stock of cigarettes for the voyage and bought some Dutch currency notes. The former were put in a trunk marked "wanted on the voyage" but on going to the baggage room, I found it had been put in the hold. I was not the only one and many passengers said their winter clothes had been put there. The captain refused to open the hold so we could not do anything about it. I had bought my Dutch guilders at about 12 to the £ sterling and was startled to learn from one of the crew that at Port Said they could be bought at 20 to the £. So after running out, I borrowed some until we got there and then bought some with my sterling travellers cheques.

When we got to Suez the reason for the captain's reluctance to open the hold became clear. We had on board, mostly in the second class over 1,000 Dutch who had been prisoners of the Japs and had no warm clothes at all. We anchored on the south west extremity of the bay opposite a camp with long sheds built near the shore. Two landing craft came off to the ship and all those with no winter clothes were invited to go ashore and get some. When they returned each had a white kit bag, full up and we learned that a modest outfit of one suit, two shirts, underwear, pyjamas, socks, etc., with appropriate items for the ladies, had been issued to everyone from huge stocks of all sizes in the sheds and no charge was made for them at all. It was organised by the allies for those who had been in prison camps in the Far East—a good piece of work.

The *Oranji* arrived at Southampton in the afternoon of 3rd December and Cook's representative who rejoiced in the name of Christopher Wren, a pleasant man, told me a room was booked for me in London, and their man would meet me at Waterloo.

Next morning I reported at head office. In the last six months the Labour government had passed a bill to nationalise the company by compulsory purchase of all the shares by the Treasury, operative on 1st January, 1947. Edmonds, the staff manager, was retiring on that date and had already gone on terminal leave, so I saw Mockett who was taking over from him. I spent two days there seeing various departments. When talking to Mr Vallancy, the assistant secretary, I showed him a map of Cocos Island about 30 inches square and pressed on him the request for the company to pay for the radiogram and records to be ordered for Cocos. He said, "I had no idea it was such a lonely sort of place and will do my best to get them a radiogram." In the end we got them a very good (RGD) one but as direct current ones were not then obtainable, a small motor generator was supplied. Later I chose about three dozen records at the HMV shop in Oxford Street; the whole lot was paid for by head office and shipped to Singapore for sending on by *The Islander* on her next visit.

I left London by train for Newcastle early on 6th December and reached Warkworth at 5 p.m. to be met by Sylvia and taken to the Sun Hotel to which she had moved a couple of days earlier. I went to see my parents whom I had not seen since going to Penang before the war in 1938.

CHAPTER SEVENTEEN

West African Tour—Accra, Freetown and Lagos

We had a cold and wintry leave in England. The first thing was to get ration books at Alnwick though we were lucky as there seemed to be few shortages at the Sun Hotel at Warkworth.

While in South Africa during the war we arranged for food parcels to be sent to my parents and sent some to our bank manager in Hampstead. Later when Stubbs returned to Australia from Cocos, it was arranged with him to send more food parcels to them from there.

There was snow, ice and frosty weather from 13th December onwards. We were lucky that, having been mostly in hot countries during the war, we still had the warm tweed clothing which had been bought in Gibraltar in 1938 and did not need to rely on our clothing rations.

On 20th December head office told me of my appointment to Accra in the Gold Coast as manager from 1st April.

We had our Christmas dinner with my parents, and there was a dance in the hotel on Boxing Day.

At the end of January we went by train to Scotland to see Colonel and Mrs Fielding whom we had known in Penang when he was adjutant of the Volunteers. They were now at Comrie in Perthshire where he was OC of a prisoner of war camp for Germans who had not yet been repatriated. On 10th February we went to Edinburgh by train and stayed for four days during which we saw most of the sights; Holyrood Palace, the castle, Princes Street, etc. We then returned to Warkworth just in time for a severe blizzard which cut it off almost completely with roads full of snow six feet deep.

Just after this my brother, Miles and his wife, Sybil, arrived and stayed at the Sun Hotel. When India was declared independent in 1945 he had retired from the Indian Army after twenty-five years service.

At the end of March we went to London and I spent a couple of days in head office where I met the new managing director, Mr John Innes. On taking over Cable & Wireless Ltd, on 1st January, the Treasury had appointed their own directors. There were five of them: Sir Stanley Angwin, the chairman, was a retired chief engineer of the Post Office; Mr Innes had also been an assistant chief engineer there, but during the war had served with the Ministry of Fuel & Power; Major General Sir Leslie Nicholls who had been Eisenhower's chief signal officer in Algiers and later in Europe; the other two were part time: Mr Gallie, a member of the Trade Union Council; and Mr Black, an accountant, both Scotsmen. The only ones I met were Mr Innes and General Nicholls who later succeeded the former as managing director.

I learned in the engineer-in-chief's department that a radio-telephone service would soon start from my new station, Accra to London, so I asked them to arrange for me to visit the GPO overseas telephone exchange and later went to St Martin's le Grand and Faraday House.

Mockett, now staff manager, told me I was booked to sail on the troopship *Almanzora* from Southampton about 26th April, but they could not get a passage for Sylvia and she would have to wait for another ship later. Sylvia wrote to Mrs Joy, the colonel's wife whom we had known in Malaya whose home was in Bournemouth, and it was arranged she should stay at an hotel near Mrs Joy until she could come to Accra to join me.

We visited the large HMV shop in Oxford Street to choose the gramophone records for Cocos. I sent them a list to choose from by airmail to Mr Smith, our manager in Perth, Australia, who passed it to them on the cable, and their choice was ordered by the stores department in head office. Years later I wrote and told Roy Plomley about this with the list of the records. He must have contacted our head office, as soon after he did a *Desert Island Discs* programme by radio-telephone with Ascension Island. A. R. Harrison, now manager, introduced his staff to Roy and each chose a record and it was broadcast by the BBC.

Dan Griffin arrived in London from Cocos having paid his own fare as normally he would have gone to Australia. When in Cocos he had asked me to recommend him to head office for an engineering course at the London Training School, now housed on the top floor of the new Electra House on the Victoria Embankment, but his application was turned down. He now renewed it in person and came to see us and we had a party with him and Mary Cooper, the ex-naval nursing sister, whom we had known in Malta and Gibraltar.

We went to one or two theatres and saw *The Winslow Boy* and Noel Coward himself in his play *Present Laughter*. On 24th April Sylvia left by train for Bournemouth and the following afternoon I caught the boat train for Southampton to join the *Almanzora* and she sailed the next morning.

She was a Royal Mail Lines ship of 20,000 tons completed in 1914 at the beginning of World War I. Between the wars she ran between the UK and South America but was now old having been a troopship in the second war. I found myself in a two-berth cabin with J. C. P. Wells, aged twenty-six whom I had not met before as he had only worked in London cable station but was now posted to Lagos.

I had learnt that D. (Bertie) Banks who had been assistant manager in Penang and a prisoner of war of the Japs, was now manager in Freetown, Sierra Leone, and wanted to see him, so asked the purser whether we would be allowed ashore there. He was rather off-hand and said he had no idea, so next day when I saw the captain going to his cabin after the noon sights ritual on the bridge, I followed him and asked if I could speak to him. Captain Carr said: "Yes, of course, come

Manager's New House, Dodowah Road, Accra.

in and have a pink gin." He told me he had met many of our men in the Western Telegraph Co travelling to and from South America and knew all about us. He said there would be no difficulty about going ashore at Freetown. To return his hospitality I asked him to join Wells and I one evening for drinks in the lounge before dinner.

The ship's wireless officer sent a note to Banks from me via the company's Freetown radio station, and a naval officer disembarking gave me a lift in his launch. Bertie Banks, looking a bit thin, welcomed me and took me and Verral, his No. 2, for lunch at his bungalow at Hill Station. He was busy having it re-decorated and seemed cheerful enough after his ordeal during the war. He was in a ship in 1942 with many of our men (among them the divisional manager, Singapore) which was sunk by the Japs, and the survivors imprisoned. Nineteen of our men died, including the divisional manager. His wife had not accompanied him to Freetown.

The *Almanzora* sailed in the evening and reached Takoradi on 8th May where I was met by J. W. Millest and his wife who had motored from Accra.

Next day I started to take over from Millest. A. T. Wood was assistant manager. He had done two consecutive tours there, first arriving just after our departure in 1944. A red haired Irishman, J. (Ginger) Hayden and C. V. Lawson were the other members of the staff. Lawson was completing a new wireless station at Abubuasi, about eight miles outside Accra, where there was a bungalow which had been recently built. A. R. Harrison had installed a wireless station in the cable office in 1943. After 1945 the company had acquired this new site at Abubuasi and all the wireless equipment including the aerial towers had been moved there and additional transmitters, receivers, power plant, etc. installed. It was connected to the cable office by underground landlines laid for us by the post office. The new station was working to London as before, but some of the other equipment intended for telephony and facsimile had not yet been completed.

On the departure of the Millests a week later, I took over the flat at the west end of the office which Sylvia and I had occupied during the war. Wood had a motor bike which he kindly lent me while I was at the hotel but a car was needed so I bought a new Ford Prefect.

Sylvia wrote to tell me she had sorted our household effects which had been sent from South Africa to a store in Southampton, selling what we did not need, and that head office had booked her passage, also in the *Almanzora*, sailing early in June. So I wrote to Captain Carr and told him my wife was coming out in his ship and asked him to look after her.

I got on well with Wood. He was a capable man and very keen on his work. His wife and daughter were in England. He asked me if he could go out now and then to Abubuasi to learn from Lawson as much as possible about the running of the wireless station and said frankly that Millest had not allowed this. I told him he could go provided he promised not to neglect his work in the office, and this arrangement proved satisfactory.

Sylvia sailed on the *Almanzora* on 11th June and was given a place at the captain's table. She met Mrs John Rutter and small son on board, en route to join her husband who was assistant manager at Lagos. The ship arrived at Takoradi on the afternoon of 23rd June.

Mrs Wynne Joy, near whose home in Bournemouth Sylvia had been staying, had a brother who was Collector of Customs at Takoradi. He offered to put us up for a night or so, so I motored there the day before and we stayed one night with Johnson after Sylvia's arrival, driving back to Accra the next day.

So here we were, back in the same flat we had occupied in 1942/44. A new bungalow was being built for the manager on a large plot of land in the Dodowah Road on the Ridge about two miles away. Various materials for this bungalow got lost or mislaid en route from the UK and the construction was held up for months. It was never finished while we were there, but photos reached us after we had left.

Our friend Kesby who had been on Lord Swinton's staff in Achimota, near Accra, during the war, was back here running what was known as Wagon (from its telegraphic address). This was the West African Governor's Conference to co-ordinate their policies in peacetime, following Lord Swinton's similar work during the war. Kesby's wife, Doris, was now with him. We had not met her before, but became great friends and have foregathered with them many times since we retired.

In our office the working arrangements were the same as when we had left, that is a high speed morse wireless circuit to London, and the cables to Sierra Leone and Nigeria. But we now closed down at 9 p.m. opening the next morning at 8 a.m., so there was no night duty. But the cable relays were connected at night to a bell in the mess, so that Freetown or Lagos could call us in an emergency and we could raise them in the same way.

I learned that there had been two cases recently when cash from the counter had been stolen—not very large amounts, about ten or twenty pounds each time. No one had been suspected or caught. I decided that this was not satisfactory and instructed Mr Roberts, the chief counter clerk, to bring all the cash in hand, except £5 change, to me at noon and again at 4 p.m. when it was put into my safe instead of remaining overnight in the counter safe. No stealing occurred during my time there.

My previous experience as a manager having only been at Cocos where there were no banks or cash, I now came into contact with our local bank, the British Bank of West Africa, whose office was on the other side of the road from us. A new company manager is introduced by the man he is relieving but authority for him to sign cheques was notified from our head office through the bank's head office in London. The company had a few simple rules about accounts to keep a check on their managers. All money received had to be paid into the bank and all payments made either by cheque or from the petty cash which was re-imbursed by cheque each month. The bank sent a copy of the bank statements direct to our head office. The manager was only allowed to draw so much each month from the company's account, this being fixed by head office and controlled by the local bank manager. If the manager needed more in any month, he telegraphed to our HO who advised the bank through their HO.

In small stations the manager did the accounts, occasionally with assistance from a local clerk. I trained a clerk here and in Lagos to do most of the paper work. In larger branches there was an accountant or accounts clerk, European in big places, otherwise local staff. To keep a check on him, the rule was that he had to be sent on three weeks' or a month's leave annually and the work done by a senior member of the European staff.

I had more than once been annoyed by actions of some managers when I was a junior, and I determined that if I ever became a manager I would try to avoid such things. The company's rules said that the relations between them and the occupants of staff houses were to be those of landlord and tenant. This implied that if the manager wished to inspect a house, he should arrange it beforehand at a convenient time. And there were smaller matters, such as posting the promotions of junior foreign staff on the office notice board, showing that their salaries were in some cases lower than those of local staff under them. Promotions and matters affecting salaries should be notified to him privately by letter.

Experience showed that the essence of good management is foresight and in management of men to be tactful and, not only fair, but seen to be fair. One of the African operators called Quarshie was selected to be my clerk in Accra. As there was no separate office available, he worked at a large table in my office. I decided there was far too much secrecy about how management worked. Of course, some matters have to be confidential, but it is much better if the staff understand why things are done. So I rarely had to send Quarshie to another room when discussing staff matters with the assistant manager and others, and he was thus able to hear, and no doubt tell others, that decisions were only made after careful consideration, thus making fair treatment to be seen to be done.

I suggested to head office a start should be made to train Africans in electrical work. Up to now they had only been trained as operators and in clerical work. It was proposed that a school for mechanics should be established at Freetown to which two or three young Africans could be sent from Accra, Lagos and perhaps Bathurst in the Gambia. This was eventually done, I believe. I warned my senior African staff that this innovation could not affect them but would be open to young men only, perhaps their sons, and they accepted this.

As already related, we could bathe from our own beach where the cables landed, and regularly did so while we were in Accra. Early in July we went to a garden party given by the governor and his wife, Sir Alan and Lady Burns, at Christianborg Castle about two miles east of us along the coast.

A young assistant engineer, Preece, arrived and we took him by car to Aburi, in the low hills to the north, to meet Miss Sutherland and her staff of the Scottish Mission there. We had two minor earth tremors towards the end of July but no damage was done. Our houseboys did not like them and bolted to the open air. We were never in a really severe earthquake but there is no doubt they are very frightening as I learned later in Manila when experiencing a bad shake at the top of a six storey building.

Lawson was transferred to Barbados and was relieved by Byrne. Head office told me to send Byrne to Freetown to advise regarding the site of the proposed wireless station there, and he left by air. Shortly

*Messengers: Montol, Sam and
Commodore.*

afterwards we had a letter from our old friend Sandham, the ship's
wireless operator whom we had known in Malaya, telling us he was
coming to Takoradi as chief operator of the mailship. Byrne was
booked to return on the same vessel, so Sylvia and I drove to Takoradi
to see Tom Sandham and bring Byrne back. It made a week-end
holiday for us and we found Sandham as cheery as ever. Some months
later he came out again and his ship called at Accra and we put him up
on shore for a few days and took him to Abubuasi to see the wireless
station.

Mrs Byrne arrived and went to live with him at the bungalow at the
wireless station. We had an office telephone to them on one of the spare
landlines but it was not connected to the public system. So I arranged
for the post office to install a telephone at Abubuasi which was
connected to our office switchboard as an extension. So through the
switchboard, they could phone anyone in Accra.

Byrne had a couple of African operators at Abubuasi to train them to
do watchkeeping on the wireless transmitters and receivers. It was what

is know as "common site" working, with the transmitters and receivers each in a separate building connected by a covered way, with an emergency diesel engine. The transmitter aerial towers were close by, but the receiving aerials on masts were about 1,000 yards away with underground feeder cables to the receiver room.

We met the Bishop of Accra, John Aglionby, who lived next door to us on the west side in a large compound with his church and bungalow. He was an Irishman, a bachelor, and did not mix very much with the European community but devoted most of his time to his African flock. He was a tall, rather gaunt man, but very genial.

Mockett at head office sent a circular letter to managers saying the company would be prepared to buy suitable houses for married staff if available, as he knew that at many places there were not enough, and this was a major hardship for married men. In Accra Hobson and his wife had no house when I arrived, and she had at once asked me if there was any chance of getting one. They got a house temporarily but it was not a satisfactory situation.

We met a man who worked for John Holt & Co and he told us they were buying a house on the Ridge. Soon after he said that John Holt had backed out of the sale; we went to see it and I interviewed the builder. It had only just been finished and the garden was not yet fenced. He quoted me the price so I wrote to head office who at once approved the purchase.

In October we got authority to buy carpets and curtain materials for the new manager's bungalow in Dodowah Road. We chose what was needed at the United Africa Coy's shop called Kingsway and the manager agreed to store it until the house was ready.

Arthur Wood went on leave and his relief, David Cox, arrived a fortnight later. When he got home Wood wrote me a nice letter, saying he had enjoyed serving under me, and hoped we should meet again. I was able later in some sort to repay this kind thought.

Colonel Clapp, the chief signal officer at GHQ invited me and my senior staff to a demonstration of the army's signal organisation. Cox and Byrne came with me, and General Irwin and his staff officers were there. Col Clapp gave a short talk and then showed us their signal office except the cipher room which could not be shown to civilians. General Irwin told me that Field Marshal Montgomery was to visit them shortly as he was now chief of the Imperial General Staff.

During his visit an evening military tattoo was staged on the race course and everybody went to see it—and Monty. It was very well done and included a pageant depicting St George slaying the dragon, a splendid one which spat flames and smoke. Monty arrived before the start, driving down the race course in a car which stopped in front of the governor's box. At the finish the car came back to pick him up. He got in and then realised the spectators beyond the governor's box had not been able to see him closely, so he got out on the other side and walked up the course in front of them, waving to loud applause—a typical bit of "Montyism" but quite appropriate as he was really part of the show, and we all wanted to see the great man.

As she had done during the war Sylvia kept open house for anyone who wished to come and have morning tea with us, and we gave small dinner parties and invited the men in the mess and other friends. Our new house in Osu Avenue was nearly ready and head office authorised the purchase of furniture, etc. for it.

It was a nice house with dining room and sitting room down below, and upstairs two bedrooms with balconies overlooking a large garden. One had a beautiful sunken bath and toilet en suite and the other a shower and toilet. Near the house and overlooking the garden was a summerhouse with porch where one could sit out for teas or drinks in the evening. I let Mrs Hobson choose most of the furnishings, and they made a nice home of it, and started getting the garden laid out.

We took regular exercise in the form of walking or cycling after tea, and also bathed a lot from our beach. There was quite fair surfing which is fun and good exercise.

Sir Gerald Creasy, Kesby's boss at Wagon had been appointed as the new governor of the Gold Coast and arrived in January. We went to see the swearing in ceremony in the Legislative Assembly building. The chief justice made a very witty and amusing speech of welcome before the ceremony which helped to enliven the solemnity of the occasion.

Colonel Clapp had gone on transfer and was relieved by Colonel Mac-Ostrich who came to dinner with us. He said he had been in Malaya when the Japs arrived, and had been one of those sent to work on the infamous Siam Railway.

Since the war ended there had been an acute shortage of manufactured goods such as clothing, cotton goods, canned food, etc. The price of raw cocoa, the chief export of the Gold Coast had risen enormously. To try and prevent inflation and wastage, the government set up a cocoa marketing board which bought from the growers all the cocoa at a fixed price, and sold it on the world market at a considerable profit. This was put into a fund for a rainy day and also to finance a campaign to eradicate a disease of the trees called swollen shoot. Nevertheless, prices of goods were rising and there was considerable discontent, mainly in the towns. In Accra this was accentuated by the demobilisation of thousands of African ex-servicemen many of whom had served in Burmah during the war, and were reluctant to return to their villages but could not get jobs.

In January there was a small riot when a mob looted the Kingsway shop of the United Africa Co. This was easily controlled by the police, African rank and file with British officers. However, some Africans including Kwame Nkrumah, Dr Danquah (a barrister), and others had started an agitation for self government.

I went to see the post master general and enquired what the local law was in case the government had to introduce censorship. Later he sent me a copy of the ordinance dealing with this.

At the end of February arrangements were made for a rally of African ex-servicemen on a Saturday afternoon on the old cricket ground about a quarter of a mile east of our office, followed by a march around the town. The organisers announced they wished to march to Christianborg Castle to present a petition to the governor about lack of employment. The governor refused and said they could send a deputation to the secretariat building which would be received by a senior official. This was not in accordance with African custom. The police warned that the march must keep strictly to an agreed route and not go to the castle.

On the previous Thursday, O'Neill, a Canadian newspaper man, called on us and said he thought there would be trouble on Saturday. We had been invited out to dinner so I told Sylvia to be prepared to stay at home.

I did not personally see what happened on the Saturday afternoon but heard clear accounts later. The driver of our station wagon belonging to the wireless station was an African ex-serviceman—a quiet, reliable man and he told me that he went to the rally and that the leaders announced when it was over they would now march to the castle to see the governor *who had invited them to do so*. About a quarter mile short of it they were stopped by a police patrol with a European superintendent. Our driver did not see exactly what happened as he was in the rear, but other accounts agreed that the large mob fanned out on either side and violently stoned the police. The latter fired warning shots overhead and when this had no effect, the superintendent fired about five shots into the crowd and killed one or two men. The mob then fled back towards the town.

We saw the crowd streaming past the office about 4 p.m. and went out to see what was happening. After hearing there had been shooting I told our staff to come inside and stay there. O'Neill telephoned us and asked if we could take press messages on the phone which we did, using headphones and a typewriter rigged up in the counter. He was the only European newspaper man in Accra and he drove round all the evening, telephoning in his reports, so that we had a picture of what was happening outside. Smoke began to rise from the town as the mob started looting shops and warehouses. A truck load of police came past but it was clear they had lost control and eventually had to withdraw.

I telephoned the castle and asked if they wished us to stay open all night. They said, "Yes, please, remain open." So we advised London, Sierra Leone and Lagos. It was decided to send all the African staff home at 9 p.m. The European staff from the mess would have one man on duty all night to handle government messages to and from the castle by telephone. The latter had already sent several, to the Colonial Office in London and also to Lagos and Freetown.

Just before we closed the counter at 9 p.m. on looking through the traffic, I saw one or two messages from local African correspondents to London national newspapers which contained libellous lies about the governor. I decided that this was a special situation in which he should be told, so I rang the castle and said to a secretary that libellous telegrams were being sent. In a few minutes the governor himself came on the line and I told him about it. The main lie was that the ex-servicemen had gone to the castle *at the governor's request* and had then been fired on. I told him of my recent talk to the post master general who had informed me that the governor could legally set up a censorship of cablegrams by special warrant, issued to me. I said that we had a European supervisor on duty all the time and if he wished would arrange for any doubtful messages to be referred to the castle by phone before despatch, but he must promise to send me the warrant authorising this. He said he would have to consult the attorney general, but agreed to my suggestion and would confirm it later. We therefore commenced this limited form of censorship forthwith.

About 11 p.m. one or two rifle shots were heard coming from the bishop's compound next to us, so one of our servants climbed the fence to see if he was all right. Soon afterwards he walked into our compound and said he was quite safe. During the following day, Sunday, he walked about the town and was the only European who could do so with impunity. The Africans regarded his *juju*, i.e., magic, as so powerful that no one would dare to molest him.

"Ginger" Hayden was listed for night duty and I visited him in the office before going to bed about 1 a.m. and found him armed with a large hammer in case of accidents.

Soon after 3 a.m. we were awakened by a noise and found that it was a detachment of troops sent to guard us; there were twenty or so African soldiers with an officer and two NCOs, the last three Europeans. They were from the school of infantry, at Teshi, a few miles east of Accra. We had two empty rooms on the ground floor which had held wireless equipment during the war, so we put them in there. They posted sentries at our two road entrances, and another to guard the cable landing at the rear of the buildings. Sylvia made sandwiches for the Europeans and our messengers gave food for the Africans as they had none with them. After settling them in, we managed to get a couple of hours more sleep. Smoke was still rising from parts of the town and there were noises.

Next morning, Sunday, the counter was very busy. Being on the very edge of the town people could reach us in cars without going into the main streets which were still without police, and many Europeans came to send cablegrams home. It was decided to open the counter again at 2 p.m. instead of 4 p.m., normal on Sundays.

As I was leaving my office to go upstairs for lunch six Africans who had found the counter closed, appeared and asked if they could file some long messages. I took them into my office and explained that it would take time to count and charge them, but I would take them and their offer of £10 on account. Among them was Kwami Nkrumah and Dr Danquah, the barrister.

Just after they had gone, a Mr Kerr from the government secretariat arrived with my censorship warrant signed by the governor. After putting it in the safe, I showed him the messages that Kwami Nkrumah had left with me. They were to the United Nations and various left-wing politicians in England and said the senders wished to take over the government as the governor had lost control. Kerr hurried back with copies to the castle. The castle telephoned and told us to send the

Accra staff, May 1948.

messages on. It was known by the government that these leaders had
stirred up the riots and next day Kwami Nkrumah and four others were
arrested under the war time 18B law, and sent to detention in the
northern provinces.

During the whole of Sunday the rioters looted the town and burned
several shops. We saw fights among Africans over loot and later heard
that several had been killed.

On Monday, at my request, the governor sent two officers from the
secretariat to do the censorship work. A force of Nigerian troops which
had been flown in, cleared the town of rioters and restored order. They
made house to house searches and recovered a lot of loot which was
taken to the airport and laid out in a large hanger. A curfew from dusk
to dawn was proclaimed and troops patrolled the streets.

No Europeans were hurt, but a senior official who was going by car
on Saturday afternoon to see his wife in the Gold Coast hospital was
attacked and only saved by an African friend who hid him. Hobson had
to hide in a car to get home to his new house, and could not get in for
duty till the Monday. None of us went into the town for three or four
days. Later we went to the broadcasting station on the ridge to get food
as the town shops were unusable, many being burned out. Rations
organised by the United Africa Co were obtainable at the station.

The castle had instructed me not to reveal that there was a cable
censorship. Head office had been informed by coded telegrams of all

that was going on. Due to a press telegram from O'Neill missing publication deadline one evening, he became suspicious and asked me if messages were being censored. I referred him to the castle but he said they would not tell him and I refused to say anything.

A secretary at the castle told me by telephone that they had advised the Secretary of State that telegrams were subject to delays, implying that this was due to us. Head office was informed and told that we were not causing any delays.

Our African staff behaved very well throughout the troubles, and there were no cases of absenteeism though conditions were difficult for them especially during the curfew. Head office sent them a message of commendation which some ignorant person put into code, so it had to be paraphrased before publication to avoid compromising the code.

Gradually things got back to normal and a Commission of Enquiry was appointed to investigate and report on the disturbances. As some of the furnishings bought for the new manager's house had been left with the Kingsway store and looted, we went to the airport to see if any of them were there but only found strips of carpet which had been cut up by the thieves. Fortunately they were covered by the store's insurance.

On 25th March head office instructed me to hand over to Byrne and proceed at once to Freetown to relieve D. (Bertie) Banks. I took Byrne to call on Mr Robert Scott, the Colonial Secretary, and he thanked us for our assistance during the riots. The Commission was still sitting when we left. We heard that the police superintendent who fired on the mob was cleared of blame.

Sylvia started packing up and we were given farewell parties by the bishop and two of the army messes at Achimota as well as by our own mess. Our African staff wanted a group photograph taken and sent me a copy.

We left for Takoradi in the station wagon from Abubuasi. Thirty-two miles out it broke down and neither the driver nor I could restart it. It was the ignition coil which had packed up. We waited at an African house, the inmates of whom were most kind and provided us with chairs under the trees. Then we hailed a passing light truck, nearly empty and the driver said he could take us to Swedru, the next town where he had to turn off north. I telephoned Accra to send a breakdown truck for the station wagon and we started bargaining with taxi drivers to take us to Takoradi. But when the truck driver heard what they wanted for the trip, he said he would take us for less (£12), in spite of his obligation to go elsewhere. So we continued in the truck, Sylvia and I sitting next to the driver and his companion riding in the back with our luggage.

Next day we sailed on the new Elder Dempster passenger ship *Accra* of 11,600 tons. She was a good vessel but the deck space was not so extensive as on some of their pre-war liners.

We arrived at Freetown and were met by Banks. A. W. Brown with whom I had been friendly at the Hampstead School in 1928/29 was assistant manager. The office had the bachelors' mess over it and overlooked the river estuary with the cable tanks below on the water front. Between were two wireless towers for the coast station for ship communications.

Our efficient African chief clerk, Mr Fraser, met us at the pier and dealt with the Customs over our baggage saving us much trouble.

We found the Hill Station bungalow in poor condition, the paintwork being dirty in several of the rooms. It had a large square lounge with nine windows. Being built on a sloping hillside, one entered by going up covered steps about twelve feet high, but the rear was level with the ground. There were several rooms at the back which were not used, having been originally intended as a week-end house for the staff from the mess. So we set to work to renovate it, had several rooms painted, and Sylvia made eighteen new curtains and got it into good order.

Besides Brown, there were three assistant engineers, C. A. Freeman, W. M. Wright and P. A. Wolfe. The first two had their wives there. The Freemans had a rented house at a place called King Tom, and the Wrights lived in a not very good house about a mile from the office. He had a small sports car. There were about twenty African staff and some messengers including two or three girls who worked in the abstracts. Freetown, as its name implies, had been largely populated by repatriated slaves.

Freetown was a second Grade station, a relic of being the main branch of the old African Direct Telegraph Company, so I drew the minimum salary of that grade. A few days after we arrived a letter came from head office telling me that we were to go on leave on Bank's return; but hardly had I got it, than there was a service telegram cancelling this letter and saying I was to go to Lagos to relieve R. R. Byrant.

Sylvia had learnt from Mrs Brown that Banks had done little to entertain the staff, so she asked the whole lot to dinner one night and it proved a successful evening as everybody seemed to get on well together. We subsequently were entertained by them and had other parties at our house.

Owing to our distance from the office I worked there from 8 a.m. to 2 p.m. and did not go in the afternoon. One was always in touch by telephone in case anything important turned up. An extra copy of the company's code book was kept at Hill Station so that I could read coded service messages.

Our garden needed attention and Sylvia got it in good order. Some mealies were planted as we liked "corn on the cob". Soon after they were ripe, Sylvia heard a fearful noise and on going out was just in time to see a herd of monkeys making off with most of the cobs. Things grew very quickly. Our garage door needed a "door-stop" so a piece of tree stump about two inches in diameter was sharpened and driven in the ground. By the time we left it had sprouted and looked like becoming a tree.

We soon met Mr and Mrs J. Gibson. He had been in the Eastern Telegraph Co in Malta in 1919 when I was in *Levant II* but had been axed and was assistant director of supplies in the government. His wife came from Mauritius and was charming. The had a house about half a mile from us on the next hillock.

I found that we were not complying with a Labour Ordinance which obliged employers to have a fixed percentage of ex-servicemen on their staffs unless they had a dispensation. So I went to see Mr Bell, the Labour Commissioner, and after explaining that our trained staff had been exempted from military service, obtained this dispensation. We had two or three men who had served in the army including Wright who had taken part in the ill-starred Norwegian expedition in 1940.

At the end of May a severe tornado came over Freetown and across Hill Station about 2 a.m. in the morning. Our head boy, John, appeared about 7 a.m. and said, "No morning tea." Sylvia went to the kitchen and found a tree had fallen onto it, bringing the roof down. We had heard the noise of the storm during the night but did not realise its severity. Later we learnt that it had crossed the hillock where the Gibsons lived and taken off the roof of their house. Large sheets of galvanised iron roofing were littered all around. The storm then went down the hill to Lumley Beach and cut the tops off a row of casuarina trees near the Golf Club as neatly as if it had been done with a scythe.

At the end of July a French cableship, the *Alsace,* arrived after doing

Trees blown down by a tornado in May 1948, Sierre Leone.

a repair for us. We had Captain Fanau and the chief cable engineer, Monsieur Mangon and the chief engineer to lunch, and Mrs Gibson who spoke fluent French came to help entertain them. Sylvia and I had lunch on board the ship.

In August the English staff gave us a farewell party and Mrs (Topsy) Freeman exercised her talents in making some drawings of real and apocryphal African scenes including one of me as an African chief complete with top hat, with which to decorate the dinner table.

Banks and his wife arrived in the mailboat *Accra* and as there was no need to overlap, we left for Lagos on the same ship.

We got to Lagos on the 18th August to be met by Bryant at the Apapa wharf on the far side of the harbour.

Besides him the foreign service staff consisted of John Rutter with wife and small boy, S. C. Griffin, J. C. P. Wells, L. L. F. Harding and later H. S. Shaw who was an ex-Indo-European Telegraph Co's man. When this company which had landlines across Europe and through Persia to India packed up after the war, our company had taken on some of their staff. There was an African staff of about twenty-five men, and some messengers.

The office and quarters which had been built in 1922 (just as I was leaving the cableship *Transmitter* there) was on the Marina, a long avenue facing the harbour and entrance. It was on a corner site where a side road ran inland, and next to us, across the side road, was Government House in extensive grounds where the governor, Sir John Macpherson lived. Sir Hugh Foot (now Lord Caradon) was chief

Invitation cards by Mrs C. A. "Topsy" Freeman, August 1948.

secretary. After we had retired, Sir John became chairman of Cable and Wireless Ltd.

Our two-storied building was L-shaped and the upper floor at the top of the L had a flat for the Rutters, then the mess, and our flat was at the lower part of it which ran along the side road. There were two 100 foot towers for the wireless aerials for services to ships and London. In addition to the cable to Accra, there was one to the French at Cotonou in Dahomey.

Bryant said he had been looking for a site outside the town for a wireless station but nothing suitable had been found. He took us for a drive ten miles or so inland to a possible place but it had no services, i.e. electricity, water, etc. There was a house being built for the manager at a new residential suburb called Ikoyi. Lagos was practically an island with a large lake to the east, with the harbour and long entrance on the west. To the north, beyond the town, there was a bridge over an arm of the lake, and the sea was at the south end. Near here was a beach where we went to bathe.

All along the Marina avenue were houses and gardens with green lawns studded with trees, and it was a pleasant place to live. There were a few good shops including the United Africa Co's new big one called (as in Accra) Kingsway.

A week after our arrival Bryant departed for England. He left us his Vauxhall car to sell when we left.

At the end of August we ordered a new Prefect car from the Ford agents, to be delivered in England early in 1949 when we expected to be on leave. I had been told that E. H. Webb would relieve me in January.

Our head clerk was an African called J. A. George who was a tribal chief and he was a pleasant capable man. His daughter got married soon after our arrival and we were invited to the wedding which was celebrated in European style.

The two principal tribes in Southern Nigeria were the Yorubas and the Ibos, the latter living mostly in the eastern provinces. It will be remembered that after the country got its independence, there was a civil war between them. One of our operators complained that most of the staff were harassing him. I found he was an Ibo and the others were Yorubas. He even said that Wells and Griffin were against Ibos! As he could not be pacified, this young African insisted that his written complaint be forwarded to head office which was done in accordance with the company's rules, adding my remarks to the effect he seemed to have a chip on his shoulder. Head office replied that they had taken notice of his complaint but they could find no substance in it; and there the matter rested.

While on the subject of Africans, I had a vivid demonstration that even the apparently civilised ones have a wild streak. Rutter was installing a telephone terminal for radio-telephony and not having any well-trained mechanics, had to do a lot of the work himself including wiring it up. I was in my office one morning when I heard a most appalling noise of shouting, and on opening the door saw all the African clerks pouring into the corridor, yelling at the top of their voices. So I shouted very loudly: "Everybody shut up and go back to your work." They stopped and sheepishly returned to their jobs. What had happened was that Rutter was soldering up an earth lead when he got quite a severe electric shock and burn from a faulty cable to his soldering iron. He fell over and the African assistant mechanic who was helping him, rushed into the main office, yelling blue murder. Whereupon all the staff lost their heads and did the same.

We took Rutter upstairs to his flat and called the doctor.

A suggestion was mooted that we should share a wireless site near the airport, several miles north of the town, with the Posts and Telegraphs, and the chief engineer took us out there to see it. I suggested to the government Lands Department that we should be given reclaimed land at Ikoyi but was told there was none to spare. I heard after we left, that this was where it was finally built. Pressure was probably put on the Lagos Government through the Colonial Office to give us room there.

We always did our best to help customers, whoever they were. Before we left Accra, Bryant wired me one Saturday lunchtime saying an

The Cable Office, Lagos, upper floor left the mess and right the manager's flat.

American businessman wanted to fly to Accra that afternoon and a request by cable for a visa had just been sent to our police. So I telephoned the chief of police and he promised to send someone immediately after lunch to deal with it, and the American got his visa promptly.

Colonel Wellingham, with whom I had been friends at the Hampstead School in 1928/29, was now Manager of our London station and he sent me a note by cable asking me to inquire of the Lagos Hospital about a man seriously ill. This was done by phone, and Wellingham got the reply in ten minutes—probably for some customer, and I hope he was impressed.

We opened a radio-telephone service with Accra and it was arranged that the governors of the two colonies and a number of businessmen should inaugurate the service, followed by light refreshments in our flat. Sir John MacPherson was away but his deputy came to speak to the governor of the Gold Coast.

Owing to serious shortages of replacement spares one of the power stations had to shut down, and there were power cuts on alternate evenings in different parts of the town. We had the usual emergency engine in our building and were thus enabled to be a blaze of light when Government House and others nearby were all in darkness.

Rutter was extremely hardworking and conscientious and at Christmas I had difficulty in getting him to leave the office early and go upstairs to be with his wife. Early in January they left for leave in England.

Mr and Mrs Webb arrived and we fixed them up in an hotel not far from the office.

We were due to sail on 17th January in the *Apapa* and the mess had invited us to a farewell party on the Saturday. But the day before I ran a temperature and could not go. It was malaria and on the Sunday we got the doctor who lived nearby and he recommended we should sail if at all possible. I felt better next morning and we got away. The ship made the usual calls at Takoradi, Freetown and the Canaries but throughout the voyage my temperature went up and down and I took quinine regularly.

We arrived at Liverpool at the crack of dawn on a wet morning but my temperature was up and I could hardly stand, so Sylvia called the ship's doctor. They got an ambulance and I was put on a stretcher and carried ashore and whisked off to the Royal Liverpool Infirmary. The port authorities and customs did all they could to help Sylvia and she said they were splendid. After getting ashore and seeing me at the hospital, she went to our office in Liverpool and saw John Ellison, the manager, who, pulling out a cheque book, asked her how much money she wanted. She explained that what she needed was an hotel, not money as she had travellers' cheques. He sent her off with his chief clerk, Mr Wilson to the Lord Nelson Hotel, near Lime Street railway station, who fixed her up for the next few nights.

I was a week in the Tropical ward of the Infirmary and they turned on all the works to find out what was wrong with me—I had already said it was malaria—but I soon began to recover. We left by train for Warkworth and put up at the Sun Hotel near to my parents. Ellison had notified head office and Mockett wrote Sylvia a nice letter, and said I should only come to London when quite better.

Rationing was still on in England and we had brought home a side of bacon and two cheeses which we divided between my parents and my brother who was living with his wife at Dalry in Scotland.

Dr Robertson came to visit me as I had been instructed to see my local doctor and said all was well, but he thought Sylvia looked the sick one, and after examination, diagnosed severe anaemia. He prescribed for her and said she must go very slowly. So we had a quiet time in the hotel with visits to my parents and friends. Just after my birthday Fords advised our car was ready for delivery.

I went to London by train and stayed at Oddeninos Hotel in Regent Street and went to head office. When one reached managerial rank, one reported to the staff department and they advised all the other departments who might want to interview you.

I collected our Prefect car from the Ford showrooms in Regent Street and drove to Upminster in Essex where the Kesbys now lived after their return from Accra and they put me up for the night. Next day I continued on my way home and arrived at Warkworth in the evening. Sylvia was still far from well but we went for a drive the next day to Seahouses, near Bamburgh, so that she could try out the new car.

Dr Robertson said that Sylvia should have an operation, so early in April we drove to Newcastle and she saw the surgeon, Mr Hodgson, at the Windsor Nursing Home just outside the town and it was arranged that she should go there in two days time.

Sylvia had the operation and soon made good progress. Before it started, the surgeon said she should not worry as everything would be all right.

On the 20th the Doctor said she could go out for a drive so I took her to see *Annie Get Your Gun* which was acted with great verve by a provincial company. The next day we returned to the Sun Hotel at Warkworth.

While in Newcastle I went to the Swan Hunter shipyard and visited the cableship *Edward Wilshaw* being built for the company and was shown round her by Captain Milne.

We left Warkworth by car for Dalry in Ayrshire to see my brother and his wife who had bought a house there.

With brother Miles and Sybil, we had drives in the country round about to Stewart Newton, Castle Douglas and Ayr, the latter through very wild moors and hills. I remember going along the Solway Firth with the woods near the road full of bluebells looking like a blue mist, interspersed with pink campion.

A letter from Mockett at Head Office arrived, appointing me to Ascension Island as assistant manager/engineer. I wrote to him and asked whether it was possible to change to some place which was not exclusively populated by company's men, pointing out that I had already done one lonely island stint at Cocos. He wrote back and kindly offered me the managership of our Manila branch in the Philippines which I accepted at once. This was a second grade station and the most easterly in the company's system.

We left Dalry for Warkworth taking my brother with us as he wanted to visit our parents.

Four days later we left Warkworth by road for London, calling at Newcastle on the way for Sylvia to see Mr Hodgson who pronounced her much better.

We had a busy time in London seeing friends and having various inoculations at the Tropical Hospital, and visiting head office. Sylvia wanted to get some silver fittings for the handsome crocodile skin dressing case brought in Batavia in 1941, so we went to Mappin & Webbs for them.

Colonel Wellingham entertained us to lunch at the Norfolk Hotel close to our new head office on the Embankment, and Everred from the staff department took us to the Philippine Consulate in Hans Place to get visas for our passports.

On 4th June we motored to Liverpool and put up at the Lord Nelson Hotel. We had arranged for our Prefect car to be shipped to Manila by the Blue Funnel Line in whose ship, the *Autolycus* we were to embark.

When at head office I was surprised to learn the company had a car in Manila for the manager as this was very unusual; it had been bought when the station was re-opened after the war, and there was no public transport. We decided to take our own car as it had been obtained without purchase tax on condition it was exported within six months. A permit had also to be obtained to take it outside the sterling area without payment in hard currency.

On 8th June we went on board the *Autolycus* and sailed in the evening for Hong Kong en route for Manila.

CHAPTER EIGHTEEN

Manila

The *Autolycus*, a Blue Funnel motor cargo ship of 7,704 tons, 15 knots, was on her maiden voyage. On the forward well deck there were five racehorses in wooden stalls, bound for Singapore. We had a large cabin with toilet, shower and two beds which were very comfortable. Captain Broad was the master, a rather thick-set pleasant man, and we sat at his table in the saloon on either side of him. He asked whether we would mind attending a funeral and said it was a member of the company who had asked for his ashes to be buried at sea.

We had rough weather in the Bay and one of the horses was very seasick. He lay down in his stall and when Sylvia went in to comfort him—rather to the trepidation of the groom accompanying them—he put his head in her lap and groaned.

We passed Gibraltar and not long after the ship's engines stopped for a few hours. There was trouble in the engine room. Two days later we passed the islands of Pantelleria and Malta in the evening.

We arrived at Port Said and I went to call on E. L. Carr, our manager. Meanwhile the engineers did some tinkering with our engines and at 2 a.m. next day we entered the Canal but only got as far as the Great Bitter Lake where we broke down again.

A gang of fitters arrived by launch from Port Said and another Blue Funnel ship, the *Aenaeus* stopped and sent over to us what looked like a cylinder liner. The fitters at last departed and we left the Bitter Lake, passed Suez and entered the Red Sea where it was even hotter and sultry with fog at times.

We arrived at Aden early but did not go alongside for fuel until noon. Bruford, our manager, took us to his house for lunch where we met his wife and daughter. He had been the inventor of the system by which cablecode signals could be transmitted on wireless circuits and relayed by means of the regenerator into a cable.

We left Aden and finally arrived at Port Swettenham on 11th July where we stayed until the evening. We drove to Klang and saw the Sultan of Selangor's rather delapidated Istana (palace). The countryside all around was very green and pretty.

Next day the ship reached Singapore and tied up alongside in Keppel Harbour. The following day I had lunch with G. T. Edwards, the divisional manager, in his enormous house. His wife had recently left for a visit to Rio de Janeiro. Edwards had been a Western man and this was his first time in the Far East.

We had rough weather in the China Sea but finally arrived at Hong Kong, and were met by Bryant, and taken to the Gloucester Hotel. I went to the office where I saw Mackie, the manager, and the elder Lynn-Robinson who was engineer. We were a week in Hong Kong and had quite a gay time. Mrs Mackie gave a lunch party of wives for Sylvia, the bachelors' mess, led by "Ginger" Hayden, asked us to a dinner party and Bryant took us to Aberdeen where we dined on board a junk and chose our dinner from fish alive in tanks.

On 27th July we left Hong Kong for Manila on the Dutch passenger/cargo ship *Tasman*, 6,000 tons. We had rather a small cabin and the weather was rough. The bridge and passenger accommodation had iron grills all around and there was an armed guard against Chinese pirates. The ship arrived in Manila Bay in the evening of 29th and anchored. This bay, about twenty miles across, is almost land-locked and at the entrance is the fortress, Corregidor Island, (The Guardian) where General MacArthur was holed up by the Japanese in 1941. We found that MacArthur is much revered by the Filipinos and his famous words on leaving Corregidor, "I will return," have never been forgotten.

Our ship docked the next day and we were met by Pat Sladden, a tall New Zealander, who was acting manager. Six months before our arrival, Harry Moss (whom I had relieved in Cocos) had taken over from Heath when the latter went on leave. Moss had left Manila a couple of weeks before we got there to go to Penang leaving Sladden temporarily in charge. There was one other foreign service man called Brophy.

After going through the customs Sladden took us in the company's car to our house about four miles from the city centre in a southern suburb called Pasay City. A very long street called Taft Avenue went straight from Manila to and through Pasay City. Sladden's house and ours (numbered 3606E Taft Avenue) were in a short cul-de-sac off the east side of the avenue. It was a two-storeyed building, cement block walls for the lower floor and weather boarding for the upper. The ground floor had a large sitting room with arch opening into a big dining room, and behind were a kitchen, two store rooms and the usual offices. At the rear of the house was a garage and servants' rooms. Upstairs there were three bedrooms with two bathrooms, a verandah and a boxroom. It had a small garden around it. There were four house servants, a cook (man), housemaid, lavendera (wash girl), and garden boy. Pedro, the car driver, lived out.

Next day Sunday we spent doing a lot of unpacking. On the Monday we went to the immigration office and were finger printed. To enter the Philippines for residence one had to have an immigration permit. They were issued on an annual quota basis and at that time the quota for the British was 500 so there was not much difficulty in getting ours which had been obtained by Moss before our arrival. After finger printing and filling in forms, we were issued with an Alien Certificate of Registration and an Immigration Certificate of Residence both of which bore photographs and thumb prints.

Everyone in the Philippines had to have every year what was known as a Residence Certificate A costing half a peso and bearing a right hand thumb print, and, if earning money, a Residence Certificate B costing one tenth of one percent of your annual earnings. Companies had likewise a Residence Certificate C. When signing a legal or government document, one was obliged to produce these certificates and quote their numbers. The Philippine unit of currency, called the peso divided into one hundred centavos, was worth just under half a crown when we first arrived. In September the pound was devalued and the peso was then worth three shillings and sevenpence.

British people—but not Americans—coming to the Philippines for the first time were sometimes puzzled by a heading on government questionnaires which asked them to enter your civilian status. The answer is either married or single.

We found that our Ford Prefect car was not due until 8th August and when it turned up we had to pay about £100 customs duty on it and get it licensed. Thereafter it was kept in our garage and the company's car, a six cylinder two-door Chevrolet, in Sladden's garage. It took us both to the office daily but Sladden had the use of it in the evenings and weekends unless we needed it with driver for special occasions.

Instrument Room, Manila.

Our office was on the top floor of the five storey plus mezzanine Uy Chaco Building in a square called Plaza Cervantes which was right in the business centre with the stock exchange, banks and other offices all around. The whole top floor was rented jointly by us and the Commercial Pacific Cable Company. We only had one cable to Hong Kong and the CPC one, via Guam, Midway Island, and Honolulu to San Francisco. The CPC was half owned by the Eastern Telegraph Company with a quarter each belonging to the Great Northern Telegraph Company of Denmark and the Commercial Cable Co of the USA where it was registered. This Pacific cable had been laid in 1903 and, up to World War II, they had had a cable to Shanghai.

We handed all our American traffic from Hong Kong, etc. to them. Mr. George Perry, a tall San Franciscan with a hard head, was manager.

In addition to our public counter on the ground floor of the building with a pneumatic tube to the instrument room upstairs, there were two branch counters, one in the port area and another in the suburb of

Binondo (known as China Town). There were several million Chinese or Filipino-Chinese in the country.

In our instrument room there was a small telephone type switchboard on which were terminated a number of lines to important clients whom we provided (free of charge) with teleprinters for sending and receiving cables. The lines were rented from the Philippine Long Distance Telephone Company who operated the telephone system in Manila and other towns.

Our cable to Hong Kong was worked regenerator cable code with automatic printing; about two years later it was made a through circuit to Singapore, with drop facilities for Hong Kong messages. We had timing machines which I had not seen before; of which there were two types, the best having a slot into which the edge of the telegram form was inserted, whereupon the date and time were printed on it, a very sensitive switch being operated by the edge of the paper.

The Philippine Islands—there are about seven thousand of them, mostly small—cover an area not unlike that of England, Scotland and Wales. The city of Manila on Luzon Island, one of the largest, had a population in 1949 of about a million and was a large sprawling area covering with suburbs about fifty square miles. Public transport was by buses but as many had been destroyed during the war, they were re-inforced by thousands of Jeeps originally brought in by the US army and either sold or stolen and converted to small buses each carrying eight passengers. They were known as *jitneys* and many were flamboyantly painted in bright colours and fitted with curtains and even fairy lights. The result was some tremendous traffic jams near the city centre during rush hours.

The river Pasig flows through this centre where it is about 300 yards wide. When the US army recaptured the town from the Japs the north side did not suffer as much damage as the south, but the latter together with the old Spanish walled city, known as Intromuros had nearly all its buildings near the river completely demolished and many including the Congress and other public buildings had not been re-built when we arrived.

The events leading up to this destruction were very dramatic as related to us by people who were there at the time. When the Japs invaded the Philippines in 1941 all the American and European civilians, men, women and children, were incarcerated in the Santo Tomas University buildings a couple of miles north of the city centre.

Later the single men were removed to a prison camp at a place called Los Baños on the shores of a lake about thirty-five miles south of the city. When the Americans returned in 1944 they first captured the island of Leyte some 340 miles to the south of Luzon Island. They then landed on Luzon Island in the Lingayan Gulf, a bay on the north west coast about 100 miles north of Manila and started to march towards the city.

MacArthur had learned from his intelligence and the Filipino resistance fighters that the Japanese intended to kill all the civilian prisoners if they were attacked in Manila. So he mounted a spectacular rescue operation. The US First Cavalry Regiment were sent in armoured cars down the main road to the town carefully timed to arrive at the Santo Tomas University at 1 a.m. in the morning. They shot all the guards except a handful in one building, and captured the place freeing practically all the prisoners. They let a few guards go in exchange for some hostages they were holding. These guards are believed to have been killed later by resistance fighters, but word had reached the Japanese HQ who, believing the whole US army had arrived, retreated across the river, blowing up buildings and all the bridges. The Japs had to be winkled out of the buildings on the other side of the river as most fought to the death.

Meanwhile MacArthur had sent a number of troops in DUKWs (amphibious vehicles) right round the east side of the town to the shore of the lake and across it to Los Baños. Just before they got there parachutists were dropped on the prison camp by Dakota aircraft. They seized it, the DUKWs arrived and were loaded up with everybody and they all escaped back across the lake. Eye-witnesses told me it was a marvellous exploit, like a scene from a movie.

As well as the Commercial Pacific Cable Co with their cable to the USA, there were three other American telegraph companies who worked wireless circuits to America and other places. Radio Corporation of America was the largest having communications also to Bangkok in Siam, and Djakarta in Indonesia as well as radio-telephony. Then there was Mackay Radio, part of the Commercial Cable Company's group, and Globe Wireless. The latter was a newcomer having been started by Mr Stanley Dollar of the Dollar Line of steamers, originally to communicate with his ships, but later getting a licence to handle messages from the Philippines to Honolulu and California. They were all in fierce competition with each other and us; and as they could forward cablegrams to Europe via the USA we had to keep on our toes.

*Cable Office on fourth
floor Chaco Building,
Manila.*

So there was a continuous struggle to get as many customers as possible from the business community. I had not come across this before as it was mainly in South America that our company was in competition with other telegraph companies. However, Sladden was highly competent in this sort of situation and soon briefed me about it. He had a wall graph in his office which showed our monthly receipts and they had been steadily rising. He kept a sharp eye on all our regular customers and their accounts to see that they did not backslide and he canvassed them and potential new ones. Except for Sladden, Brophy and myself, all our staff, numbering about seventy, were Filipinos.

Our general overseer, Casimiro Barawidan, was a hardworking capable man and I got on well with him and we still write to each other in retirement. He also canvassed the Spanish and Filipino firms, being tri-lingual in English, Spanish and Tagàlog (strong accent on the second syllable). This was the third official language of the Philippines, being the native tongue of a great many folk in Luzon Island. There are a number of other languages in use in various parts but Tagàlog is the official one. We had another clerk called Bernabe who canvassed the Chinese firms and looked after their business. Reyes was the senior overseer in the instrument room.

There were about half a dozen clubs in Manila for Europeans and

Americans and their entrance fees about £20 to £25 each (worth many times what it is now) precluded us from joining many, so on Sladden's advice we joined the Manila Club and the Polo Club. The former is really the British club as, though anyone can join, only British subjects can vote at the general meetings. It had a splendid clubhouse in a residential area with a small cricket ground and tennis courts; and there was a day time branch in the city centre open for coffee, drinks and lunches.

The Polo Club, mainly American but with a British manager, was about six miles inland surrounded by polo fields, swimming pool, tennis and badminton courts, bowling alley, etc., and was what is usually called a gymkhana club.

The Sladdens, who had two children, gave a dinner party soon after our arrival for us to meet some of their friends. These included a Dutch family called De Jong. He was manager of the shipping office of the Royal Inter-Ocean Lines. The De Jongs became great friends and have visited us in England several times since we retired.

Our bank manager (Chartered Bank) called Watty had a large house in a residential area called New Manila and he and his wife gave bathing parties by their swimming pool.

Sylvia discovered that friends from Penang in Malaya had recently arrived in Manila. They were Mr and Mrs Goldman, and while she escaped to Colombo, he had been captured by the Japs and sent to work on the infamous Siam Railway. Being a tall tough man, he was very keen on rowing, he had survived where so many had died and was now local manager for his firm, a Canadian insurance company.

So we soon had many friends and exchanged dinner parties with them. Manila was a sociable place and one could go out to a cocktail or dinner party every night if one could afford it, and had the inclination, and stamina. The company allowed me an entertainment allowance of a thousand pesos a year (£178) and I had to write a confidential report every six months, giving rough details of how it was spent, i.e. club subscriptions, names of persons entertained and their businesses. But living and entertaining costs were very high and we found giving cocktail parties, except on special occasions such as visits of VIPs was much too expensive for us. So we gave dinner parties for about four to six people, sometimes more, as having a cook and two maids this was not difficult and much more economical.

In September the pound sterling was devalued. This only affected

Sladden, Brophy and myself as the Filipino staff were on peso rates of pay, the peso being pegged at two to the US dollar. Head office gave us an exchange allowance of 43% of all salaries, allowances, etc., based on sterling. This brought our local currency receipts back to what they had been before devaluation.

It was discovered by the foreign community that the government would allow one to remit up to $200 a month to a dependent relative, e.g. father or mother, so we all developed dependent relatives!

My take home pay in Manila was good because though only in the second grade, there were numerous allowances, i.e. foreign service, charge, expatriate, foreign exchange, servant and entertainment allowances. We could live on our allowances with care and save most of my salary. This was essential as we had to provide for buying a house and furniture when we retired. In fact I received more than some men in first grade jobs, but it was earned as Manila was a strenuous place.

Sladden and I went to the office about 7.45 a.m. and came home for lunch at 1.00 p.m. We returned for work at 2.30 p.m. to 5.00 p.m. Manila being in latitude 14½° North had a tropical climate and it was pretty hot, especially from February to July. Later in the year there were torrential rains and now and then typhoons which did a lot of damage to the flimsy houses in some of the suburbs.

We were also in a bad earthquake zone and occasionally got shocks which caused damage. There was a severe shock one morning and up on our top floor the metal sunblind supports rattled against the side of the building and I thought for a moment we were going to collapse into Plaza Cervantes. A large slab of concrete became detached from the top of the building opposite and fell with a crash into a car park, just missing several automobiles.

As already mentioned, all the Pasig river bridges were destroyed by the Japs and the American Army brought in Bailey bridges. In 1949 two or three of the river bridges had been rebuilt but the one near us, known as the Jones Bridge, was still under construction and our landlines, together with several telephone cables, crossed the river supported by steel cables strung between stout poles on each bank. We had arranged with the Telephone Co to share ducts in the new bridge and when it was ready lines were laid in them.

As well as no bridges, there was no electricity (or water) when the Americans captured the city so they brought in two specially made power stations on enormous barges which were moored in the river and connected by cables to the shore. Though power stations had been repaired and new ones built, demand was so great that one barge station was still in use in 1949.

In October the Goldmans took us for a Sunday lunch to Taygaytay about forty miles south of Manila on the edge of the Taal lake. This had been an enormous volcanic crater fifteen miles or more across with an island in the middle which still smokes at times. We had lunch at a restaurant on a cliff overlooking the lake where there was a magnificent view.

On 8th November there was a presidential election and Elpideo Querino was re-elected president. He had come into the office when he was vice-president and his predecessor President Roxas (pronounced Rohas), had died suddenly. The Philippine constitution is the same as the American with a president elected every four years, and two Houses of Congress and a Supreme Court.

Head office informed me that Mr F. S. Coote, on leave from Hong Kong where he had been manager, was appointed divisional manager, Hong Kong that I was to come under his jurisdiction, and he would visit me shortly. I was to continue to correspond direct with London but send copies of letters to him. A year or two later when Mr Edwards retired from Singapore, Coote became divisional manager Far East which included Malaya.

On 7th December he arrived by sea and came to lunch with us the next day and I gave a stag party at the Manila Club for him to meet various heads of British firms, etc. It was soon evident that he was a capable executive and had a gift for nosing out and becoming friends with influential people both in government and business. We discussed the renewal of the company's concession with the Philippines and Coote had consultations with Mr Antonio Carascoso of the American/Filipino firm of Ross, Selph, Carascoso and Janda, our lawyers, as it was necessary to promote a Bill in Congress to secure a franchise to operate a public telegraph service.

The historical background is interesting. In 1879 the Eastern Extension Australasia & China Telegraph Company (under Sir John Pender) had been granted a concession for forty years by the Spanish government to lay a cable from Hong Kong to the Philippines and this was done the following year. It was landed at a small town called Bolinao which is on the left hand tip of the Lingayan Gulf about 110 miles north-west of Manila with which messages were exchanged by government landline. In 1898 a Spanish Decree allowed the cable to be brought to Manila direct and the concession was extended for another twenty years, i.e. to May 1940. This was done in 1897 when our Manila office was opened. At the same time three cables were laid from Manila to the islands of Panay, Negros and Cebu for which the company received an annual subsidy of £4,500 for twenty years.

In 1898 during the Spanish-American war, the former's fleet was defeated in Manila Bay by Admiral Dewey and the Philippines were captured and declared an American possession by the Treaty of Paris. Our cable was cut during the military operations but soon restored as it was the only means of communication with the outside world. Our Spanish concession, however, was never recognised by the American government which refused to pay the subsidy for the island cables which were accordingly picked up. We were allowed to continue operating, probably because to throw us out would have led to retaliatory action by the British government when the renewal was due for the concessions of the landing in the United Kingdom of the American-owned Atlantic cables. A direct cable from Manila to the USA was laid in 1903 by the Commercial Pacific Cable Co, largely financed by us.

In 1936 the US Government granted what was known as "Commonwealth" (i.e. partial) self-government to the Philippines with a promise of complete independence in 1946. No action was taken by our company or the Americans in 1940 when the Spanish concession expired, probably because the war with Germany had started. After the war the Americans intimated that we must get a new concession from the independent Republic of the Philippines and Alan Heath on his return to Manila as manager in 1946 interviewed the President Osmena. He was promised a temporary permit to re-commence operations, but the new constitution stated that franchises to operate public utilities within that country could be granted only to Filipino citizens or local corporations with 60% Filipino capital. It was contended by our lawyers that we did not do business *within* the Philippines but Osmena's government did not accept this.

In May 1946 Osmena was defeated in the presidential election and the new president, Roxas, said he agreed with our contention that we could obtain a franchise. On the 4th July, 1946 independence was proclaimed and on 30th September the president granted us a permit to operate under the conditions of our Spanish concession until a franchise was obtained from Congress.

In 1947 the president told us to postpone presenting our franchise bill to Congress as it was too busy to bother about us. Meanwhile the Hong Kong cable was restored and our office re-opened for traffic. Most of our old staff turned up and were only too pleased to be re-engaged. Pensioners were paid their pensions back to the Jap invasion. Nothing was done in 1948 as Congress was still busy and we had our permit to operate, but in April President Roxas died and was succeeded by Vice-President Querino who stated that our permit would continue to be recognised.

Early in 1949 there was a political wrangle between President Querino and the President of the Senate and the work of Congress ceased, the president governing by decree under emergency powers, until the election in November 1949—thus bringing the story up to Coote's first visit to me.

He told me that head office wished the matter to be pressed on as soon as possible. Our franchise bill had been drafted in the name of the old company, but in 1947 head office said that it wanted it in the name of Cable & Wireless Ltd, and the lawyers agreed that it would be all right. Coote, however, found that a franchise bill in the new name stood little chance of passing Congress and it was altered back to the name of the Eastern Extension Co. Nothing could be done until the spring of 1950 when Congress met for 100 days each year, so Coote returned to Hong Kong by air.

On 30th December we attended the inauguration ceremony of President Querino which was held in a big public square, the Luneta, mostly grassed over. A rostrum and stands had been erected with a canvas awning over the seats for the invited spectators, but it was barely finished before the ceremony started, and some of the paint on the awning poles was not dry.

In February we had an interruption to the Hong Kong cable. When this happened RCA opened a wireless circuit to our office in Hong Kong and the traffic went through them. The cableship *Recorder* arrived to repair the cable. Captain Henry Lawrence, the chief cable engineer P. Cousins, and two other officers had dinner with us.

Coote paid us a visit and stayed about a week during which our franchise bill was drafted and our lawyers arranged for two members of the Lower House of Congress to introduce it during the spring session. Mr Carascoso who was handling it came to dinner with us and also gave a dinner himself at the Manila Hotel for his clients.

Corns, Sladden's relief, his wife and I made up a tennis four with an American, J. H. Thomas, the assistant general manager of the Manila Electric Co and played regularly at the Polo Club. Thomas was a first generation American, his parents having settled there about the time he was born. Mrs Corns was a very good tennis and badminton player, able to hold her own in a men's four at either game.

At the end of the month Coote came to Manila to help with our franchise bill and spent much time lobbying members of Congress to persuade them to vote for it. He was good at this, but it involved much night-clubbing which I could not cope with financially or physically.

We went to a party at the Dutch Legation where we met the minister, Mr Steenstra-Toussaint and also the Indonesian ambassador Mr Maramis who later dined with us. His wife was Dutch and we liked them both, and went to dinner with them. I was able to get them to send all their official cables by our route rather than the RCA. It was contacts of this sort that built up goodwill which helped us compete with the other telegraph companies.

Their managers were on good terms with us and with each other and, while we competed, we had an unofficial arrangement by which if anything occurred affecting our interests, e.g. some new law in Congress or alteration of charges, etc., we had a meeting to discuss it and decide on a common line of action. Our head offices also kept in touch in London and New York, and sometimes made agreements of which we were notified. One was about advertising; our bosses agreed that none of us should advertise in the daily newspapers but only marginally in such things as telephone directories. We all had large illuminated advertising signs outside our offices for which we had to pay a tax to the municipality.

Brophy had been relieved by a young man called Shannon and we took him on various drives and I had some games of tennis with him. Brophy had been doing the station accounts and it was decided that a pretty Filipino girl called Fé Asnar who had been the manager's secretary and typist should take over, so she was trained by him before he left. She proved extremely capable and did the accounts without a single mistake the whole of the time I was there. Head office approved a special allowance for this job at my suggestion. As the manager had to sign all the accounts and was responsible for them, it was necessary to do checks when they were completed. It was not difficult to ensure proper control as all cheques were signed by him.

A service message from our manager in Havana informed us that an important client of theirs called Macfarlane was visiting Manila and he and his wife and a friend, a US Senator's wife arrived at the end of June in the American round the world liner SS *President Polk*. We met them, they had dinner with us and we showed them some of the local sights. He was head of an engineering firm in Cuba and their friend had been in Korea not long before.

In July who should arrive from Australia but our old friend Admiral Moore and his daughter Barbara, and later Mrs Moore. He had retired from the navy and was appointed minister in charge of the Australian legation. We were very glad to see them. Later Lord Casey the Australian Foreign Minister paid Admiral Moore a visit and, at a cocktail party, I had a talk with him about Cocos Island which was being transferred from British to Australian sovereignty.

The company was subpoenaed to produce a cablegram from Hong Kong needed as evidence in a diamond smuggling case and, thinking it might be interesting, I went as a witness though I could have sent Barawidan. There was no jury, only a judge who was a very experienced man. Juries are not satisfactory in the Philippines as there is danger of intimidation, but the judges are capable men who conducted trials very fairly. In this case the smuggled diamonds were produced in court with a guard armed with a sub-machine gun, but as soon as they had been identified, the judge told him to take them away at once in case of accidents. As I was not called by lunchtime, I asked to see the Judge and explained that being a busy man it would be convenient if he could call me after lunch as my evidence was only formal. He agreed at once and I produced the telegram with receipt gummed to the back which was normal practice. I quoted from the International Telegraph Regulations the section which authorises delivery to whoever took the cable in at the address and signed for it.

We met the manager of the Canton Insurance Co, Mr D. Wilson and his wife, and got to know them well. He had been in the Gallipoli campaign in World War I and since then had served in Shanghai, Tientsin, etc. We had decided to take some station leave and go to Baguio the hill station in the northern mountains about 150 miles from Manila and the Wilsons said they would come with us. The best place to stay was the Country Club so I asked Mr Ross the American senior partner of our lawyers if he would sponsor me as a temporary member.

It was better to motor in company as there were bandits in the countryside known as Huk Bahalaps (or Huks for short) who sometimes attacked travellers. They had originally been guerillas fighting the Japanese but when the war ended they would not return to normal life but preyed on people in country districts. So on 3rd November the Wilsons in their car, and we in our little Ford Prefect, set out for Baguio. When we came to the mountains we went up a long valley rising gently, finally coming to the head of it, and then faced a steep road for several miles. Eventually we arrived at Baguio and the club.

The town is not very big but nearby is a large US Army rest camp and many bungalows scattered about amongst thousands of tall pine trees so that it is known as the City of Pines. There are parks and gardens, and a golf course, and it is very pretty.

Stephen Crawford, the manager of the Shell Co, and his wife were also there and he and I went on several long walks together. He told me the trouble he had had to get foreign exchange out of the Bank of England after the war to buy petrol pumps and other apparatus when he was re-starting operations which would bring in plenty of dollars in return. Our company were also dollar earners, and we used to remit regularly to head office, but when exchange control was imposed it often took some time to get authority from the Central Bank of the Philippines. An occasional bottle of Scotch to the officials helped matters.

After ten days we returned home by going down a steep zig-zag road to a place called Naguilan on the coast due west of Baguio, and thence along the Linguyan Gulf where both the Japs and Americans had invaded, and down the main road to Manila.

Coote advised me that Major General Sir Leslie Nichols, the new managing director, would come with him to visit us and I was instructed to give a big cocktail party in the Manila Hotel which had a large ballroom, and ask everybody of importance from the president downwards. This was arranged and about 1,000 invitations were issued. However, Hong Kong had a typhoon and all aircraft were grounded so the MD and Coote did not arrive before the party. It could not be cancelled so Sylvia and I had to receive all the guests—about 500 turned up—and explain the non-arrival of Sir Leslie.

I had got a photograph of the MD from Harold Wilson, the Public Relations Officer in London and copies were published by newspapers in Manila with his potted biography, mentioning that he had been chief signal officer to General Eisenhower in Algiers and Germany. A note about him was typed to give to newspaper men who met VIPs at the airport.

They arrived the next day and we took them to the hotel and later to the Polo Club and they had dinner with us that night. They talked some shop and mentioned that the Commercial Pacific Cable Co was to be closed down in about six months time. I had been told this by Coote and warned to keep it under my hat, so Sylvia did not know, and I told her it was top secret.

We had found out that the Ayala Company a Spanish-Filipino family business firm was promoting a new high class residential estate on land surrounding the Polo Club about six and a half miles from the city centre. One had to buy a plot and erect a house or bungalow costing at least P35,000.

We had been plagued with noisy people and dogs barking at our house in Pasay so I went to see the Ayala Company and they said they would be prepared to build two bungalows for us to rent on a three years lease. Foreigners could not buy land because of a recent judgement of the Supreme Court. When the new constitution was drafted it was laid down that foreigners could not buy *agricultural* land. This was directed at the Chinese of whom there were about three or four million. But when a test case about a house near Manila was brought in the Supreme Court, the latter ruled that *all* land was agricultural—clearly wrong, and not intended by the framers of the constitution, but it became the law thenceforth. Some foreigners evaded it in various ways, such as two Englishmen who had American wives in whose names the land and house was held. All USA citizens had the same rights as Filipinos for the next twenty-five years under an agreement forced on the government by the Americans before the latter would give them $1,000 million war damages compensation. The same agreement tied the peso at two to the dollar unless the American president agreed to a change.

So we told Sir Leslie Nichols about it, and he went and had a look at the site and then instructed me to write to head office and he would support it.

He asked to meet the managers of the American Telegraph Companies so I arranged with them to come to his hotel for drinks before lunch. They all came and he chatted to them and then sent messages to their bosses whom he knew in the USA. I think they were much impressed. Nichols, Coote and I then went to a lunch party arranged by Barawidan for all our staff to meet the managing director. This was a great success as he talked to many of them before lunch and afterwards made a very good speech and a group photo was taken which was later printed on the cover of *Zodiac,* the staff magazine.

In the evening Nichols, Coote, Sylvia and I went to a dinner party given by Spanish friends of Coote called Mr and Mrs Descals who was the head of a large firm which grew tobacco and made cigarettes and cigars.

We had our usual Christmas dinner party, and on 29th December went to a presidential evening reception at Malacanan Palace. It had been built in Spanish times and was surrounded by extensive grounds which ran down to the Pasig river, and was a long rambling building of three stories, most of the reception rooms being on the first floor. The American governor had lived there, and it was now the presidential residence and office.

At receptions one's car arrived at an entrance at one end and inside there was a lobby which led to a wide staircase to the 1st floor. The crowd of guests had to slowly climb these stairs with many halts as at the top they had to proceed in single file past an ADC who took their cards and announced the names to the president who shook hands, and then there was the vice-president and his wife beyond. After that one could wander about the reception rooms or go downstairs and walk in the garden which was illuminated with fairy lights. There were bars and a buffet supper on both floors where one could get refreshments, and small tables at which to sit.

President Querino was a widower with one daughter. His wife and son had been shot in the street during the last days of the fighting in Manila, when the Japanese went about shooting everyone on sight, and about 20,000 persons were killed. As can be imagined the Japanese were not popular at this time.

The men at these receptions wore dark tails or dinner jackets, but Mr Foulds, the British minister, wore a white mess jacket when the weather was warm, so I did the same the second time we went and, lo and behold, the president was wearing one too. The copying of fashions is complimentary and when the president's daughter got married he asked the British legation for details of the wedding of Prince Philip and Princess Elizabeth, as she then was, so they could make similar arrangements.

Mr Carrascoso took me to see Mr Balmaceda, the government Minister for Commerce and Industry as he thought it might help in our franchise legislation. After conversation, the minister said he understood that the British government "had an interest" in our company and I agreed. Filipinos, following American practice, were not fond of nationalised companies, so one had to be tactful about it.

Mr Naylor, the new manager of the Philippine Long Distance Telephone Company invited me with other managers of commercial firms to a 10 a.m. to 4 p.m. symposium on their telephone service. He gave us an interesting talk on telephone working and their service in particular and we were shown a film illustrating how to use the phone to the best advantage, with some amusing examples of how *not* to use it; for instance, being shunted from one department to another in a big office so that you had to repeat yourself several times before reaching the man you wanted, causing much waste of time. Sladden had trained most of our staff on how to answer the phone and take messages from clients with the minimum of time wasting, and Richards, Reuters correspondent, told me they were very good whenever he rang up.

Head office advised that we could have the two bungalows at Forbes Park on a five years' lease, and we inspected the sites proposed by the proprietors; that for us in a road called Narra Avenue, and for Corns in Bauhinia Road (all names of local trees) about half a mile from us. Each bungalow had a large lounge/dining room with kitchen, garage, and servants' quarters beyond, and at the other end with access from a passage, three bedrooms, one with bathroom en suite and another bathroom between the other two.

Mr and Mrs Faulds (British Minister) left for the UK in February. Later their reliefs, Mr and Mrs Frank Gibbs arrived, and we got to know and like them. Before we left Manila the legation was raised in rank to an embassy and Mr Gibbs was knighted and became Sir Frank Gibbs.

At various times we met all the members of the British legation and Sylvia found that the wife of the vice-consul, W. H. Smith, had the same maiden name as herself (Cairncross) and they became very friendly. After we had both retired we went to see the Smiths who lived in Dumfriesshire.

In March G. C. Gately arrived from Hong Kong to reinforce our staff. He was a cheerful chap and we liked him and invited him many times to our house. In April our friends the Wilsons left to retire in

South Africa where we saw them later.

Coote came from Hong Kong for the spring session of Congress and our Franchise Bill was presented and passed by the Lower House. But when it was to come up in the Senate Carrascoso lost his nerve, thinking it would be defeated and did not present it before the session ended, to Coote's annoyance.

At the end of June our new bungalow was finished and we moved in. There was a fair sized garden and Sylvia had it partly laid out before the bungalow was finished, but it took some time to get it in good order. Sylvia had been persuaded by a neighbour, Mrs Ferguson, to buy some raffle tickets for a charity. Soon after she phoned and said Sylvia had won a prize and to bring her car with a bucket and some ropes to the Manila Hotel. On arrival she found it was a six foot diameter steel pond with water lilies. So the lilies were put in the bucket and the pond tied on top of the car which was gingerly driven home by Pedro as it was blowing half a typhoon. It was dug into the garden in front of the house and looked very nice.

Corn's bungalow was not finished until a month later, when they moved in with the help of the company's car and Pedro.

The Forbes Park Estate had a system of good roads all around the central area occupied by the Polo Club which was on a slight hill and a few more houses had been built. The Ayala Company managed it well. Water, electricity, telephones and storm drains had been put in, and sewerage was by individual septic tanks. Being right away from the town it was quiet and pleasant.

Beyond Forbes Park was Fort McKinley which had been an American military camp, and near it was a large cemetery with hundreds of graves of American soldiers, killed in the fighting to free the Philippines from the Japs—a grim reminder of the war.

One of my business friends was Peter Richards, Reuter's correspondent. He had lived there for some years and was married to a Spanish girl called Dolly who worked at the British legation as a translator. We had an arrangement by which we each told the other about the arrival of visiting newspaper correspondents whom he wanted to contact for news and I for their cablegrams. Head office advised me of impending visits as they issued cable credit cards so they could send messages to their newspapers who paid for them at their end.

The income tax system in the Philippines was similar to that in the USA. Every year you had to fill in a form and in conformity with the

Bungalow at Forbes Park, near Manila.

instructions on it, you assessed what tax you had to pay. You then made another copy and sent the two, by messenger, to the Bureau of Internal Revenue with a cheque for the amount of the tax. They stamped the second copy which you kept as proof of payment. Later PAYE was introduced for salaries and wages, and I had to work it all out and instruct Fé Aznar how to calculate it. There were no coding tables as the only allowances were for children, so it was fairly simple, but in the case of foreign service staff whose tax was paid by the company a formula had to be algebraically worked out, as tax had to be paid on tax.

The same procedure applied to the company's income tax, and this had to be done by a certain date and if payment was late a fine of ten per cent was exacted. Not being used to such deadlines I filed the company's return too late, so I paid the fine myself as it was undoubtedly my fault. It cost me £84. So I started a "Manager's Information Book". This was a hardback foolscap index book into which was entered alphabetically all the notes which might be needed in the administration of the branch, e.g. date all payments were due—with weekly, monthly and annual summary—details of property leases, and dozens of other things which were added as they cropped up. It was not only very useful to me, but to anyone who relieved me, and I brought it up to date before I left.

As much of the cash we took in for cablegrams related to transmission over other companies' or government lines, our income was calculated by a statistical formula which related our messages to the total of the whole system, and distinguished whether they were terminal or transmit messages. This was accepted by the Internal Revenue and was indeed the only practicable way of assessing our revenue, as the cost of doing it for each message was prohibitive. Later, when we got a franchise, we ceased to pay income tax—only franchise tax as will be explained further on.

The Internal Revenue decided to check our accounts and sent a succession of clerks to do this—quite a waste of time as they could find nothing wrong. One or other of them sat at a table in my office for about two months. Later the Congress passed a law that all company accounts had to be audited by certified public accountants (similar to our chartered accountants). Our neighbour in Taft Avenue was Mr

One of our Raleigh Bicycles.

Ferguson, head of a British firm of chartered and certified accountants, called Fleming and Williamson, so it was arranged that they should audit our accounts. He was a Scot and very hardworking. He and his wife and three daughters had been interned in the Santo Tomas camp for nearly four years so his loss of income was onerous.

The Director of Telecommunications. was a Mr F. Cuaderno, and I had paid him more than one call. I also met their chief engineer, Mr Alfonso, a very able man, and Mr A. Angustia, head of the traffic division. The latter became a particular friend of mine as we liked each other, and I negotiated with him a simplified system of payment of accounts. We used to pay them for messages handed over and they us by separate cheques, so it was agreed that one account should be deducted from the other, so that only one payment was needed. This was to our advantage as they always owed us a net amount and were slow payers.

A large number of Filipinos had Spanish names and it was thought that this was due to intermarriage; but, after reading a book on their history by a former American lieutenant governor, it was learnt that this came about in the seventeenth century when the Spaniards issued a decree saying that all Filipinos must adopt Spanish surnames, and lists were posted on church doors for people to choose their names.

The majority of the people are Roman Catholics, except in the southernmost islands where there is a large number of Muslims. But there is also a breakaway catholic church which claims about three million adherents.

Manila had an active amateur dramatic society whose members were mostly British and American and they gave performances regularly.

The company had a Filipino pensioner called F. Gardoqué who was over eighty years of age. One of my jobs was to certify that men in receipt of pensions were still alive, and I visited them now and then if they could not come to the office. Gardoqué had served years ago in the Philippine revolutionary army under the rebel leader Aguinaldo who had fought first against the Spanish and later against the Americans for a time after they captured the country. Aguinaldo was still alive, and I saw him once at a celebration rally in memory of his rebellion. Gardoqué had become an ardent stamp collector so I put him in touch with my mother who had started collecting during the war, and they exchanged a number of stamps by mail.

Our Hong Kong office had started a public radio-telephone service with Canton using VHF ex-American army equipment, and found that there was such a demand from the Chinese for it that several channels were needed. Coote asked me if I could obtain any of the VHF sets in Manila so enquiries were made of a firm called Bolinao Electronics whose manager was an American called Chaney. He obtained two sets and Coote told me to buy them and get an export permit. A few days later Chaney telephoned me and said that a Filipino army officer and some of his men had appeared and demanded that the sets should be handed over to them. Chaney was very angry and wished to call his (or our) lawyers and the police to protest at this high-handed behaviour. Coote was contacted and told me to let the army have the sets.

There was another incident with the Filipino military when an intelligence officer called and demanded production of a telegram which he alleged someone had filed. I told him that this could only be done on production of a subpoena from either a judge or the National Bureau of Investigation (the local equivalent of the American FBI) who were authorised by law to issue them. He said if he asked the NBI for an order the matter might be leaked, and was told politely that that was his problem. He then hinted that the military might raid our office but I refused to budge.

One local British businessman told me how to fiddle income tax. As already described, you assessed yourself and paid tax. The assessment went into a file in the Bureau of Internal Revenue, and later—usually a year or two—as they were always behind, it might be investigated to find out if you had declared all your income. So you bribed a clerk in the office to remove and destroy your file and hey presto, you were in the clear.

There was a good deal of nepotism, curruption and general fiddling in the Philippines. Congressmen, for instance, had to pay out about P30,000 in expenses to get into the legislature. Lots of people wanted franchises to run bus and other public services which needed bills in Congress. So you had to pay to get your bill through and there was "log-rolling" between the members.

Policemen were not immune and occasionally would pull up your driver (or you) for some alleged minor traffic infraction and only let you off for a five peso note. At Christmas it was the custom, as in some South American countries, for gifts like bottles of wine, biscuits, fruit, etc. to be given to the traffic police on point duty where they stood on an upturned tub in the centre of the street surrounded by their gifts while they waved the cars on. There was one tall traffic policeman whom I passed everyday and was soon given a salute. He suddenly appeared in our office and asked to see me. Could I give a cousin of his a job? It was explained to him that my bosses did not allow me to create jobs but that next time there was a vacancy, I would let him know, but his cousin might have to start at the bottom in competition with others. About eight months later our office sweeper was promoted to messenger, with higher pay, so I sent for the policeman who appeared very quickly, sent his cousin round and he was given the job. Well, it turned out for the best as he was a good worker and showed such aptitude for mechanics that he was made assistant to our head mechanic, Pascual, for training, and when we left was becoming very proficient. So I was sure of the goodwill of one traffic cop.

In case the reader should only see the mote in the Filipino eye, and not in his or her own, it should be mentioned that we *never* heard of any battered wives or children, though we regularly read two newspapers daily; nor any bank robberies or muggings. Our relatively small payroll was collected by two or three of our clerks who put all the money in their pockets and we never lost any. I once passed the Central Bank when a security van was unloading cash or bullion and there was an army jeep nearby and four soldiers with sub-machine guns deployed by the roadside.

At the beginning of 1952 the Commercial Pacific Cable Company closed down after a long period during which their cable to Guam had been interrupted. Mr Stroup, the manager was not told until the last minute which made it awkward for us. And for Sylvia who was consulted by his wife about buying some new equipment for their house.

Head office instructed that traffic from Hong Kong and the Philippines for the USA was now to be handed to Mackay Radio. Their manager, Mr Farrugia was pleased, I liked him and we got on well together.

It was arranged that we should take over the CPC share of the top floor of the Uy Chaco building. We needed more space as for some months I had rented a room on the mezzanine floor for my personal office to make space upstairs for additional apparatus.

We heard that A. T. Wood who had been my deputy in Accra in 1947 had arrived at Jesselton where the company were opening a new branch instead of the old station on Labuan Island. The cables from

Singapore and Hong Kong would now come ashore at Jesselton, the capital of British North Borneo (now called Sabah). Coote asked me if I knew Wood and what he was like, and I told him he was a very capable man. After he had met Wood he also liked him, and years later Wood became manager at Singapore and then divisional manager at Hong Kong.

Head office asked me to inspect a cargo ship calling at Manila and report on its suitability for shipping some cable from Singapore to Bamfield on Vancouver Island. This was done, but a month later they said the ship was not going to Singapore and wanted a report on another one. The agents told me the latter was not calling at Manila but going to Iloilo in the island of Panay about 300 miles away to the south. Head office was told and instructed me to go there. Sylvia said she would come, so we flew there in a Dakota of Philippines Air Lines and stayed three days. The ship's agents were very attentive and took us for drives in the countryside, and we lunched on board the ship one day.

There was a great deal of tuberculosis in the country which had been caused by malnutrition during the Japanese occupation when many people starved because the Japs shipped large quantities of rice to their own country. One of our local clerks, a member of a family several of whom had been on our staff, was affected and he was given six months sick leave on full pay. Dr Lissner said he would give him a course of treatment but after that he was still not well and was given another three months leave. The doctor told me he did not come for treatment and he was not pleased with him, so I gave him a warning. Finally, as he still did not do as the doctor told him, I reported to head office that he should be retired, but to my surprise the company told me to give him another three months leave. And I am glad to say that he did eventually recover and was still working for us when I left Manila.

It will be seen that managing our Manila branch was a pretty busy job and I could have done with a good secretary, as all really confidential matters including special reports to Coote and head office on political subjects had even to be typed by me. My Dutch friend, De Jong, suggested that his nineteen-year-old daughter who was very intelligent should work for me, but the family was not going to be long in the Philippines and it was no good training and then losing her soon after; when this was explained to him he agreed.

Coote engaged a new firm of lawyers to handle our franchise bill. They were Balcoff and Poblador whose sleeping partner was Senator

Paredes, then President of the Senate. Mr Balcoff was an American and they were more used to political matters than Carrascoso.

On 6th February we were at the Polo Club with some friends when Hector Maclean, the manager, appeared and said I was wanted on the phone. It was Corns and he said, "The King has died." He added that Peter Richards was annoyed because his telegram from Reuters had arrived after he heard the news from the Americans. Corns complained to our London Station who said they were sorry but they had a large number of such messages planked on them, and ours got delayed.

Coote came to Manila soon after to be there when our bill came before the Senate and stayed with the Philippine Foreign Minister, Mr Elizalde, in his penthouse flat—another example of his flair for having VIP friends.

Coote also got to know Senator Don Vicenté Madrigal, a wealthy businessman who said he would help us. It was learned that our bill had been sent to a committee of the house and shelved. Don Vicenté who was chairman of this committee resurrected it, and got it recommended to the Senate. Meanwhile Coote continued lobbying senators to vote for it. He pointed out to them that if it was rejected, the Americans would control the whole of the country's external communications, and this argument carried much weight.

It was decided that the Manila Club should have a memorial service for King George VI. There was no British padré available so it was arranged for an American Anglican clergyman to conduct it, and it was held out of doors on the cricket ground after office hours one afternoon. Most of the British community attended with many Americans and a few of other nationalities.

After the service Coote told me that he wanted to have a hundred copies of our Franchise Bill printed as the Congress office had not got enough for him to give to Senators, and could I get it done by 9 a.m. tomorrow morning? It was then about 6 p.m. so I said I would try, and we drove to Barawidan's house in Pasay. There was a Chinese printing works which did newspapers, and we had employed them for some years to print our local telegram forms.

Barawidan said they could do it, and he delivered them to Coote at 9 a.m.

Well, to cut a long story short, the bill was passed by the Senate and signed by the President on 7th June, 1952. It was really a triumph for Coote who had worked so hard to get it. He told me that in conversation with President Querino, he asked him what was thought about the British in the Philippines and the President replied: "Oh they are nice quiet people and never give any trouble."

Not long before, Coote had got worried about the cost of it all, so I prepared a statement for him to send home showing the financial advantages which were quite considerable, e.g. instead of telegraph tax of 2% plus income tax, under a franchise one paid 5% of gross receipts and were free of all other taxes including customs, etc., duties and, best of all, the 17% tax on home remittances. We recovered all our expenses in a year or two.

Head office advised that W. M. Wright accompanied by his wife, was sailing shortly to relieve Corns, who was then to take over from me for furlough. Coote had discussed a suggestion that although I would reach retiring age in two years, I should return to Manila after leave, and this was confirmed. By the time I got back, Corns would be due for leave.

As Sylvia had not seen her sisters since 1946 we decided to spend three months of our leave in Cape Town and head office agreed; so we booked our passages on the Dutch liner *Ruys* via Singapore and Durban. The company's Chevrolet car was getting old and head office wanted to scrap it and give the manager and his assistant car allowances. So we ordered from Vauxhalls in England a new left hand drive six cylinder Velox car for delivery on our arrival. Our Prefect had right hand drive as when we got it we had no idea it was going to Manila. Before the war everyone drove on the left side of the road but when the American army recaptured the place, they were the only people who had any motor transport and said: "Hell, we are not going to keep to the left . . . " so driving on the right became compulsory.

Senator Madrigal's secretary telephoned one morning and said his boss was flying to Hong Kong and would Coote have lunch with him tomorrow at the Hong Kong Hotel? I told him Coote was in England but Mr H. C. Baker was acting in his place and would the Senator like to meet him? The secretary said: "Yes", so I told Baker over the cable and it was arranged.

Mackay Radio had a strike of their operators engineered by a union which tried to recruit some of our staff. A few were members of the English union (Association of Scientific Workers) which had been recognised by Cable & Wireless Ltd. The difficulty was that under local labour laws, only registered unions could officially represent staff. I advised Barawidan to tell our staff that if they joined the local union they might be called out on a sympathy strike when they did not wish to strike at all.

On 6th July we gave a farewell dinner to the Filipino staff at a local restaurant. Barawidan made the arrangements and I paid the bill, about £1 per head, very reasonable by local standards. The *Ruys* was due to sail from Manila a few days before the Wrights arrived so we did not see them until we got back. Arrangements were made for entry permits for them and re-entry ones for ourselves, and we applied to take an allowance of foreign (dollar) currency, all of which was approved by the government.

So on 12th July we embarked on the *Ruys*, a motor ship of 14,000 tons, where we had a double cabin with bathroom. After three days and 1,100 miles she called at Sibu in Sarawak and moored to a buoy a mile or more from the shore. A pipeline from the refinery was attached to the buoy and we stayed all day taking on diesel fuel.

We reached Mauritius on 2nd August, leaving the same day. We went ashore for a walk and met Gilbride at our office. Our next stop was at Lourenço Marques (now Maputu). The ship left early next day and we

Farewell party to Mr and Mrs J. F. Stray.

reached Durban on 10th August. We were met by our friends the Wilsons who drove us about twenty-five miles to Pietermaritzburg where Sylvia's brother Douglas and his wife Edna were living, and where we put up at the Imperial Hotel.

We stayed there for three days and they came back to Durban with us and had lunch on board before we sailed for Port Elizabeth where we stayed a day and a half and saw Derick Dillon, the brother of my shipmate in the cableship *Britannia* in 1920.

On 17th July we arrived at Cape Town and were met by Sylvia's sister Gertrude with a neighbour called Bobs Pope who brought her in his car.

We were driven to Pinelands where Gertrude lived with her elder sister Mercy, and later to our hotel, the Majestic at Kalk Bay on the shores of False Bay on the eastern side of the Cape Peninsula. We stayed there for three and half months. It is a pleasant place facing the bay with the imposing Hottentot Hollands mountains on the further shore. A good deal of our time was spent at Sylvia's sisters' house. As we had no car we used to go on the electric suburban railway where there were frequent trains which also ran into the centre of Cape Town.

I went to the United States Consulate who acted for the Philippines which had no consulates in South Africa. Corns advised that there was a query about my re-entry permit but this was soon put right. So we had a pleasant holiday and then sailed on the *Bloemfontein Castle* for England. She was a one class ship of 18,000 tons, but being in the off season there were only fifty passengers out of the 700 which she could carry. We had two single cabins and there was a plethora of stewards to wait on us. She was a fine vessel and had an outdoor swimming pool on the upper deck aft which was well patronised in the tropics.

It was very rough in the Bay of Biscay and we arrived at Tilbury on 23rd November and went by special train to St Pancras and the Regent Palace Hotel.

We called on our bank manager at Hampstead and went to Mappin and Webbs as Sylvia wanted to get some silver. I spent about two or three days in head office and presented General Nicholls with a box of Philippine cigars to remind him of some he had been given while in Manila.

Mockett said I should do another year in Manila and then the question of a further one could be decided. Also there was no chance of my being promoted to the first grade before retirement—which was pretty obvious anyway.

We went to the Exiles Club at Twickenham and had dinner there with David Cox and his wife and the Philippine embassy and consulate now installed in "Millionaire's Row" in Kensington Gardens. There the final arrangements for our re-entry permits were made and we called on the ambassador and his wife, Mr and Mrs Romero. He was out but we were received by Mrs Romero and chatted to her about Manila.

There was some snow later but on the whole the weather was not too bad. Just before Christmas we went to Alnwick to see the Percy Hunt meet near the Castle, and three days later my brother Miles and his wife arrived by train from Wiltshire where they had a cottage at East Knoyle. They stayed with us at Warkworth House Hotel and we gave a party there for our parents on Christmas Day.

On 21st January we left Warkworth and drove to Bournemouth, where Sylvia visited her friends the Joys while I went to East Knoyle to stay for a couple of days with my brother.

After spending two days at head office we left by car for Liverpool where we embarked on the Blue Funnel ship *Patroclus* for Manila.

CHAPTER NINETEEN

Manila Again

The *Patroclus* was a so-called "P" class Blue Funnel ship of 10,000 tons with a speed of 20 knots, and did a three monthly round trip to Japan via Singapore, Hong Kong and Manila carrying cargo and thirty passengers. The ship went to load at Rotterdam where she stayed six days and we were able to visit The Hague, Amsterdam and the seaside resort of Scheveningen.

We passed Gibraltar, arrived at Port Said and went through the canal the next day. We took oil fuel, the ship had steam turbines, at Aden and arrived at Singapore on 6th March, having stopped in the Malacca Straits on a very calm morning and practised life-boat drill followed by putting a couple of lifeboats in the water for a row around by the crew, while the passengers took photographs.

We were met by Bryant and Captain Henry and Mrs Lawrence, and during the four and a half days there had a rather hectic round of parties including dinner on board Lawrence's ship, the CS *Stanley Angwin* and lunch at the Tanglin Club.

My birthday on the 12th was celebrated at sea, and the next day we arrived at Manila and were met by Corns and Wright and their wives.

Before leaving England we had bought two Raleigh bicycles, an Eddystone short wave wireless receiver and another miniature receiver for Sylvia's bedside, and these, together with our Vauxhall car, had to be processed through the Customs and duty paid which meant an exhausting morning. One also had to go through the usual fingerprinting exercise as the Filipinos made a point of treating everyone the same, from a company executive to a Chinese coolie.

Next day Sylvia discovered there had been a flood and a trunk full of her clothes and some packing cases with books, etc., stored under the house were full of water and everything in them was ruined. We got on to Lloyds agent and he sent a surveyor to verify the loss and they paid up insurance of about £150.

In April Coote paid us a week's visit. He was proposing a scheme whereby the Jesselton to Hong Kong cable should be diverted into Manila using the old shore ends of the Commercial Pacific Cable Co's cables to Guam and Shanghai which came into the cablehouse on Dewey Boulevard shared with us. He said we should need more trained electrical staff and told me to engage one or two young Filipino university graduates in electrical engineering. So I passed the word around through Barawidan and soon had several applicants.

To evaluate them, a questionnaire was drawn up for use when doing interviews and each was asked orally various questions to elucidate their background and training and, finally my assessment of their suitability which information was noted down against each. This system worked well, as on studying the dossiers obtained, it was easy to select two or three of the most suitable, who were interviewed again to get the final choice. A young man called Manuel Luber was chosen. Later another called Villamarzo and a third called Blancoflor were engaged. Wright asked me if he could interview the later ones using my questionnaire and when he did so it was found that we agreed on the best ones to employ.

Wright proved to be a good and hard working assistant manager and we got on well together. He and his wife liked their bungalow and enjoyed being in Manila though they found it expensive for his salary. We often used to go together to the city premises of the Manila Club for morning coffee. There was a large round table in the bar room and people from British and foreign firms used to sit there; so one kept in touch with all the local business and other gossip.

Howard Cavender, the manager of Globe Wireless, and his wife Betsy gave a dinner party at a Chinese restaurant to two visiting officials of the Taiwan (Formosa) Government communications department and invited us to meet them. It was an entertaining occasion and the two Chinese who spoke American English, were amusing about their country's customs.

On June 2nd Queen Elizabeth was crowned and the British community gave a coronation reception at the Manila Hotel where the ballroom was decorated. There were also decorations at the Manila Club. Guests were received by the British Ambassador, the Australian Minister, and the Consuls-General of Canada and India. Firms and individuals subscribed to pay for the celebration. We were able to listen to the commentary on the procession and service in Westminster Abbey on our Eddystone short wave receiver, and Howard Cavender kindly had the programme picked up at the Globe Wireless receiving station and relayed to the Manila Club during the afternoon and evening. Amplifiers and loudspeakers at the club were set up by Wise & Co a British firm who had been in Manila since 1809.

When Blancoflor, the third Filipino assistant engineer was being engaged, it was found that one applicant was already employed by the Government Radio Control Division, whose chief, Mr G. Canon, was known to me and much liked. This employee appeared to be very able, being older than others applying. Wright and I agreed that he was good but it was likely that he might not stay with us, and had more chance of promotion in his present job. Mr Canon was consulted about him and said he did not wish to lose him and that he had a bright future, so we did not engage him.

When there was heavy rain in Manila the River Pasig used to rise and flood parts of the business centre near us, and Plaza Cervantes several times had a foot or so of water in it which went into our entrance and counter on the ground floor. On arriving in the morning we had to remove our shoes and socks and roll up our trousers before getting out of the car.

A Filipino called Palma came to see me and said he had just come from Shanghai where he had previously been employed in our office before it was shut down by the Japs and the Chinese communists. He asked if there was any chance of a job as he was a cableman of twelve years experience. I liked the look of him and after consulting Barawidan, he was engaged on a temporary basis as we were rather short of operators. As he proved efficient he was eventually given a permanent position on the staff at a point appropriate to his original seniority.

When engaging the new assistant engineers, they were warned about "throwing their weight about" with our existing staff, but told that if they worked hard to learn our ways, there was good chance of promotion to responsible jobs. Eventually they were sent one at a time to Hong Kong for a few months' experience there and all did well. Our senior local staff men were told it was not possible to train them as engineers as this could only be done with young men who had been to university. The Shell Company had a serious strike by their office staff when they engaged Filipino engineers for training as junior executives, and I wished to avoid anything like that happening.

Our friend Sacha Goldman invited me as a guest to attend a Rotary luncheon being given at the bottle making factory of a company directed by the Filipino financier Colonel Andrés Soriano. This new building on the river above Manila was to serve Col Soriano's brewery and Coco-Cola plant, and had just been completed with one glass furnace and space for another.

A South African, E. J. R. Blake, came to our office having been sent by our embassy and we had him to dinner and took him to the Polo Club. He was a tall good looking man who lived at Constantia where the wine is grown near Cape Town and represented a firm of trawler fisheries who were looking for overseas markets.

Television had been started in the Philippines by a local company in association with the Radio Corporation of America. It was promoted by a brother of President Querino, but the receivers were rather expensive and the programmes not very good except for some films. The Polo Club bought a set and we watched it once or twice.

Every now and then our car would be sent to fetch Sylvia about 4 p.m. and she would come to town, meet me and have tea at a store and we would go to the cinema before returning home for dinner.

A presidential election was held and Querino who stood for another term of office was beaten by a new man, called Magsaysay sponsored by the opposition Nationalista party. Magsaysay's success was a new phenomenon in Filipino history. Most of their political leaders had come from the upper, well educated classes, many of them lawyers. The new president might be described as a man of the people, as he came from lower down, having been a motor mechanic in his youth. He was also a new broom dedicated to cleaning up some of the corruption which Querino had tended to turn a blind eye to amongst his friends and supporters.

It had become necessary to impose import controls on account of a lack of foreign exchange and the government office administering them had been heavily implicated in the dubious granting of licences to political figures. Unfortunately the new president was killed in an air crash not long after we left Manila.

Hector Maclean, the manager of the Polo Club, produced a quite original decoration on the occasion of a large ball being held when the weather was rather hot. He obtained some sprays of pink roses (probably flown from California) and with the co-operation of Colonel Soriano's brewery who made ice, each spray was frozen into an ice block a foot thick and about three feet tall and wide. These blocks were then placed end up with the rose spray vertical in shallow trays on each window ledge at the entrance and round the dance floor. The effect was most striking and the ice helped to cool the air coming in. They lasted for about a week.

Head office had shipped out half a mile of new multi-core polythene insulated and steel armoured cable. This was to replace the beachpiece of our Hong Kong cable where it left the cablehouse and crossed under Dewey Boulevard on the sea front. The beach at that point had got heavily silted up with sand 20 to 30 feet thick above our cable. In December, having obtained all the government permits needed, we engaged an American engineering firm to lay it for us. A large concrete manhole was made just inside the sea wall about 300 yards south of the existing landing with a entry hole in the wall. From the manhole a trench was dug along the sidewalk just inside the wall to a point opposite the cablehouse and thence across the double carriageway boulevard. When all was ready the new cable was laid in, using a large lorry with the reel on it, tested and the ends sealed. Wright and I took turns in supervising these operations.

We arranged to go to Baguio from 29th December to 14th January, as I felt rather sick. We could not get into the Country Club at first and stayed five days at the Pines Hotel which was comfortable, and then went into a detached two bedroomed bungalow at the club. We motored there and back and our stay was uneventful and I felt somewhat better but not fully recovered.

A cable was received from my stepfather saying my mother had died of a heart attack. She was eighty-two-and-a-half years old. It was possible to fly from Manila to London in twenty-four hours but even if head office had agreed, it was very expensive and could not be afforded.

In February Coote came from Hong Kong and stayed for seventeen days. He wanted to get permission to bring the Jesselton to Hong Kong cable into Manila from the Minister for Public Works and Communications, Mr Vicente Orosa, and avoid having to go to Congress to amend our Franchise Act. I took him to see Mr F. Cuaderno, the Director of Telecommunications, who was very friendly and Coote said that we seemed to be on better terms with the authorities than they were at Singapore. Some maps and a memorandum were prepared to put our case, and copies made for Coote. He produced a lawyer, Mr N. Y. Orosa, a brother of the minister, and said he had engaged him to be our legal adviser.

He asked me if I would like to be transferred to Hong Kong, presumably to relieve E. E. Story (my relief in Penang in 1941) who was assistant manager. I declined as it would have been too expensive to move shortly before retirement unless there was a chance of promotion to the first grade, i.e. to manager, Hong Kong, and Mockett had ruled such promotion out.

The minister gave us permission to bring the cable in and Coote went away quite happy.

It had been learned that the air-radio station at the airport proposed to handle telegrams for the airlines which were not of a strictly operational nature. So all the telegraph managers had a meeting and decided to approach Mr Canon (Radio Control Director) to ban this, as it encroached on the public telegraph service we were enfranchised to perform. We all went together to call on him. After discussion, he asked us to state our case in writing. I suggested to the others that I should draft the letter and they agreed. This was to get it the way I wanted it, and my draft was accepted and sent in all our names. The air-radio's proposal was subsequently dropped. Though our office was the smallest of the companies in Manila, I aways got the impression that the American companies had a hearty respect for Cable & Wireless, as they always listened to our views and took them into account.

Another matter was allowing regular customers to pay on monthly bills through credit accounts. But competition caused difficulties as some firms would fail to pay bills promptly and if their credit was stopped by one telegraph company, would get it from another, and unscrupulous ones could get nearly a year's credit by switching to a third or fourth. Radio Corporation of America suggested that if one company stopped a firm's credit after failure to pay in a month, we should all refuse credit to it. All head offices agreed to this scheme, ours rather reluctantly.

Coote said that, as he had engaged Mr Orosa as our lawyer, it would not be necessary to employ Ross, Selph, Carascoso and Janda, and I was to sack them in the next few months. I was not happy about this as they had given much good advice in the previous four years and I liked them. We no longer retained Balcoff and Poblador as they had been engaged to obtain our franchise.

Having read Arthur Bryant's books about Samuel Pepys, it was remembered how the latter said you should convey unpleasant news to someone. You should write to them and then call on them a few days later. You are not there when they feel most hurt and perhaps angry, and the call dispels the impression that you are afraid to face them, but by that time their anger has cooled off somewhat. This technique was tried and it worked as the lawyers' services were terminated without any lasting feeling of annoyance.

When talking to Bryant at Singapore on the voyage out, I told him that the managing director had not responded kindly to my request for an air-conditioner for my office. Bryant said, "The way is to get the company's doctor to recommend it as necessary for your health." So I spoke to Dr Lissner and he agreed it was needed and, sure enough, head office wrote and said it could be installed. My room abutted on a verandah so a room air-conditioner was fitted through the wall with the air intake there.

We still had difficulty in getting permission to remit money to head office so when it was reported that the government would give foreign exchange for new equipment for firms to expand, application was made for a remittance to pay for new relays, etc., being sent by head office for the bringing in of the Jesselton-Hong Kong cables, and this was approved. The bank issued a letter of credit for the money, this was the approved procedure, and then asked who was insuring the goods, as they were technically their property until they arrived and we were debited with the cost. For some years the company had been themselves insuring shipments to branches, so we had to sign an indemnity for the bank.

While I was on leave the Union of Telegraph Operators which had earlier called a strike at Mackay Radio had recruited a good many of our staff and their leader came to see me about one of our operators. While generally their speed and accuracy gradually increases with practice up to a normal limit, one occasionally finds a man who appears unable to reach the usual standards, and there is nothing one can do about it. In this case the man had lost his annual increments owing to this sort of inability, so he had been transferred to the abstracts department where he could earn increases of pay, though the maximum there was slightly lower than that for operators.

Another problem arose regarding our franchise tax on the income we received from "transit" messages, i.e., those handed to us by the American companies for onward transmission to places like India, Singapore, Hong Kong, etc. Under the Bermuda Agreement with the

USA there was a flat rate for telegrams from the USA to the British Commonwealth (and also to Indonesia, I do not know why), so that our share of the charges varied according to destination. After argument with the Bureau of Inland Revenue, we got them to agree to a statistical average transit charge for all such messages as it was too costly to evaluate each message separately. As was pointed out to them, these messages *could* be sent via the Atlantic, in which case they would get no tax at all. This kind of diversion was actually practised with one country which demanded exorbitant transit taxes.

As I was still not at all well and Sylvia also had been attended by the doctor who was giving her injections, I wrote to Mockett and asked if he could send a relief for me to retire, and in May he advised me that A. G. (Jebel) Hill who had been my assistant in Port Sudan and was manager at Djakarta, would be sent at the end of August to relieve me.

We wrote to Bournemouth to get various house agents to send us particulars of bungalows in the area, as we decided that this was the best place to live, and they sent us details. We ordered from the agents for the British Ford company a small Anglia car for delivery on our arrival. The Chartered Bank lent me a file of details of the impact of British income tax on going to the UK for permanent residence, so that mistakes in moving funds could be avoided.

We decided it would be a good idea to visit Japan on the way home.

In June the Hong Kong cable became interrupted close to the beach at Manila and the Danish Great Northern Telegraph Company's ship *Store Nordiske* was sent to repair it. We were lucky to have recently laid in the new cable and made the manhole on the sea front, as the ship was able quickly to divert the shore end to it. Captain Petersen was entertained at our house. The joke about this ship was that about half the ship's officers were called Petersen or Pedersen and he said it was a fact that there were four or five officers with this name.

We had trouble restoring the duplex balance after this repair. I spent a whole Sunday having a go and got it nearly right, but failed to detect that a resistance box had gone faulty, so Coote sent the deputy engineer, Saunders, from Hong Kong and he spotted the fault at once and had it right in a few minutes.

It was announced that a conference of the South East Asia nations was to be convened at Baguio to make a defence treaty afterwards known as SEATO and it was expected that the British Foreign Secretary, Anthony Eden, would attend with other VIPs. The

Philippine Long Distance Telephone Company called a meeting of carriers (as the telegraph companies were known), the broadcasting people and some newspaper agency men, and it became apparent that Baguio lacked facilities, only three or four telephone lines being available. This must have been impressed on the government as well as inadequacies in hotel accommodation as it was decided to change the venue to Manila and it would be held in the Congress building as its members were in recess.

Wright and I inspected the building. There were numerous rooms normally used as members' offices and we asked for two to provide counter and operating space for acceptance and despatch of press telegrams. Coote said he would send two men from Hong Kong, an engineer and a public relations man, and high speed apparatus to work to our office.

In the event Lord Reading came in place of Anthony Eden and our arrangements worked smoothly. Mr Bonham-Carter, the British Foreign Office conference organiser, came to see me and said they had engaged a whole floor of the Manila Hotel where their cipher office would be and could they have a teleprinter line to our office? I said, to his surprise, that it would be free as we usually provided such facilities to our best customers. Later he asked me for a second one which we were able to let him have. Lines were arranged by the telephone company. Every evening they sent long telegrams, but only to Singapore whence they were sent to London by Foreign Office wireless. Owing to differences in time, they could get replies during the night, in time for the next day's session of the conference.

Meanwhile Sylvia had been busy packing our belongings, though she was feeling far from well, being very run down. Barawidan invited us to his house for a buffet supper with his family and we had a pleasant evening.

We went to the Japanese consulate for visas and had to be fingerprinted again. About a year earlier the first Japanese ship to visit Manila since the war had arrived but so strong was the public feeling against the Japs over the atrocities which had been committed during the war, that the crew were afraid to go ashore. This feeling had now abated somewhat, and the government had agreed to the opening of the consulate.

On 27th August Hill arrived and I took him to visit the Manila Club. We gave a cocktail party at the Polo Club for him to meet friends and clients of the company, and there was a large staff farewell party. He said he had sent a note to Croger (who had been with me in Cocos and was now in Djakarta) to tell him that Manila was a most strenuous place to be in. Hill was later sent back to Djakarta and replaced by Henderson from Hong Kong.

On 11th September Sylvia and I sailed on the Blue Funnel cargo liner *Pyrrhus* and arrived at Hong Kong two days later.

The next day Sylvia felt better and we had dinner at the Peninsula Hotel at Kowloon which was very good, and on 16th September the ship left for Japan.

The voyage was uneventful except that a military aircraft, presumably Chinese, came and inspected us, roaring past the ship at mast height. On 19th September we arrived at Otaru in the northern Japanese island of Hokkaido where the ship loaded timber, called Japanese oak, and we had some walks ashore and bought some excellent apples. The country round about was very arid and rocky, and it was rather cold.

On 21st we sailed for Yokohama passing through the straits of Tsugaru where a ferry boat crossing from Hokkaido to Honshu nearly ran into us, and arrived on 23rd.

We stayed four days in Yokohama and visited Tokyo and did some shopping. We were not much impressed with the capital city. It was noisy and seemed to have gone American in the centre. There were not many motor cars about but plenty of trams and buses and a large number of odd three wheeled motor cars with a large motor-cycle type engine mounted over the front single wheel.

We arrived at Nagoya on 28th getting good views of Mount Fujiyama on route. On 30th the ship docked at Kobe where we stayed until 3rd October. We went to Kyoto by fast electric train and saw numerous temples and gardens, very pretty.

Hong Kong was reached on 6th and we left the evening of the same day and arrived at Singapore on 10th where at the office we saw Cumbe, the brother-in-law of the George Eastwoods. The ship called at Port Swettenham and then went on to Penang, where we were met by "Happy" Hampton who gave us dinner at the Penang Club. Harold Cox and his wife of the Chartered Bank who had come from Manila, said we must stay the night with them in their enormous house—the largest bank manager's house ever seen; it was very comfortable and they were charming hosts.

*On our last voyage home Sylvia embroidered in coloured silks a tablecloth with
nineteen scenes from the places we went to.*

On arrival at Aden we were met by our manager, Kime, who took us
for a drive to Little Aden and round about, and gave us lunch and we
sailed after tea. We got to Suez on 30th and passed through the canal
during the night.

In the Mediterranean news was received that there was a dock strike
at Liverpool, so the captain slowed down as there seemed no point in
arriving while it was on. We had booked hotel rooms in London for 8th
November so wirelessed to say we would be a day late. But then
suddenly the strike ended and we reached Liverpool on the 8th
November after all. So we stayed the night at the Lord Nelson Hotel
there and went on to London next day to the Regent Palace Hotel.

*Our bungalow
at Barton-on-Sea.*

We collected our new Ford Anglia car and I did the usual round of the departments in head office for the last time. On 17th we drove to Bournemouth where we stayed at the Cliff End Hotel. We then went house hunting and found the bungalow at Barton-on-Sea, ten miles east of Bournemouth. We bought it with possession in January and commenced shopping for heavy furniture and other things needed.

The bungalow has a small garden front and back, and proved very satisfactory and we have been in it ever since.

Since retiring we have spent short holidays in various parts of England and Scotland and made two trips to Cape Town by sea to visit Sylvia's brother and sister-in-law. But we have no wish to do any more travelling abroad.

We think our life abroad in the company's service has been very interesting and would not have wished to do anything different. It has, however, made us rather sceptical of those who pontificate about what other countries should do, on the strength of relatively short visits. It is believed that to know anything about an overseas country you should live and work there for a year or more.

Looking back, the company's management of its branches and staff abroad seems to have worked well, and certainly much better than that of many other firms; the staff really have a very close family feeling for one another. We have since met some we had not come across before, and felt at home with them at once.

My furlough finished on 28th February, 1955 and I retired officially on 1st March which was just one month short of forty years since joining the London Training School in April 1915.

INDEX

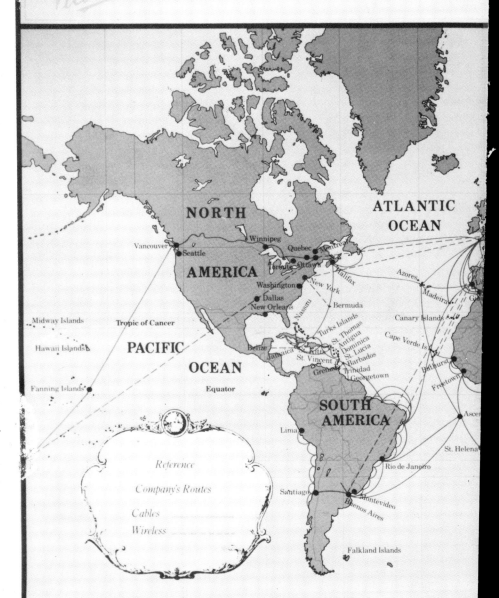